DISMANTLING
THE WEST

Also by Janusz Bugajski

Atlantic Bridges:
America's New European Allies (with Ilona Teleki)

Cold Peace:
Russia's New Imperialism

Political Parties of Eastern Europe:
A Guide to Politics in the Post-Communist Era

Ethnic Politics in Eastern Europe:
A Guide to Nationality Policies, Organizations, and Parties

Nations in Turmoil:
Conflict and Cooperation in Eastern Europe

East European Fault Lines:
Dissent, Opposition, and Social Activism

Czechoslovakia:
Charter 77's Decade of Dissent

Related Titles from Potomac Books, Inc.

Persian Dreams: Moscow and Tehran Since the Fall of the Shah
—John W. Parker

Kremlin Rising: Vladimir Putin's Russia and
the End of Revolution, Updated Edition
—Peter Baker and Susan Glasser

Russia and Postmodern Deterrence:
Military Power and Its Challenges for Security
—Stephen J. Cimbala and Peter Jacob Rainow

DISMANTLING THE WEST

Russia's Atlantic Agenda

JANUSZ BUGAJSKI

Potomac Books, Inc.
Washington, D.C.

Library of Congress Cataloging-in-Publication Data
Bugajski, Janusz, 1954–
  Dismantling the West : Russia's Atlantic agenda / Janusz Bugajski. — 1st ed.
    p. cm.
  Includes bibliographical references and index.
  ISBN 978-1-59797-210-9 (hardcover : alk. paper)
  1. Russia (Federation)—Foreign relations—Western countries. 2. Western countries—Foreign relations—Russia (Federation) 3. Russia (Federation)—Strategic aspects. 4. Russia (Federation)—Foreign relations—Europe. 5. Europe—Foreign relations—Russia (Federation) 6. Russia (Federation)—Foreign relations—United States. 7. United States—Foreign relations—Russia (Federation) I. Title.
  D2025.5.R8B84 2009
  327.470182'1—dc22

                                              2009015026

Printed in the United States of America on acid-free paper that meets the American National Standards Institute Z39-48 Standard.

Potomac Books, Inc.
22841 Quicksilver Drive
Dulles, Virginia 20166

First Edition

10 9 8 7 6 5 4 3 2 1

To the kids:
Simona, Petar, and Nevena

Contents

Russia's European Energy Web

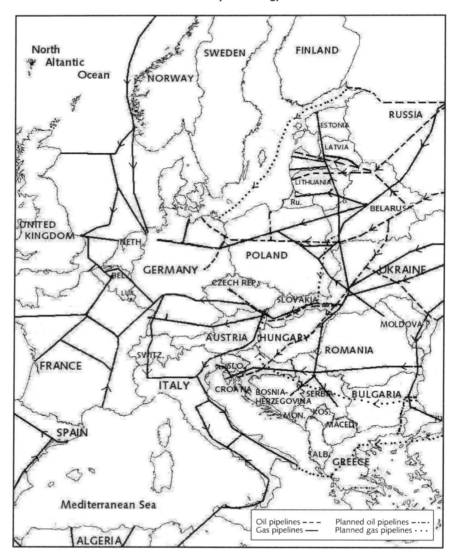

Source: Janusz Bugajski, *Expanding Eurasia: Russia's European Ambitions* (Washington, D.C.: CSIS Press, 2008);
map created by Besian Bocka. Used with permission.

Russia's European Ambitions: Establishing Influence Zones

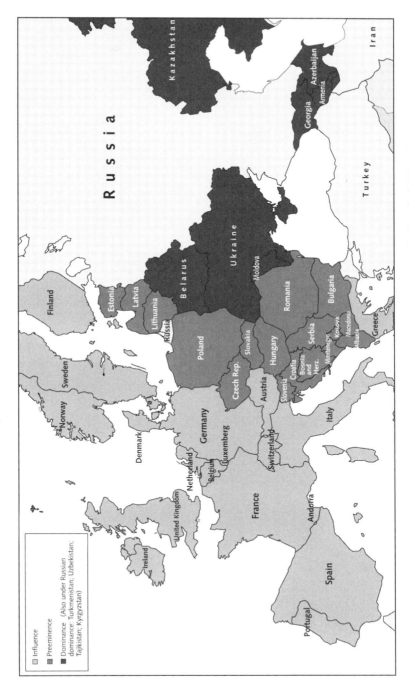

Source: Janusz Bugajski, *Expanding Eurasia: Russia's European Ambitions* (Washington, D.C.: CSIS Press, 2008); map created by Besian Bocka. Used with permission.

Introduction: Moscow's Challenge

Moscow's overarching goal toward the Western world is to reverse the global predominance of the United States by transforming "unipolarity" into "multipolarity" in which Russia exerts increasing international leverage and political influence. To achieve this long-range policy objective, the Kremlin is intent on expanding the Eurasian space in which Russia is the dominant political player and causing the Western or Euro-Atlantic zone of security to become increasingly fractured and neutralized. In this strategic struggle, "Eurasianism" for Moscow involves two interconnected approaches: transforming Europe into an appendage of the Russian sphere of influence and debilitating Euro-Atlanticism by undercutting Europe's connections with the United States.

In pursuit of its long-range objectives, the Kremlin employs a number of interlinked strategies. The most significant involve *discrediting the West*, in which Russia is depicted as the stalwart bastion against America's neo-imperialism; *international posturing*, whereby Moscow poses as a defender of international law, national independence, and political stability; *expanding spheres of influence,* through which Russia's regime defines its national interests at the expense of its neighbors; *dividing and dominating*, where Moscow fosters international divisions to disrupt the emergence of a unified policy and exposes individual states to intense pressures; *promoting political indispensability*, in which Russia poses as an essential partner in global security issues and engages in strategic blackmail by threatening to terminate its assistance; *neutralizing through dependence,* in which Moscow escalates Europe's energy dependence to mute any challenges to its expansionist policies; and *playing security chess*, whereby Russia manufactures security disputes in order to gain advantages vis-à-vis other security questions.

Within the context of these strategies, Russia deploys a range of weaponry to curtail the further expansion of the North Atlantic Treaty Organization

(NATO)–European Union (EU) sphere and to weaken the coherence and effectiveness of Atlanticism. These include divisive diplomacy, political subversion, informational warfare, institutional manipulation, and military threats. A primary instrument is energy entrapment, whereby Russia pursues a monopolistic position as Europe's energy supplier and converts energy dependence into intergovernmental influence. Moscow is also gaining major economic inroads in Europe through targeted investments and the purchase of strategic assets that enable it to entice politicians and leverage major businesses to support Russia's broader interests.

The European Union occupies a pivotal position in Russia's strategy, as it can either strengthen or weaken the Kremlin's approach toward the West. Russian leaders view a unified EU foreign policy, synchronized with Washington, that undercuts Russia's aspirations as a threat to their ambitions. Alternatively, EU institutions or specific member states can help buttress Russia's policies. The absence of a common EU strategy toward Russia, accompanied by division and indecision in both the Union and the NATO alliance, has several negative consequences for Western interests.

First, it enables Moscow to fracture the EU by bilateralizing or nationalizing relations with individual states and providing diplomatic and economic incentives to some capitals while exerting political pressure on others. Second, EU divergence generates disputes over the approach of specific member states toward Russia and undermines the development of a common EU and NATO foreign and security policy on a broad range of issues. Third, European disunity and an overly accommodating approach toward Moscow, exhibited by some Western European capitals, further restricts EU and NATO enlargement eastward. This can unsettle the reformist prospects of aspirant states in Eastern Europe and the Black Sea region. And fourth, EU divisions and political acquiescence toward Moscow may undermine relations with the United States and disable the pursuit of a joint Western strategy.

The argument posited by some analysts that Russia is too weak to implement its strategies and achieve its objectives can be answered through three observations with regard to growing capabilities, relative strength, and persistent divisions among adversaries. First, the Russian state has been significantly centralized and strengthened under the Putin presidency, while the Kremlin has steadily expanded its strategic objectives and sharpened its economic, political, diplomatic, and military tools.

Second, Russia is substantially stronger than each of its postcommunist neighbors. The relative weakness of the former Soviet republics should be measured by not only their military capabilities but also their dependence on Russian energy and trade and their vulnerability to various forms of influence and pressure from Moscow.

And third, Russia relies on strategic divisions between the Western powers and their inability to devise a single coherent policy approach toward Moscow. This enables Russia's leaders to more effectively pursue their agenda by exploiting weaknesses and fractures among their adversaries and partners. This does not mean that all of Russia's ambitions can be steadily achieved. Indeed, the Kremlin has confronted some notable setbacks to its Eurasian agenda, such as the enlargement of NATO and the democratic upheavals in Ukraine and Georgia. Nonetheless, Moscow views these as temporary retreats rather than as permanent strategic defeats.

This book offers a detailed assessment of Russia's ambitions to undermine Western multinational institutions and to dismantle common Western interests by examining several components of the international strategy Moscow developed under Putinism.

Chapter 1 outlines Russia's development under Putinism and describes how the rebuilding of state power coincided with the expansion of state interests. A primary purpose of political centralization was to transform Russia into a global power and a counterpoint to the United States and the transatlantic alliance. The political structure established under Putinism can be understood as "authoritarian statism," a system controlled by a narrow clique of security officials who fused their political ambitions, economic interests, and imperial aspirations. For the Putinist post-KGB network, profit and politics intersected in a strategic calculation, combining national authoritarianism, corporate statism, and imperial nostalgia.

Chapter 2 discusses how Moscow focuses on undermining the global interests of the United States through selective confrontation with Washington. While Russia exploited Kosova's independence to undermine the West, it simultaneously used the "Kosova precedent" to justify its invasion and partition of Georgia. The purpose of this scenario was to undermine and eventually remove U.S. and Western influences from the Caucasian region. In a wider geostrategic framework, the chapter pinpoints how Russia's leaders pursue global anti-American alliances in order to challenge U.S. interests and distract Western attention from their neo-imperial agenda within Eurasia and toward Europe.

Chapter 3 assesses in detail Russia's strategy toward NATO and its attempts to weaken the transatlantic link and undermine U.S. preponderance. This is accomplished by forging bilateral ties with selected NATO states, manipulating anti-Americanism, and discrediting the role of NATO in global security. To dismantle the alliance and reduce its effectiveness, Moscow depicts NATO as the all-purpose enemy controlled by the United States in the pursuit of world dominance; exploits various arms control arrangements; reasserts its military power as a counterpart to NATO; and berates the alleged expansion of U.S military infrastructure in Central-Eastern Europe (CEE).

Chapter 4 focuses on Moscow's strategy to establish expanding zones of influence, including political dominance over the post-Soviet republics and pre-eminence among Russia's former CEE satellites. By examining these distinct international spheres and specifying the major foreign policy tools at the Kremlin's disposal, ranging from diplomatic offensives and informational warfare to energy blackmail and the purchase of political influence, one can assess Europe's position in Moscow's grander strategic ambitions.

Chapter 5 examines how Moscow seeks to divide and weaken the Western European state by developing bilateral ties with targeted capitals and preventing the European Union from assuming an effective foreign and security policy. Moscow capitalizes on unresolved international disputes or manufactures regional or bilateral conflicts to drive wedges between EU countries and between Europe and the United States. Such disputes have included the planned U.S. missile defense shield in Central Europe, the parameters of energy security, and the validity of various arms control treaties.

Aggressive diplomacy, negative propaganda, and the promotion of pan-European altercations also amplify the Kremlin's drive to marginalize troublesome new EU and NATO members that are critical of Moscow. Furthermore, by courting particular European capitals and estranging others, Moscow can more easily divide and dominate, by weakening EU and NATO consensus while developing interest groups and political supporters who will favor or comply with important ingredients of Russia's foreign policy.

Chapter 6 appraises Russia's manipulation of energy supplies as a geostrategic weapon that fosters European economic dependence and promotes political acquiescence. Energy is one of Moscow's primary tools for foreign policy influence and dominance, and the Kremlin has systematically undertaken to become a leading energy superpower and to use its monopolistic position as a political and strategic weapon. Russia seeks to play a major role not only as an energy superstate but also as an international financial center that would allegedly break the monopoly of the U.S. dollar and the Euro currency and establish an allegedly more stable multipolar world.

Chapter 7 examines Russia's extensive economic investments and asset purchases in various parts of the wider Europe and what this portends for Moscow's political ambitions. Under the Putin administration, the most productive large-scale sectors of the Russian economy were transformed into tools of government policy as Moscow nationalized the major energy concerns and other strategic industries. These holdings enabled the Kremlin to pursue an increasingly vigorous foreign policy with economic instruments and thereby to more systematically influence policymaking in targeted countries.

In conclusion, chapter 8 considers how Europe and the United States lack a common strategy to deal with Russia's empire building. A loose coalition of larger Western European countries are apprehensive about provoking disruptive disputes with Moscow. They are willing to overlook negative trends in Russia's domestic foreign policies and even to sacrifice some basic European or Western values and interests. For Berlin, Paris, and Rome in particular, short-term commercial pragmatism generally prevails over long-term geostrategic calculation.

The concluding chapter also offers several concrete and practical recommendations for the Western alliance to reinvigorate its cohesion and defend its security interests by counteracting the damaging strategic impact of a restorationist Russia. The most effective and realistic long-term Western strategy toward Russia needs to combine practical engagement with strategic assertiveness. Practical engagement focuses on the pursuit of cooperative relations in areas where Western and Russian interests coincide, as in countering international terrorism and the proliferation of weapons of mass destruction or in the resolution of regional conflicts where Moscow can play a more constructive role.

"Strategic assertiveness," as an essential complementary approach, must focus on vital long-range Western interests where the EU and NATO, working in tandem to strengthen transatlanticism, can effectively counter Russia's negative policies. As a primary principle, all NATO-EU allies must avoid compromising core interests through agreements with Russia that sacrifice one Western security priority to gain Kremlin support in another arena. For instance, the effective defense of a NATO member state cannot be sacrificed for Russia's evident agreement to cooperate in combating jihadist terrorism. Such compromises not only undermine Europe's commitment to expanding and safeguarding democratic governments, but they also permit Russia to pursue its agenda to dismantle "the West" as a coherent security community.

1

Russia's Revival

With the demise of the post–Cold War era, the West and Russia are embroiled in a new strategic confrontation, primarily in the Eurasian landmass. Russia is reasserting its global reach by seeking to contain the further expansion of the Western or Euro-Atlantic zone of influence and by reversing the global predominance of the United States. Russian analysts believe that the United States has passed its zenith as a global power and that Pax Americana is inevitably on the decline. This provides a valuable opportunity for a resurgent Russia to terminate Western dominance of global affairs by extending Moscow's influences in key regions adjacent to its territory where it asserts privileged interests, particularly throughout the wider Europe. According to a Hungarian member of the European Parliament, "Russian tradition has little appreciation for the notion of equality of nations, which is the fundamental principle that governs Europe today. On the contrary, Russia believes in the hierarchy of raw power through which the Kremlin is trying to restore its status in the world."[1]

Russia's assertive strategy and imperial renaissance is more threatening than one based on ethno-nationalism and the pursuit of monoethnic or monoreligious states. It revolves around the creation of an expansive multinational state without specific ethnic boundaries in which statism and imperial control rather than narrow ethno-religious identity predominates.[2] This resembles the continuation of the traditional historical strategy pursued by the czarist empire in absorbing territory, assimilating and Russifying adjacent nations, and neutralizing states that resist incorporation in a Russia-dominated empire. In the words of one Polish analyst, "Russia has created a model of a multiethnic empire, with a long and particularly effective tradition of expansionism, strong (absolute) central power and a consistent policy of centralization, and finally, with a long string of ideologies giving divine legitimacy to that power and its expansion."[3]

Russia's Objectives and Strategies

Russia's primary objectives toward Europe and the United States are focused on expanding the Eurasian zone in which Russia is the dominant political player and dismantling the West as an effective model of security and development. Regardless of the ideological heritage, doctrinal diversity, and cultural underpinnings of Russian "Eurasianism," in practical terms for Moscow "Eurasianization" has two interconnected strategic meanings: (1) transforming Europe into an appendage of the Russian sphere of influence and (2) debilitating Euro-Atlanticism by undercutting Europe's connections with the United States. Russia dismisses the notion that it is a European periphery and instead views itself as the pivotal power on the Eurasian landmass, larger and more globally significant than Europe itself.[4]

Russia's newly installed president, Dmitry Medvedev, succinctly highlighted the two strategic objectives during his visit to Berlin in June 2008, when he proposed the creation of a pan-European security pact that would sideline or absorb the North Atlantic Treaty Organization (NATO) and steadily enfeeble U.S. influence. In Medvedev's words, "Atlanticism as a sole historical principle has already had its day. NATO has failed to give new purpose to its existence."[5] Hence, for Russia's leaders Eurasianism has become a useful geostrategic counterpoint to Atlanticism.

Medvedev followed up his proposal for a new European security framework during the World Policy Conference in Evian, France, on October 8, 2008.[6] In elaborating on the initial plan, he posited the notion of equal security, in which Russia would maintain a veto on any further NATO enlargement and where no state or international organization would possess exclusive rights in providing peace and stability in Europe. In effect, Moscow would be in a position to block any moves by the Central-Eastern European (CEE) countries to enhance their own security and obstruct any changes in NATO's military infrastructure in Europe. The European states would need to negotiate with Russia any proposals for missile defense, weapons modernization, or peacekeeping deployments. Meanwhile, the United States would be expected to take a backseat in a process intended to weaken transatlantic ties.

Under Moscow's security plan an authoritarian and expansive Russia would become an equal partner in determining European security. The Kremlin's proposal was welcomed by the Spanish prime minister José Zapatero, while French president Nicolas Sarkozy seemed to take the Russian bait by calling for an Organization for Security and Cooperation in Europe (OSCE) conference in 2009 to open a debate on European security in which Russia would play a key role.

Some Western analysts have also acquiesced to the Kremlin's strategic objectives by contending that the West needs to be cognizant of and even sympathize with Russia's national humiliation because of its recent loss of empire.[7] This is tantamount to compensating Russia for its past imperial failures and serves to gloss over or even justify imperialism, colonialism, enforced Russification, and the panoply of Soviet communist repression as understandable national interests. Such an accommodating stance can also become a cover for tolerating the re-creation of a new Russian imperium in Eurasia in which anti-Americanism and the dismantling of any effective Western alliance plays an important political role.

Historical anti-Westernism is deeply ingrained in Russian political calcula-tions. During the previous five centuries, Russia built its empire in opposition and in competition primarily with Western powers. At the same time it claimed a purer heritage of Christianity and viewed itself as the defender of Europe against the allegedly barbarian east and south. Even Russia's modernizers envisaged reforms as tools to strengthen Russia's reach and dominance and not as an integrative process with the West. Moscow became more ambitious in the eighteenth and nineteenth centuries as its empire expanded. Under the czars Russia challenged the West as the bearer of a superior culture and civilization. Under the Bolsheviks, following their coup d'etat in October 1917, Moscow combated the West on the basis of ideology, socioeconomic determinism, and historical destiny.

The statist and neo-imperialist essence of Putinism again challenges the West, primarily as an alternative center or fulcrum of independent statehood, international protection, and economic development. It specifically confronts the concept of American preeminence or "Atlantic-centrism" in which the world is allegedly welded to a single axis controlled from Washington. In building a new global order, Moscow strives to renew itself as a major pole of power by re-creating its dominant role in a revamped empire, beginning with the "post-Soviet space," which has become a euphemism for Russia's imperial space.[8]

Observers wonder to what degree the Kremlin pursues a grand strategy to achieve its stated or disguised objectives. The answer seems self-evident. Under Putinism, decision-making has been centralized in all sectors of government and a narrow clique in the Kremlin has captured the state apparatus and the economy to serve specific policy objectives. There is little reason to doubt that the Putinist inner circle tightly coordinates foreign policy, even though the degree to which any specific strategy is applied toward any particular country depends on the position it occupies on Moscow's geopolitical canvas. In pursuit of their long-term transcontinental objectives, Russia's leaders employ several interlinked strategies that can be encapsulated as follows:

Discrediting the West: Moscow charges the West in general and the United States in particular with "democratic messianism" in which Western values and political systems are evidently forced on victimized and defenseless states.[9] Washington is accused of a multitude of imperialist designs, including political unilateralism, aggressive militarism, disregarding international institutions and international law, undermining state sovereignty, overthrowing governments, and breaking up independent states. Russian leaders thereby seek to promulgate anti-Americanism and anti-Westernism while depicting Russia as the stalwart bastion against America's neo-imperialist encroachments and its plans to dominate the globalization process.

International posturing: The Russian state poses as a stalwart defender of international law and of the international system embodied in the United Nations, in contradistinction to the West. It selectively highlights evidence of its multilateralism and its alleged determination to work through international institutions, particularly the UN Security Council (UNSC). Moscow postures as the spokesperson for the national independence, political stability, and territorial integrity of all sovereign states regardless of their political structures and human rights records. Moreover, Russia's self-defined "sovereign democracy" is depicted as a valid independent model that should be emulated more widely.[10] At the same time, Moscow disguises its unilateral, noninstitutional, and aggressive record toward Georgia, Moldova, Ukraine, and other neighboring states whose security it seeks to control.

Expanding spheres of influence: The Russian regime defines its national interests at the expense of its neighbors. Putinist foreign policy focuses on establishing several zones of expanding influence among immediate neighbors and former satellites where Western influence needs to be curtailed or comprehensively eliminated. This can be described as an essentially zero-sum calculation. For Moscow, realpolitik consists of advancing state objectives in line with its capabilities and Western weaknesses. In the Kremlin's approach smaller European countries are not accorded the status of fully sovereign states but must have their security interests dictated either by Moscow or by Washington or remain neutral by remaining outside of NATO. Hence, Russia pursues political dominance over the post-Soviet republics and political preeminence among former Central-Eastern European satellites. It employs a broad range of tools to achieve these ambitions, ranging from diplomatic offensives and informational warfare to energy blackmail, ethnic conflict, military threats, and the purchase of political influence.

Dividing and dominating: Moscow sparks conflicts with specific states to test the reaction of the larger powers and multinational organizations, including the European Union and NATO. It thereby seeks to foster and develop cleavages between Western countries and disrupt the emergence of a unified security and foreign policy toward Russia. By periodically acting in an aggressive manner toward countries such as Estonia, Latvia, or Poland, Moscow probes and gauges NATO and EU reactions. It is encouraged by a weak and divided Western response to expand the parameters of its assertive foreign policy posture. Provoking a fractured and ineffective Western reaction is also designed to demonstrate the limitations of Western security guarantees and the vulnerability of individual states to Moscow's pressures.

Promoting strategic indispensability: Rather than posing as a superior ideological, political, and economic alternative to the West, as during the Cold War, the Kremlin now depicts Russia as an essential player in global affairs. In this schema, the Europeans and Americans must be convinced that Moscow's cooperation is necessary to resolve problems that Russia has in fact contributed to creating. In this way, Moscow poses as an indispensable partner on issues ranging from Iran's nuclear program to the spread of jihadist terrorism and the proliferation of weapons of mass destruction (WMDs). To underscore their indispensability, Russian officials also engage in strategic blackmail by asserting that they can terminate their assistance in Western negotiations with Iran or in allowing supplies across Russian territory to NATO troops in Afghanistan. Moscow calculates that increasing dependence on Russia's diplomacy and practical collaboration will undercut an assertive Western response to its expansionist policies.

Neutralizing through dependence: Moscow pursues several projects to escalate Europe's direct dependence on Russia. These assist in fracturing the European Union and undercutting a more activist Western policy in challenging the Kremlin's political expansionism. Most notably, this strategy includes growing hydrocarbon energy supplies and increasing trade and business interconnections. Energy dependence is manipulated as a means of political pressure, whether through pricing policies, supply disruptions, or infrastructure ownership. Additionally, lucrative investment deals are offered by Russian officials to those states, corporations, and politicians that are perceived as Russia-friendly, particularly on occasions when political disputes with several other Western governments are sharpened, as was the case following Moscow's military intervention in Georgia in August 2008.

Playing security chess: The Kremlin purposively manufactures security disputes with the United States, NATO, and the EU to gain advantages for its positions vis-à-vis other security questions. Its negotiating strategy is to engineer a crisis and exploit the ensuing attention to secure beneficial concessions from its adversaries. Numerous examples of this process include NATO's incorporation of the CEE countries; the U.S. missile defense system, elements of which are planned to be constructed in Poland and the Czech Republic; and Kosova's final status as an independent state. All three have been presented as threats to Russia's national interests, and the West is pressured to make concessions. Additionally, Moscow foments bilateral disputes with individual countries, whether over trade or market access, or some pressing political question, and uses these as bargaining chips to gain the neutrality of targeted capitals vis-à-vis some broader conflict with the EU or NATO.

Two steps forward, one step back: Russia's leaders seek advantages by partially stepping back from an initially aggressive stance and pushing the West to make concessions by accepting some of its gains. Several Western leaders then herald their evident success at averting a larger international crisis. Russia's invasion of Georgia in August 2008 can be seen in the light of such calculations, whereby the EU focused its attention on dispatching monitors to the buffer zones created by Russian forces deeper in Georgian territory rather than to the disputed regions of South Ossetia and Abkhazia, which Moscow recognized as independent states in its de facto partition of Georgia. Moscow refused to admit the European Union's Monitoring Mission (EUMM) into the two territories; it emplaced a large number of additional troops in Abkhazia and South Ossetia, prepared to establish permanent military bases, and seized additional areas that Tbilisi had controlled prior to the August war.

Mixing messages: Russia's regime periodically sends mixed messages with regard to its foreign policy intentions in order to confuse and disarm Western capitals. For instance, while it claims to be working for a peaceful and amicable resolution to a bilateral dispute, as with the "frozen conflicts" in Georgia or Moldova, it may simultaneously be preparing political provocations and military responses to gain clearer advantages from the dispute. By initiating and participating in various negotiating formats, Moscow can convince some Western officials that it favors a peaceful resolution and far-reaching compromises while it is preparing alternative scenarios. A mixed message may also be intended as a veiled threat of potentially harmful actions by Moscow. This can include withdrawal from an arms treaty, the cancellation of an energy agreement, or a direct challenge to develop or deploy nuclear weapons against NATO territory. Initial combative statements serve to warn Western capitals of adverse consequences if they fail to compromise with Russia. The statements may be subsequently toned down or even denied by officials to demonstrate a softer line when the adversary appears intent on making concessions.

Beyond the Post-Cold War Era

To achieve their long-range strategic objectives, Russia's leaders first needed to restore their country as a "sovereign democracy" unfettered by outside powers.[11] During the past decade, President Vladimir Putin's administration rebuilt the power of the central government; eliminated all viable political, informational, and organizational alternatives; stifled the independent civic sector; seized the country's major economic assets; imposed control over billionaire oligarchs; and rekindled Russian state nationalism to mobilize the public.[12] The purpose was not simply to enrich a new ruling oligarchy but to transform Russia into a global power and a counterpoint to the United States and the transatlantic alliance.

The Russian leadership scripted a self-justifying myth to explain the country's relations with the West since the fall of communism. Kremlin spokesmen claim that throughout the 1990s Russia was humiliated by Western powers, particularly by the United States, and they bemoan the collapse of a powerful Soviet Union. Moscow acts as if the Cold War continues in a new guise, having allegedly resulted in a halftime draw. According to a prominent Russian analyst, "Searching for enemies and casting the West in the role of the principal foe has turned out to be the most successful method for rallying the people. . . . Anti-Western sentiment has become the new national idea, and national revival has taken the form of revisionism. . . . Anti-Western ideology has become an important factor that legitimizes the highly centralized state."[13]

In a strategically key statement at the 43rd Munich Conference on Security Policy in February 2007, President Putin listed Russia's grievances toward a range of international institutions, described the unipolar model of American hegemony as unacceptable, condemned the unilateral and illegitimate actions of the United States in international affairs, complained about the European Union and NATO acting outside the UN framework, spelled out Kremlin priorities to diminish the effectiveness of international organizations that obstruct Moscow, and warned that Russia was reviving its power on the world stage.[14]

In Russia's pursuit of a global revival, its key instruments were no longer military might and ideological messianism based on the interests of the communist movement. Its growing international assertiveness revolved principally around its divisive diplomacy, energy strategy, activist propaganda, and subversive measures to gain political influence, undermine its rivals, and consolidate alliances that undercut U.S. dominance.

There are several ways to depict Russia's emergence under Putin's rule: as a regional hegemon, as an aspiring global player, and as a neo-imperial state.[15] Avoidance of the "neo-imperialist" designation obscures the thrust of Moscow's strategy. Putinist Russia has evolved into an imperial project for two core reasons. First, it has clearly articulated ambitions to restore its global status, primarily in competition with the United States, and to undermine international institutions that hinder its aspirations. Second, Moscow's drive to dominate its former satellites, curtail the expansion of Western structures, and neutralize Europe as a security player is accomplished through a mixture of threat, subterfuge, disinformation, pressure, and economic incentives. Russia's national interests are thereby viewed as predominating over those of its smaller neighbors and European partners.

Russia's imperialism can be described as "neo" because it no longer relies primarily on traditional instruments such as military might and the implanting of political proxies in subject states. Instead, Moscow employs an assortment of diplomatic, political, informational, economic, and security tools to encourage the evolution of pliant governments that either remain neutral or actively promote Moscow's strategic agenda. The precise political colorations and ideologies of any compliant government are less important for the Kremlin. However, if these subversive strategies prove unsuccessful, military force may also be employed to destabilize a neighboring government and fracture its territory, as the invasion of Georgia in August 2008 poignantly illustrated.

Russia is a hydrocarbon power with global ambitions. Its energy exports have been its main economic motor and have ensured an annual growth rate of some 6 percent since 1999 and accounted for over half of government revenues. During the Putin era, capitalism and economic growth have not been accompanied by progressive democratization but by the restoration of political and economic controls by a narrow clique of security officials.[16] Formal democratic processes and institutions serve as a camouflage for autocratic and bureaucratic controls over state and society. Despite the existence of a parliament (Duma), the ruling political party, United Russia, dominates proceedings and is controlled by Kremlin officials. The Kremlin elite has also concentrated capital in companies that it can control, as this provides the lubricant for political patronage and an instrument of foreign policy.

There is debate among Western analysts as to how the Putinist system should be defined and how it will evolve. Rather than classifying contemporary Russia according to its economic characteristics, such as "oligarchic" or "bureaucratic capitalism," the structure established under Putinism can be understood as "authoritarian statism" or a *chekistocracy*, a system controlled by a narrow clique of security officials, commonly styled as *siloviki* (activists from the Soviet security structures), who outlived communism and fused their political ambitions, economic interests, and imperial aspirations.[17]

Russia's transformation from a quasi-democracy to a security police state has been evident in the expansion of the Federal Security Service (FSB, Federalnaya Sluzhba Bezopasnosti), the Foreign Intelligence Service (SVR, Sluzhba Vneshney Razvedki), and the Military Intelligence Service (GRU, Glavnoye Ravedy-vatelnoye Upravlenie). Under Putinism, the FSB chekist network seized control of vital political and economic sectors and supplanted the Yeltsin-era oligarchs and organized crime groups.[18] This was accomplished through a mixture of pressure, intrigue, blackmail, coercion, and other extralegal means. Profit and politics intersected in a strategic calculation, combining national authoritarianism, corporate statism, and imperial nostalgia.[19]

How durable such a system is likely to prove is a matter of speculation. With the election of President Medvedev and Putin's appointment as prime minister in May 2008, the two leaders seemed to operate in a tandem that perpetuated the Putinist strategy. Medvedev seemed to be acting as a transitional figure before

Putin's return to the presidency. Nonetheless, a struggle for power between and within competing patronage networks could intensify if economic conditions were to seriously deteriorate.[20] The least probable scenario would be the liberalization of Russian politics under Medvedev's presidency, given that the ruling elites have personal stakes in maintaining a nontransparent and authoritarian state structure not subject to internal accountability or international inspection.[21]

Moscow's public relations machinery strained to stress Medvedev's authority while depicting the new president as moderate and more accommodating to the West than Putin. His assertive stance toward Georgia in the summer of 2008 was described as an unavoidable response to Tbilisi's aggressive policies toward its separatist regions. For additional Western consumption, the customary Russian nationalist bogey figures were allegedly waiting in the shadows to undermine Medvedev if he displayed weakness.[22] In reality, a few months into Medvedev's term in office, his approach demonstrated a continuity of Putin's policies even though the new president initially sent out signals that he would be more respectful of the rule of law. Moreover, the president's foreign policy prerogatives were curtailed under the new foreign policy doctrine released in July 2008, which provided greater authority to the Putin government.[23]

Russia's internal and external developments are closely interlinked. The Putinist system has interwoven centralism and statism with imperial restoration and great power ambitions.[24] In this equation, the Kremlin's often-cited pragmatism is not a policy agenda but a means to an end, consisting principally of tactical maneuvers to achieve strategic objectives. Pragmatism in foreign policy signals variable approaches and elastic tactics for achieving specific long-range goals. However, the objectives and not the means are what ultimately define state policy.[25]

Officials assert that a strong centralized Russian state is necessary for stability, prosperity, security, and Russia's international grandeur. Hence, official propaganda and Russia's educational system can overlook the "excesses" and "mistakes" of Stalinism because Stalin built a strong Soviet superstate and Russia has inherited its international status and needs to emulate its global authority.[26] Although Russia was the inheritor of the assets and international representation of the Soviet Union, unlike the post-Nazi German state, Moscow did not assume responsibility for any reparations for the international victims of Soviet repression.

Instead of confronting and expunging the Soviet past, the Putinists in line with their Stalinist predecessors diverted attention toward a new enemy, the rapacious West evidently intent on dismembering Russia. In this new version of the Cold War, the battles are "fought with cash, natural resources, diplomacy, and propaganda."[27] For the Kremlin, the West has again become the primary adversary both for domestic consumption and to justify its global ambitions. Russia's leaders have consistently claimed victimization by the West.[28] Allegedly, the United States and its closest NATO allies have never treated Russia as a real partner and have sought to keep the country weak, divided, and self-absorbed.

> Maintaining Russia's superpower ambitions and its domination of the former Soviet space are now crucial to the reproduction or continuity of its political system and the self-perpetuation of power. In short, Russia's foreign policy has become an important tool for achieving the Kremlin's domestic objectives. And a key foreign policy objective is to create the image of a hostile international environment in which Russia is besieged while demonstrating a strong state reaction that legitimizes the hyper-centralization of Kremlin power, top-down governance, and its crackdown on political pluralism.[29]

During a visit to Moscow in October 2007, U.S. secretary of state Condoleezza Rice claimed that Russia and the West were not embroiled in a new cold war. She was correct in the sense that the escalating West-East confrontation may actually be less predictable than the Cold War standoff. During the Cold War, the battle lines between the Soviet Union and the Western allies were clearly drawn through Europe and Asia. The two adversaries were sharply differentiated according to ideology, political structure, and economic system. Both were capable of annihilating one another, and their stockpiles of nuclear weapons were an effective deterrent, styled as mutually assured destruction, that froze any potential military conflict.

The Cold War had its ebbs and flows, its warmer periods of détente and accommodation and its frosty conflicts over Cuba, Vietnam, Korea, Afghanistan, Angola, Nicaragua, and other third-world states. However, both sides understood each other's strategies and objectives and sought to prevent the spread of their rival's system, especially within their respective spheres of influence. The Soviet Union and its core imperialist state, Russia, lost the Cold War to the West when communism disintegrated and the Soviet bloc unraveled in the early 1990s. Soviet-communist political and economic structures could no longer compete with America and Europe.

While the West endeavored to spread the virtues of democracy and free markets, a new imperial Russia gradually arose from the rubble of communism and the shortcomings of postcommunist Russian democracy. Since the beginning of the Putin presidency in 2000, Moscow has reappraised the past, claiming that the disappearance of the Union of Soviet Socialist Republics (USSR) was a major twentieth-century tragedy and that the Cold War ended in a stalemate. Kremlin officials also affirm that having withstood Western humiliation, Russia was now strong enough to reassert itself as a global power and challenge its former adversaries.

As a result, the post–post–Cold War era may prove more disruptive than the Cold War itself for three principal reasons: *strategic confusion*, *operational cunning*, and *new weaponry*.

First, strategic confusion is evident in the West because the nature of the adversary is less clear-cut. Moscow does not pose as an ideological foe but as a political counterweight and practical alternative to the West. Russia's distinct agenda to establish spheres of dominance along its lengthy borders is depicted as the defense of national interests, while Kremlin intentions to neutralize the EU and to reduce U.S. influence are underplayed or misunderstood by many Western governments. It is difficult for Washington and Brussels to respond to a novel strategic struggle when much of the West does not understand the kind of threat that Russia poses and is not actively engaged in countering such a challenge.

Some analysts contend that Russia primarily seeks to be an equal of the United States. However, this raises several vexing questions about Moscow's ambitions. For instance, what does the Kremlin understand equality with Washington in international relations to be? Russian leaders view American unipolarity as endowing Russia with essentially second-class status. Equality would signify a revived superpower position commensurate with that of the United States and encompassing re-created zones of influence in nearby regions, including Europe. Equality with Washington will encourage Moscow to feel entitled to act as a dominant player toward former satellites and to pursue balances of power with Washington. Equality would also have significance for Russia's position in international institutions. Invariably, Moscow would seek an elevated status vis-à-vis countries that it considered to be less than equal or even subordinate.

In an illustration of strategic confusion, the notion that Russia's anti-Westernism is primarily intended for internal consumption is highly misleading. Anti-Westernism and anti-Americanism certainly help to mobilize the public and discredit opposition to the regime, but they also have direct external consequences. Anti-American propaganda offensives justify Moscow's foreign policy assertiveness as the defense of Russia's state interests. They also contribute to solidifying alliances with anti-Western governments who feel threatened by democracy promotion or other forms of "Western penetration." Conversely, the terms "anti-Russian" and "Russophobe" are increasingly attributed to critics of Putinism, thus deliberately conflating regime with nation. It is reminiscent of the "anti-socialist" and "anti-Soviet" labels once affixed to domestic dissidents and foreign critics of Communist Party rule.

The second difference with the Cold War era is that Russia is operationally stealthier than the Soviet regime was prior to its collapse. Without declaring any ideologically motivated global mission and by claiming that it is pursuing pragmatic national interests, the Kremlin engages in asymmetrical offensives by interjecting itself in its neighbor's affairs, capturing important sectors of local economies, subverting vulnerable political systems, corrupting or discrediting national leaders, and systematically undermining Western unity.

Moscow's stealth tactics have persuaded some analysts to believe that Moscow's geoeconomic goals prevail over geostrategic imperial objectives and that power holders in the Kremlin are focused on profit rather than politics. The contention that private and corporate interests motivate Moscow's policy decisions is highly contentious.[30] This Russia Inc. argument does not answer important questions about Kremlin policy: in particular, how are the private interests of state officials separated from state interests? Russia has traditionally been governed by arbitrary rulers who controlled the economy and whose private interests overlapped with their ideological predispositions and imperial ambitions. Moreover, the expansion of Russia's power and influence actually serves the private interests of Kremlin leaders; getting rich and making Russia strong are now largely synonymous. Centralized control over growing energy revenues has enabled the Kremlin to accelerate the pursuit of both objectives.

The third contrast with the Cold War is evident in the deployment of novel tools for subversion, disinformation, and domination. In particular, Moscow's growing monopolization of energy supplies from within Russia and the Caspian Basin to Europe buttresses its power projection for as long as the price of hydrocarbons remains high on world markets. Europe's dependence on external energy supplies and Russia's accumulative purchases of energy infrastructure and other assets in targeted states reinforce the latter's political influence.

U.S. policy during the George W. Bush administration has also provided a bonanza for the Kremlin. The surge in anti-Americanism, stimulated largely by the Iraq War, which caused much of the European public to view the United States as a greater menace to peace and stability than Russia, has been welcomed in Moscow. Kremlin leaders deliberately exacerbate such fears by depicting Washington as a unilateralist aggressor imposing itself in all corners of the globe.

To deflect criticisms of its expansionism, Moscow claims that U.S. policymakers are driven by a Cold War mentality. It berates the "victory in the Cold War syndrome" and accuses Washington of preserving "dividing lines" in world politics by co-opting new members in the "sphere of Western influence."[31] Putin himself attacked senior American strategists for purportedly seeking to militarily disarm and territorially divide Russia.[32] Kremlin officials condemn several political leaders in the West as "cold warriors" and regularly recycle Cold War stereotypes about American imperialism.[33] The objective is to increase criticisms of Washington in EU capitals, divert attention from Moscow's policies, and raise Russia's stature as a vital counterpart to the United States and NATO. This allows the Kremlin a freer hand to implement its agenda under the cover of pragmatism, commercialism, and the defense of national interests. According to Harvey Sicherman, "The Russian Prime Minister and his circle do not regard the post–Cold War settlement in Europe as legitimate. They mean to contain and then roll back Western influence, preferably through diplomatic and economic pressure and, failing that, if possible, by the threat or use of military force. Putin's demand for greater respect of Russian interests has become the Cold War by other means—and sometimes by the same means."[34]

Moscow's Western Agenda

As Putin's Russia restores its great power status and rebuilds its zones of influence, it can seriously undermine Western interests. Moscow possesses a broad arsenal of tools to use in pursuit of its ambitious agenda to undermine Western unity, obstruct democratic development along its borders, and curtail the further enlargement of the NATO-EU sphere. Putinism has reanimated Russia as a muscular state that is increasingly recognized as an important global player. It has developed an assertive foreign policy with several key targets: to rein in wayward neighbors within its ambit, to neutralize the EU as an Atlanticist pole of influence, to establish strategic global alliances to project Russian power, and to undermine the U.S.-dominated unipolar system.

The reintegration of the "post-Soviet space" became a priority under Putinism, which elevated Russia's assertiveness as the key stabilizing factor in Eurasia. Moscow opposes any significant foreign military presence in the region and seeks to dissuade its neighbors in the Russian-dominated Commonwealth of Independent States (CIS) from inviting U.S. forces or petitioning for NATO entry. It also aims to forestall the formation of rival regional alliances that may obstruct its expansionist goals or strengthen Western policies.

A primary tool of influence is economic penetration, which is evident in strategic infrastructural purchases and targeted investments that enhance Russia's influence over a specific country's financial, trade, and investment policies. Russia also pursues a monopolistic energy position and aims to convert fossil-fuel dependence into long-term strategic influence in the wider Europe. Russian companies enable the Kremlin to engage in a policy of state capture abroad by increasing its political influence with government officials, business leaders, and political parties in a wide array of European countries.

To limit the scope of Western institutional enlargement, especially in the security arena in the CIS, Moscow obstructs the creation of alliances such as GUAM (Georgia, Ukraine, Azerbaijan, Moldova) that could block Russian inroads and deepen the region's ties with NATO. Russian officials oppose the process of security integration with NATO and focus on military integration in Moscow-dominated collective security mechanisms. Putin understood that Russia was too weak to prevent NATO's incorporation of the majority of former Soviet satellites. Instead, the Kremlin attempts to minimize the impact of NATO's growth by seeking a role in alliance decision making and by weakening its effectiveness. At the same time, it actively campaigns against NATO entry for all former Soviet republics, including Ukraine and Georgia.

Putinist strategists concentrate on several European subregions as springboards for rebuilding a larger zone of influence in the broadly defined Eurasia. The Eurasian label has been debated ad nauseam by analysts primarily concerned with whether the Putin administration adopted a Eurasian identity.[35] Such a focus displays a failure to understand Putinism as an eclectic and goal-oriented assemblage of precepts and philosophies that blends communist and czarist, nationalist and internationalist symbols together with disparate events and personalities from Russian history to demonstrate and develop Moscow's enduring dominance. Russia's neo-imperialist ideology (or system of precepts and justifications) involves a patriotic synthesis of all previous Muscovite empires, including the Soviet Union, and depicts Putinism as a means for restoring the greatness and glory of the Russian state.

Russian elites also employ Eurasianism to distinguish the allegedly unique Russian civilization from the more narrow European experience. "Eurasia" is not synonymous with either "Europe" or "Asia" but allegedly presents a unique synthesis that surpasses both. In this grand context, Putinism has never envisaged integration with the West and its various institutions as more than an opportunistic tactic to gain strategic advantage in creating a pole of power distinct from the Euro-Atlantic variant. In this sense Eurasianism is a counterpart to Euro-Atlanticism and is evident in the centuries-long struggle between Russia and the West in which communism was only one episode.[36]

In Russia's Western strategic horizon, perceptions of the European Union have undergone three main stages, with some overlap. In the early 1990s the EU was viewed as a relatively harmless organization, limited to Western Europe (WE), focused on economic cooperation and trade, and lacking a foreign policy and security dimension. By the mid- to late 1990s, the EU was increasingly perceived as a useful counterpart to NATO and U.S. influence as it assumed a growing number of "soft security" functions amid intensive internal debates about the rationale for NATO's existence.

During the Putin presidency, the EU has been perceived as encroaching on Russia's interests. By the mid-2000s the Union included most of the CEE states and became a magnet of attraction for Russia's "near abroad" that could pull a number of countries permanently out of Moscow's orbit. Several new EU members became increasingly outspoken about Russia and challenged an accommodating Union approach toward Moscow's democratic regression and external reimperialization. The EU's democratization agenda was also seen in the Kremlin as challenging Russia's policy of maintaining pliable governments in neighboring post-Soviet states. Additionally, EU standards for government accountability, business transparency, market competition, and environmental protection could increasingly endanger Russia's economic penetration, which was primarily based on opaque business practices and hidden personal or political connections.

The EU has come to occupy a pivotal position in Russia's strategic equations, as the Union can either strengthen or weaken the U.S. role in pan-European politics. A unified EU foreign policy synchronized with Washington that undercuts Russia's aspirations is viewed in Moscow as a source of threat that needs to be neutralized. Conversely, EU institutions or specific Union members can also assist Russia in developing a multipolar world and eroding U.S. influence. In this strategy, Russia-EU cooperation, whether at the institutional level or through bilateral ties with individual capitals, has evolved into a means for limiting NATO-centrism and U.S. leadership in Europe.[37]

Divided Western Responses

While Russia calculates in terms of zero-sum struggles, some Western states-men have operated according to "zero-threat" assumptions. A number of NATO and EU members, particularly France, Germany, and Italy, are apprehensive about provoking disruptive conflicts with Moscow and have been willing to overlook negative trends in Russia's domestic politics and foreign policies. Such an approach is ultimately counterproductive to European interests, as EU weakness and disunity encourage the Kremlin to be even more assertive in pursuit of its goals and selective in terms of its European partners. Russia preys on and encourages European divisiveness as this limits EU and NATO involvement in the "post-Soviet space" and undermines any pursuit of democratic standards in Russia itself. In the words of one American analyst, Russia assumes that it cannot have full security unless Europe is insecure.[38]

Policymakers in several EU countries repeat the formula that common interests between the EU and Russia will prevail and ensure interdependence as Russia allegedly seeks to be a part of Europe.[39] They undervalue the distinction between tactics and strategies, fail to question what policy objectives are disguised behind Russia's commercial interests, and assume that Moscow is intent on evolving into a mainstream European country. Underlying such an approach is a benign view of Putinism and denials that Moscow possesses any grand strategy in its foreign policy. These assumptions are challenged by the CEE capitals that have a longer and more direct experience of an assertive Kremlin.[40]

There is a fundamental difference between the EU and Russia in their political and international development as well as in their perceptions of mutual relations. The EU project is designed to reduce the role of individual states, surrender elements of state sovereignty, and increase multinational governance. In stark contrast, Putinist Russia is intent on rebuilding a strong state that is not bound by common international norms and thwarts the influence of organizations that restrict Moscow's room for maneuver. While the Russian leadership operates in terms of spheres of influence and zero-sum calculations, EU policymakers believe in mutual interests, shared sovereignty, and win-win solutions.[41]

Russia has become one of the most divisive issues in formulating or implementing a successful EU foreign policy. Union institutions have operated on the supposition that Russia can be entangled with the EU and constructively reformed through several layers of committees and procedures. In reality, because the EU is not a centralized organization, it lacks an all-encompassing policy toward Russia even though formal mechanisms exist to regulate relations with the stated objective of building a strategic partnership.[42] The key EU-generated document has been the Partnership and Cooperation Agreement (PCA), signed by the EU and Russia in April 1994 and validated in December 1997 for a ten-year period, with automatic annual renewals unless either party formally withdraws from the accord.

The PCA format has included EU-Russia summits, involving heads of state congregating twice a year to define the direction of bilateral relations; the Permanent Partnership Council (PPC) established in May 2003, enabling ministers to meet as often as necessary to discuss specific questions; the Parliamentary Cooperative Committee (PCC), involving a representative of the European Parliament and the deputy chairman of the Russian Duma; and senior experts-level meetings.

Russian officials have also called for the creation of an EU-Russia Council, similar to the NATO-Russia Council, with the intent of conducting joint military exercises and operations. The latter proposal has been resisted most vehemently by new EU members from CEE who argue that such an arrangement would encourage Moscow to press for more influence within the Union. Security dialogue between Russia and the EU remains weak: there is deep mistrust of military cooperation with the Union within the Russian military establishment as well as a sense that the EU military is less relevant as compared to NATO and the United States. Nonetheless, Moscow seeks assurances that the EU will specify the geographical scope of its European security and defense policy (ESDP) and not act without a UNSC mandate.

All the EU-Russia formats were instituted before the EU expanded to include new members from CEE in May 2004. The PCA was not renewed at the November 2006 summit in Helsinki because of the opposition of states that have a more distrustful view of Russian policy and made renewal contingent on Moscow's ratification of the 1994 Energy Charter Treaty. Poland exercised its veto against renewing the accord in November 2006 in reaction to Moscow's ban on importing Polish meat products. Warsaw also wanted all twenty-seven EU members to form a united front on the question of energy security and oppose Moscow's unfounded import bans.[43] The trade issue was resolved by early 2008, and the Polish cabinet dropped its objections to relaunching negotiations of a new PCA in time for the EU-Russia summit in Khanty Mansiisk, Siberia, in June 2008.

Lithuania insisted that any accord with Moscow include assurances about Russian oil supplies, which continued to be interrupted as a form of political pressure against Vilnius. In May 2008 EU foreign ministers approved a mandate for restarting talks with Russia on a new agreement after Lithuania dropped its objections. Discussions on a new partnership were formally launched at the summit but were expected to take several months. Moscow did not press for a comprehensive PCA that would link its access to the EU market with internal democratization and human rights. Instead, it preferred a more general framework agreement that could be loosely interpreted and give Moscow greater maneuverability.

Several concrete areas of cooperation, or four "common spaces," were approved at the EU-Russia summit in May 2005: economic transactions, justice and home affairs, education and culture, and external security. However, the EU's common strategy toward Russia, adopted in June 1999, was grounded in generalized principles that Moscow abandoned. The PCA itself asserted a joint commitment to "shared principles and objectives," including "support for democratic norms and political and economic freedoms." Indeed, the three guiding principles of EU cooperation have each proved glaringly unsuccessful: the promotion of Russia's transformation to a market democracy, the accomplishment of extensive political reforms, and Moscow's adherence to common values and Western norms.[44]

Some analysts conclude that the EU's special relationship with Russia involves "shallow collaboration, symbolic summitry, and costly standoffs."[45] EU leaders believe that such arrangements are preferable to an absence of agreements or full-blown confrontations as they provide formats for dialogue. There is also an underlying assumption that dialogue combined with economic cooperation will transform Russia into a state adhering to European standards of governance and business. However, there is no concrete conditionality involved. Hence, the official Russian document outlining the "Medium-Term Strategy for the Development of Relations between the Russian Federation and the EU (2000–2010)" envisages no direct linkage between the strategic partnership and democratic reform in Russia.

Wide divergences in Russia policy and bilateral relations have been evident within both NATO and the EU and most visible between Western European accommodationists, or pragmatists, and CEE realists. The differing approaches are not simply rooted in Cold War experiences and former East-West divisions, but increasingly they cut across all sides of the European continent. Mark Leonard and Nicu Popescu outline a fivefold categorization of EU member policies toward Russia: "Trojan Horses" (Greece, Cyprus), "Strategic Partners" (France, Germany, Italy, Spain), "Friendly Pragmatists" (Austria, Belgium, Bulgaria, Finland, Hungary, Luxembourg, Malta, Portugal, Slovakia, Slovenia), "Frosty Pragmatists" (Czech Republic, Denmark, Estonia, Ireland, Latvia, Holland, Romania, Sweden, United Kingdom), and "New Cold Warriors" (Poland, Lithuania).[46]

Such a classification is helpful as it highlights the differences in country-specific approaches. However, the schema must also allow for alterations in policy following changes of government or when an unexpected dispute with Moscow materializes. The authors conclude that in essence there are two main policy directions: the partnership paradigm, which asserts that Russia can be gradually integrated into the EU orbit, and the threat paradigm, which views Russia as a challenge to EU integrity, enlargement, and identity. Hence, the Trojan horses, strategic partners, and friendly pragmatists generally oppose any EU policies that irritate Moscow and seek to benefit commercially from Russia's economic growth. In contrast, the frosty pragmatists and new cold warriors are more openly critical of Russia's policies and seek a more assertive EU approach to counter negative Russian influences.

Some WE capitals resist the assertiveness of several states in CEE. For Berlin, Paris, and Rome, commercial pragmatism tends to trump any geostrategic calculations, thus reducing the effectiveness of the EU's long-term political impact. Their priorities include guaranteed energy provisions and a growing Russian market for EU exports. In the view of accommodationists, political stability through strong central control helps ensure these objectives regardless of the condition of Russia's democracy or its relations with immediate neighbors.

The EU is Russia's most important business partner, accounting for more than half of Russia's external trade and the majority of its foreign investment. Several EU members operate on the premise that closer economic cooperation will bind Russia closer to the Union through the adoption of European legal and democratic standards. In reality, Russia stringently opposes any significant EU involvement in either domestic Russian affairs or neighboring post-Soviet states, other than basic assistance programs such as Technical Assistance for the Commonwealth of Independent States (TACIS).

Moscow rejects any significant EU role in resolving the frozen conflicts between governments and separatist entities in Moldova and Georgia, fearful that this will impair its dominant influence. It also resists any moves by the EU or its member states to forge institutional links with regional organizations that exclude Russia, such as GUAM or the Community of Democratic Choice (CDC), initiated by Ukraine and Georgia. The EU has not dispatched officials to GUAM or CDC summits to avoid antagonizing Russia. However, several EU members from CEE have been enlisted as so-called partner countries in the GUAM-plus framework.

Russian-EU economic relations remain under question as Moscow pursues closer economic bonds in the CIS as a counterweight to the EU through the Eurasian Economic Community (EEC) and the Single Economic Space (SES). For Moscow, it is more important strategically that the CIS countries do not integrate into Western structures, including the EU, irrespective of whether they comprehensively assimilate with Russia. Moscow views the EU as a valuable market and a source of trade and investment to build up the Russian economy and elevate the country's global stature.[47] However, it applies protectionist measures against foreign capital, especially by insulating its strategic industries and assets from alien investors.

The EU has sought to expand its European Economic Area (EEA) and the Common European Economic Space (CEES) to eliminate trade barriers with Russia. The CEES was to function on the basis of the *acquis communautaire*, the entire body of European laws. Russian leaders have rejected the adoption of the *acquis*, which would surrender elements of Russia's sovereignty, while EU leaders are not willing to change CEES standards to accommodate Moscow.[48] While the EU seeks "convergence," Moscow prefers "approximation" so that it does not have to abide by the Union's legal norms and business standards.[49]

The expansion of the EU's Schengen zone has placed new restrictions on travel to the Union by Russian citizens.[50] Moscow canvassed for visa-free travel between Russia and the EU following the extension of the Schengen zone to the Baltic states. In a telling example of persistent EU divisions over Russia policy, France, Germany, and Italy signed separate bilateral visa facilitation agreements with Moscow that breached Schengen stipulations and were subsequently suspended by the European Commission. However, Russia benefited from the controversy as the EU then negotiated a visa facilitation deal with Russia ahead of several other states.[51]

Following the elections of German chancellor Angela Merkel and French president Nicolas Sarkozy in 2007, the one-dimensional Russia-first policy altered somewhat as the new leaders seemed more attuned to Moscow's disruptive policies and cognizant of its external objectives. Nevertheless, accommodationist political and business interests within their respective countries restrained both of the new governments. Several CEE capitals complain that the EU has failed to condemn persistent Russian pressures against the three Baltic members of the

Union (Estonia, Latvia, and Lithuania). This has been evident in frequent military overflight violations, periodic energy embargoes, Moscow's refusal to sign bilateral treaties with Tallinn and Riga, and direct interference in Estonian politics in reaction to the removal of a military statue in Tallinn honoring the period of Soviet occupation.

Important security developments revolving around such questions as energy supplies, the status of Kosova, and the missile defense shield indicate how an emboldened Russia is intent on disrupting the European agenda. Moscow is seeking to marginalize its former European satellites and weaken any concerted EU or NATO policy that conflicts with Russia's expansionist national interests. As Jonathan Eyal points out, "Europe is being targeted by a Russian policy that seeks to undermine the very foundations of stability in Central Europe."[52]

The Kremlin engages in a divide and rule policy outside any institutional framework by harnessing bilateral links with several larger EU states to gain advantages in trade, energy, investment, diplomacy, and security. It also uses links with individual EU presidencies to further its own agenda and disrupt continuity and consensus in Union policy. Moscow realizes that the absence of EU policy coherence is beneficial for its interests. As a result, the Kremlin is not necessarily opposed to delays in forging a new EU-Russia PCA agreement as this provides it with a freer hand to exploit bilateral connections with EU capitals.

Russia pursues a bilateral relationship with the EU as a whole and does not aspire to membership. Although they assert Russia's European identity, Kremlin officials are unwilling to surrender any significant elements of sovereignty to EU institutions or allow Russia's diverse regions any significant freedom in foreign economic activity.[53] Unsurprisingly, Moscow has also been opposed to Russia's inclusion in the EU's European Neighborhood Policy (ENP), designed to bring the post-Soviet European states closer to the EU.[54]

The Kremlin maneuvers for a strategic partnership with the EU in order to enhance its foreign policy interests, restrict international criticisms of its policies, and promote divisions in the Western alliance, while building its own regional security structure through the Collective Security Treaty Organization (CSTO). For Moscow, the ideal partnership with the Union would entail no EU interference or criticism of Russia's internal political developments or its foreign policy objectives. Russian officials complain that the EU itself is too complex and cumbersome to deal with on a predictable basis, especially as the Union cannot reach consensus on urgent foreign policy problems. They therefore seek a twenty-seven-plus-one format in negotiations. Critics argue that this would allow Russia to exploit divisions between EU members and between the European Commission and individual states.[55]

Questions have arisen about the impact that the implementation of the Treaty of Lisbon will have on EU-Russia relations. The treaty was due to come into effect in January 2009 following parliamentary ratification by all twenty-seven member states. However, it was brought into jeopardy in June 2008, when voters in the Irish Republic rejected it in a referendum and scuttled plans for its implementation. Under the treaty's provisions a new EU high representative (EUHR) for foreign affairs and security policy would be created to combine the roles of the current EUHR for common foreign and security policy, the president of the council, and the EU commissioner for external relations. The new EUHR would also be endowed with an external action service (EAS) to manage policy.[56] These institutional innovations were expected to provide more coherence in the Union's external policy.

If some variant of the Lisbon treaty is eventually adopted, the EU approach toward Russia may become more uniform. For instance, the head of the EU delegation in Moscow would report directly to the EUHR, one EU official would be mandated to deal with Russia, and there would be more centralized control over funds allocated to Russian programs. Nonetheless, it remains doubtful whether a unified EU position, or one that is in sync with U.S. and NATO policy, can be maintained. Revealingly, Russian officials affirmed that internal Union developments stemming from the Lisbon treaty will not diminish the significance of Moscow's bilateral ties with individual Western capitals.[57]

Confronting the United States

In Moscow's divisive vision of the world, Russia and the United States tradition-ally possess clearly delineated spheres of influence upon which neither should encroach. However, since the USSR's collapse in the early 1990s Washington has allegedly impinged increasingly on the Russian zone in the Eurasian region by pressuring former Soviet satellites to join NATO and forge close security ties with the United States.

According to Russian officials, Washington has engaged in a policy of en-circlement by steadily constructing an anti-Russian axis within Moscow's sphere of special interests or privileged influence among former satellites. This has avowedly involved not only the former Warsaw Pact countries of CEE but also the inner core of traditional Russian dominance in the former Soviet Union, including Ukraine, Georgia, Moldova, and Azerbaijan, as well as the Central Asian states. Washington's purported objective is to capture these countries in its security sphere and effectively isolate and marginalize Russia.[1]

Russian officials also say that Moscow withdrew its military forces from CEE and dismantled its bases in countries such as Cuba and Vietnam, expecting the United States to reciprocate by respecting Russia's primary influence in the ex-Soviet Union. However, for much of the postcommunist era, Russia was too weak to challenge American advances in these territories. With the rebuilding of Russia's capabilities during the past decade and its renewed confidence as a global actor, the Putinist Kremlin is not only challenging America's influence among the former Soviet republics, it is also using its power to undermine alleged American hegemony throughout the wider Europe and in other key regions.

Selective Confrontation

Moscow estimates that the global "correlation of forces" is steadily shifting in Russia's favor in its long-range strategy to establish a "post-American world order."[2] It envisages reducing America's global influence and containing or rolling back U.S. alliances. Cognizant of its limitations while exploiting the weaknesses of its major adversary, Moscow has approached Washington with a combination of selective cooperation and selective confrontation. Russia's elites view the United States as a power in precipitous decline. They perceive the American hegemon as losing ground in the globalization process, with its economy weakening, as evident in the financial crisis and economic recession of 2008–2009; its capability to project military power shrinking; and its authority and reputation seriously diminished. This provides Russia with opportunities to actively reduce America's global role and raise itself as a major player on the world stage.

In July 2008 President Dmitry Medvedev unveiled a revised foreign policy concept that is more assertive and anti-American than Putin's previous document issued in June 2000. It underscores that the main "positive tendency in the international situation" is the strengthening of the Russian Federation. It accuses the West of attempting to "restrain" Russia and calls on Russian diplomats to more effectively block the spread of U.S. influence.[3]

Moscow promotes itself as a benign and constructive power by interjecting in regional disputes, such as the North Korean and Iranian nuclear programs, as a problem solver. It is not always clear, however, whether the Kremlin is actively contributing to resolve a crisis or maintaining a simmering conflict to preoccupy Washington, divide the alliance, and buttress Russia's mediating role. Conflict prolongation appears to be the impetus for several lingering disputes, including the controversy over Iran's nuclear program.

In its more confrontational mode, the Kremlin vehemently opposes U.S. policy by portraying itself as a protector of international legalism, state integrity, national sovereignty, and the UN decision-making structure. This is evident in the dispute over the independence of Kosova staunchly favored by Washington and the majority of EU capitals. Russian foreign affairs minister Sergei Lavrov engages in regular propaganda assaults on U.S. policy, whether on questions of NATO enlargement, missile defense, or Washington's strategy toward the former Soviet republics.[4]

Moscow's attacks on the U.S. leadership escalated after an important speech by Vice President Dick Cheney in Vilnius, Lithuania, in May 2006, in which he underscored the democratic regression in Russia and Moscow's use of energy resources to intimidate and blackmail its neighbors. Cheney's candid and realistic speech gave the Kremlin an opportunity and pretext to claim that Washington was stoking a new cold war.[5]

Lavrov and other members of the Russian government as well as senior members of parliament have also accused the United States of creating divisions in Europe, ideologizing foreign policy, sabotaging various arms treaties, and disregarding international law. However, Moscow's unilateral recognition of the independence of Abkhazia and South Ossetia at the end of August 2008, following its military invasion of Georgia, without any attempt to work through the UN or any multinational institution, demonstrated that Russia itself no longer feels bound by international law.

Another major charge by Russian officials is that Washington is seeking to destabilize and fracture Russia itself. Following its own de facto partition of Georgia in August 2008, Moscow reanimated these accusations. Vasiliy Likhachyov, deputy chairman of the Federation Council's Committee on International Affairs, accused U.S. neoconservatives, allegedly led by Vice President Cheney, of devising a plan to encourage separatism in several Russian republics. According to Likhachev, "the next anti-Russian project can be linked with provoking conflicts between Orthodoxy and Islam" and political fractures between the central federal authorities and the regions.

> They no longer want to restrict themselves to foreign and international pressure. The incumbent and future administrations propose to pay very close attention to the Russian regions, in order to include them in the field of influence and in the field of action of the American ideological and military machine. A political project of this sort is nothing other than intervention in the internal affairs of the Russian Federation. It is a display of total disrespect for Russia's sovereignty and territorial wholeness.[6]

Although Moscow regularly charges Washington with an assortment of aggressive and destructive policies, it does not seek a full-scale confrontation but rather engages in a policy of managed instability. This could prove increasingly costly to an overstretched U.S. government in cases where Russia is able to either enlist selected EU states or encourage authoritarian and anti-American capitals to openly oppose Washington's foreign policy.[7] Moscow calculates that Washington's weakened financial and economic standing combined with its expensive and potentially unsuccessful policy in Iraq and Afghanistan will augment Russia's power projections. The Kremlin cultivates this parallel or even symbiotic process of American decline and Russian resurgence, in which Europe features as a major contested region.[8]

In Russia's overarching strategy to restore its global stature in line with its supreme national interest, Europe will either become neutralized and no longer complement U.S. strategy or it will actively promote Russia's priorities. Because it is less likely that EU institutions will work at the behest of Moscow against American interests, the Kremlin focuses on dividing Europe, promoting bilateralism, and using its economic resources to corrupt and entangle Western statesmen and business leaders who once worked to dismantle the Soviet Union but who can now help Russia to dismantle the West.

Unlike during the bipolar Cold War, Russia's current challenge to American interests does not envisage a constantly conflictive relationship in every sphere. Indeed, Moscow has been willing to enter into selective engagements and cooperative relations with Washington in order to achieve two major strategic targets. First, by acting as a partner in various crisis points, whether with regard to Iran's or North Korea's nuclear program or in countering Islamic terrorism, Russia aims to raise its stature as an indispensable global leader. For instance, on April 6, 2008, Presidents Bush and Putin agreed in Sochi to codify a U.S.-Russian strategic framework declaration. It covered cooperation on nonproliferation, missile limitations, energy, Iran and North Korea, global terrorism, and climate change.

Second, by offering cooperation to evidently resolve problems that are priorities for the United States and its allies, Moscow aims to gain advantages in other security arenas, especially in consolidating its dominance in regions close to Russia's borders. This approach was illustrated during Russia's short war with Georgia in August 2008. The Kremlin calculated that its military intervention would not be openly opposed by the West because Russia was too important a player in world affairs to resolve pressing global problems from climate change to nuclear proliferation.

The Kosova Pretext

The international dispute over Kosova's final status after NATO's 1999 military intervention in ex-Yugoslavia became a landmark occasion for the Kremlin for two major reasons. First, it enabled Russian leaders to claim that the United States was a hegemonistic and imperialist power intent on unilaterally expanding its influence at the expense of the security of European states. And second, it allowed Moscow to use the Kosova example as a pretext and alleged precedent to pursue its expansionist agenda among neighboring countries seeking closer links with Western institutions. In many respects, Kosova became a win-win dispute for Moscow. If it could block Kosova's independence, then Russia could effectively pose as a key defender of the international legal order. If it could not block de facto independence, Russia would be able to expose America's aggressive intentions while gaining international support as the leader of an alternative strategic pole.

Several strategic calculations motivated Russia's delaying tactics in UN Security Council decisions over the final status of Kosova. The Putin regime was determined to raise Russia's stature as a major international player in competition with the United States, to promote foreign policy fractures within the EU, to drive wedges between Europe and America, and to enhance Moscow's strategic position in the Balkans.

According to Russian interpretations, the dismemberment of Yugoslavia since the early 1990s and the truncation of Serbia were Western plots led by Washington to undermine Russia's influence in the Balkans. The independence of Kosova allegedly formed part of Washington's broader policy agenda to dominate Europe. Its other components included NATO enlargement in the "post-Soviet space," the arming of the three Baltic states, the building of military bases in Romania and Bulgaria, and the positioning of components of the missile defense shield in Poland and the Czech Republic.[9]

The George W. Bush administration failed to gain unanimous UNSC agreement on a plan for Kosova's supervised independence devised by the former Finnish president Martti Ahtisaari. Instead, it decided to press ahead with recognizing Kosova's statehood in February 2008 without a new UNSC resolution. Washington had concluded that seeking UNSC approval for any action meant being dependent on the agreement of Russia and China, two countries that "far from being the necessary source of international law, are the collective voice of a majority of countries who are neither democratic nor restrained by any law."[10] As a result, Kosova evolved into a valuable weapon for Moscow to boost its regional and global ambitions. By vetoing Kosova's independence in the UNSC, Russia sought to raise its international stature in several ways.

First, Moscow proclaimed that it was the vanguard defender of international legality owing to its insistence on working through the United Nations. Of course, Russia would not allow for UNSC interference in its own "strategic space" by approving a long-term UN mission in either Moldova or Georgia. Moreover, Russia itself has regularly violated the UN Charter, as in its repressive campaign in Chechnya, and stations troops in states without government approval, as in Moldova and Georgia.

Second, Russia posed as the key promoter of multilateralism, allowing the UN process to serve its interests and undercut those of the United States. Multilateral institutions such as the UN are not only slow and cumbersome in making decisions but also operate according to the lowest common denominator whereby the resistance of one capital can deny the interests of the majority.

Third, Moscow postured as a staunch protector of state sovereignty and national integrity by opposing the breakup of a UN member state, Serbia, irrespective of the genocidal policies pursued by Belgrade that led initially to NATO involvement and Kosova's separation. Russia thereby appealed to several UN members who feared separatism. At the same time, Moscow depicted the United States as an international maverick interfering in the internal affairs and state structures of allegedly vulnerable countries.

Fourth, and most significantly, Kosova formed part of a wider strategic agenda that allowed Russia to elevate its international position, to interpose in

Balkan and European affairs, to encourage splits within the EU and NATO, to aggravate weaknesses in Western decision making, and to gain veto powers over Europe's enlargement. All these objectives assist in the construction of a Eurasian pole of power as a counterbalance to Atlanticism.

Although Kosova's statehood generated some tensions in the region, the stabilization of the western Balkans was manageable as NATO, the EU, and the United States continued to work in tandem to prevent Belgrade and Moscow from exploiting ethnic divisions. Containing Russian reactions outside of the Balkans proved more problematic. In the wake of Kosova's independence, Russia pursued its imperial interests more vigorously in several neighboring regions and intensified its anti-American alliances. Moscow signaled that it would fortify its economic and political ties with Iran, seek a closer relationship with China to counter American expansionism, develop the CSTO as a competitor with NATO in Central Asia and the Caucasus, and increase pressure on all former Soviet colonies that sought inclusion in Western institutions.

In the wake of Kosova's independence, Russian authorities focused on the alleged "Kosova precedent" to undermine neighboring governments. Pressure was applied against Georgia, Ukraine, and Moldova by raising the specter of recognizing contested regions if the three capitals failed to comply with Moscow's demands. In July 2007 the Duma Foreign Affairs Committee chairman, Konstantin Kosachyov, asserted that Kosova's independence "will give Russia the right to do the same in other conflict zones and even recognize the independence of breakaway territories."[11] In reality, the multinational NATO intervention in Kosova in 1999 and the recognition of Kosova's independence by most NATO allies during 2008 did not establish any specific precedent. Russia set its own precedent by acting unilaterally in the early 1990s in sponsoring separatist movements in Georgia, Moldova, and Azerbaijan and conducting a creeping annexation of Georgian territory.

With several unsettled security questions in the Balkans, the region remains useful for Moscow in disrupting democratic expansion in the wider Europe. The Kremlin does not pursue a permanent solution for Kosova but prefers a frozen conflict or a partially recognized frozen state in the Balkans. Russia's officials also seek greater influence in Bosnia-Herzegovina through their diplomatic and business contacts with the Serbian entity. Although Bosnia has made substantial progress in its reform program under the Dayton Accords and the guidance of the Office of the High Representative (OHR), its path toward the EU has been blocked by the ambitions of nationalist politicians who threaten the country with partition. Milorad Dodik, the prime minister of Bosnia's Serb Republic, considers secession a viable option and may have been bolstered by the separation of Abkhazia and South Ossetia with Moscow's support. The fracturing of Bosnia could increase

Russia's influence in the Balkans as Russia would seek to defend the new quasi-state from Western pressure and consolidate its alliance with Serbia.

In this context, Serbia is manipulated by Russia as a valuable bridgehead within southeastern Europe to further its economic and political designs. For Moscow, Serbia has evolved into a strategic experiment in the heart of the Balkans to challenge Western encroachment and increase Russia's leverage in the region. Leaders of the largest Serbian party, the Radicals, although not in government, have called for the building of Russian military bases to strengthen Belgrade's international position.[12] While Moscow formally declined such offers, it has not excluded the possibility altogether, alongside other forms of Russian military assistance. Meanwhile, Serbia's coalition government, similarly to its Yugoslav predecessor, has flirted with Moscow in a policy designed to gain advantage by balancing Europe with Russia. The Kremlin also exploits the Kosova issue to portray NATO as incompetent and an ineffective generator of security. Russia's officials allege that the alliance engages in double standards regarding terrorism. While it expects Moscow to cooperate in combating anti-Western terrorists, these officials allege, the EU and NATO simultaneously support the "Albanian terrorists" in Kosova, and some Western capitals provide shelter to "Chechen terrorist emissaries" who have purportedly murdered innocent Russian civilians.[13]

Any Western indecisiveness over Kosova also enhances Moscow's efforts to fracture the EU. In May 2008 the EU announced that its rule of law mission (EULEX) would not be fully deployed to Kosova in June 2008 as initially anticipated. Observers suggested that disagreements between the EU and Russia over the mission's role and wrangling between the EU and UN as to which organization would have ultimate jurisdiction during Kosova's transition led to the delay.[14] Moscow wanted EULEX to operate under the joint auspices of the EU and UN and placed pressure on UN Secretary General Ban Ki-moon to be more reserved concerning the transfer of authority, as he needed Moscow's support to gain a second term in office.[15] Ban Ki-moon unveiled plans in mid-June 2008 to transfer several responsibilities of the United Nations Interim Administration Mission in Kosova (UNMIK) to EULEX, including the police sector, although the decision was delayed by several months.[16]

With the Kremlin's impetus, in May 2008 the foreign ministers of Russia, China, and India called for new talks between Belgrade and Prishtina "within the framework of international laws." Foreign Minister Lavrov informed the Duma in April 2008 that the government had done all it could to disrupt plans for a broad international recognition of Kosova and prevented the UN secretary general from consecrating the EU mission. On October 8, 2008, the UN General Assembly voted to accept Serbia's proposal to seek an advisory opinion on Kosova's independence from the International Court of Justice. Although this would not reverse Kosova's statehood, it could further paralyze Prishtina in its efforts to gain membership of several international institutions.

A decision by NATO defense ministers on June 12, 2008, cleared the way for the NATO Kosova Force (KFOR) to begin training a new security organization, the Kosova Security Force (KSF), after Kosova's new constitution was enacted on June 15, 2008. However, in signs of continuing divisions, Spain, Romania, and Slovakia, which did not recognize Kosova's independence, were not prepared to participate in NATO's program, while Turkey blocked KFOR's operational plan on cooperation with EULEX, as that could mean sharing sensitive military information with Cyprus, a member of the EU but not of NATO.[17]

The gradual integration of Kosova, together with all of its neighbors, into the EU and NATO provides the most effective strategy for long-term regional stability. The prospect of inclusion for all democratic states in the Balkan and Black Sea regions, including Ukraine and Georgia, sends two strong signals to Moscow. First, the United States and its European allies are determined to rebuild the transatlantic alliance as a unified global force that can project security to all nearby regions. And second, the value of common interests and the interests stemming from common values are more effective than Russia's attempts to subvert Europe's political leadership and divide the Western alliance.

Indecision and confusion by international players could paralyze Kosova, but instead of a frozen conflict the West's cautious policies may lead to the emergence of a novel phenomenon—a frozen state that could become the fulcrum of renewed regional insecurities. Both Belgrade and Moscow believe that Kosova's international recognition peaked during 2008 (with about fifty countries recognizing the new state), and they can stem any progress toward Prishtina's membership in international institutions. Kosova will then be suspended in an international limbo and will make minimal diplomatic or economic progress. This could lead to acts of violence or even ungovernability that could precipitate territorial partition.

If Kosova's political stability is undermined by the EU's failure to assert its role as the key body supervising Kosova's statehood, political and public frustration could mushroom, especially as neither UNMIK nor the EU have forestalled the creation of parallel Serbian municipal councils within Kosova. Prishtina has largely fulfilled its part of the arrangement with the EU, in holding general elections, forming a new government, passing a constitution, and maintaining stability inside Kosova. However, the EU remained hesitant in confronting Serbian separatists in Kosova, thus undermining the integrity of the new state.

UN Secretary General Ban Ki-moon's six-point plan for Kosova was unveiled in November 2008 and was immediately rejected by the Kosova government. It envisaged a dual authority in Kosova, with the UNMIK mission continuing to supervise the Serb minority areas in northern Kosova, which were to obtain a parallel police force, customs officers, and judges outside of Prishtina's control. Critics of the plan argued that it undermined Kosova's independence by appeasing Russia and Serbia in setting three conditions for EULEX: approval by the UN Security Council, EULEX neutrality regarding Kosova's status, and no link between EULEX and the Ahtisaari plan as the basis of Kosova's independence. EULEX, like UNMIK, would be a status-neutral mission rather than the supervisor of an independent state. Nevertheless, the UN plan approved in early December 2008 provided EULEX with a broad international mandate through UNSC legitimation. It could also pull Serbia closer toward de facto recognition of Kosova's statehood by approving the EULEX deployment. Much depends on whether EULEX proves successful in developing an integrated state or if the continuing presence of UNMIK and a dual international authority consolidates ethno-territorial partition.

Given the still unsettled security questions in the Balkans, the region remains useful for Moscow in disrupting democratic expansion in the wider Europe. The Kremlin does not pursue a permanent solution for Kosova but prefers to have a partially recognized frozen state in the Balkans. Regional instability is compounded by the bifurcated Bosnian state, in which the Serb entity could push toward independence, and the uncertain future of Macedonia, whose path to NATO and EU membership was blocked by Greece because of the perpetual dispute over the country's official name. Kosova formed part of a wider Kremlin strategy designed to keep Serbia neutral, enmesh the West in disruptive disputes, entrap Balkan political elites in energy contracts and other dependency relations, weaken NATO influence along the Black Sea region, and steadily reverse U.S. influence.

Caucasian Lessons

Russia claims that it acted legally in its military intervention in Georgia in August 2008. In reality, it violated numerous international laws including the UN Charter and UN Resolution 3314, which states that "no territorial acquisition or special advantage resulting from aggression is or shall be recognized as lawful." Russia's claims of humanitarian intervention in South Ossetia are misleading, particularly as intervention has gone far beyond establishing order in the troubled region. To justify its military intervention and the partition of Georgia, the Kremlin charges that the U.S.-led invasion of Iraq in 2003 and the acceptance of Kosova's independence in 2008 set global precedents that Russia was simply emulating. The reality is quite different when looking at Russia's policy since the collapse of Moscow's previous empire, the Soviet Union, for at least five reasons:

First, Russia itself set its own precedent for separatism within newly in-dependent states by sponsoring, arming, and funding rebel groups in Transnistria, South Ossetia, and Abkhazia in the early 1990s to severely weaken the newly emerging independent states. This was long before Kosova had evolved into a security question in the Western capitals and before the internally generated collapse of Yugoslavia had gathered momentum.

Second, NATO intervention in Kosova in 1999 was a multinational oper-ation and not a unilateral act by a single state, unlike Russia's attack on Georgia in August 2008. Although there was no clear UN mandate for the Kosova inter-vention, the majority of NATO allies approved the mission, arguing that failure to act would have given the green light to Belgrade's attempted expulsion of the majority Albanian population.

Third, the U.S. and NATO allies tried various international formats before intervening in Kosova and subsequently opting to recognize Kosova's independ-ence. This included an OSCE mission, a UN-mandated administration, and Ahtisaari's mediation to try and reconcile Kosova demands for independence with Serbia's insistence on preserving a single state. By contrast, Russia monopolized any political negotiations and maintained a permanent military presence in the separatist regions of Georgia. It recognized South Ossetia and Abkhazia shortly after its invasion of Georgia in August 2008 without any attempt at international or local mediation.

Fourth, since intervening, NATO, the UN, and now the EU have been con-structing a democratic state in Kosova with extensive minority rights, decen-tralization, and the rule of law. Indeed, the EULEX mission will formally supervise Kosova's independence for several years. By contrast, the separatist regions in Georgia are autocratic fiefdoms with criminal and FSB checkist connections that do not allow international oversight over internal governance and human rights.

And fifth, by May 2009, fifty-eight countries had recognized Kosova as an independent state, including all neighboring countries aside from Serbia. In stark contrast, it is likely that only a handful of capitals will recognize South Ossetia and Abkhazia. By May 2009 only Nicaragua had sided with Russia. Even CIS states are hesitant to support separatism within their strategic sphere that could rebound against them in their active or latent disputes with Russia.

Russia's authorities calculated that they would gain several long-term advantages from their military invasion of Georgia. Their first and primary purpose was to halt Georgia's progress into NATO as several EU states would argue that alliance membership would further provoke Moscow and degenerate Russian-European relations. Georgia's evident vulnerability stiffened the resistance of some European allies against offering membership action plans (MAPs) to either

Georgia or Ukraine at the NATO summit in April 2009. By destabilizing the pro-Western government of President Mikheil Saakashvili, which is viewed in the Kremlin as a puppet or proxy of Washington, Moscow would ensure Georgia's isolation and inability to qualify for NATO accession.

The Kremlin's second goal was to highlight the limits of American, NATO, and EU protection of a partner state in the face of Moscow's military assertiveness while displaying Russia's new power to an international audience. In effect, Russia wanted the West to acquiesce to its right to use force against an EU and NATO aspirant and to reduce Western commitments to all former Soviet republics from Ukraine to Central Asia. Through its Caucasian offensive, Russia issued a poignant challenge, calculating that neither NATO nor the EU were willing to affirm their avowed principles of supporting pro-Western states close to Russia's borders. NATO's disunity in failing to provide MAPs to Georgia and Ukraine at the April 2008 and April 2009 summits exposed Western weakness and convinced Russia that it had a valuable opportunity to press ahead with military action and the potential annexation of Georgian territory.[18]

Russia's military success in Georgia was also intended to send a warning to other countries to not place too much faith in a partnership with the United States because Washington is allegedly unreliable and unwilling to provide security assistance during a major crisis. In a demonstration of its escalating challenge to NATO following the Georgian war, Russia's Black Sea navy deployed its vessels to two Abkhazian ports. Moscow was establishing a naval or coast guard station in Sokhumi and a naval base at Ochamchire in the southern part of Abkhazia. On October 29, 2008, the Russian parliament ratified treaties with South Ossetia and Abkhazia allowing Moscow to emplace thousands of additional troops in these territories.[19] Approximately 7,600 Russian troops were deployed in the two regions on the pretext of protecting them from Georgian attacks. In an agreement signed in Moscow in May 2009, Russia was empowered to guard the borders of South Ossetia and Abkhazia with the rest of Georgia. Russia's actions were also designed to underscore persistent EU divisions, weaknesses, and susceptibility to compromise with an assertive Russia. In a note of sarcasm Russia's leaders claimed that their cooperation with the EU and President Sarkozy in particular was successful in defusing the Georgian crisis. They failed to point out that Moscow did not fulfill its pledges to the EU and actually increased its troop presence in the two disputed regions that it recognized as independent states. President Medvedev hailed such "cooperation" with the EU, where Moscow gained clear advantages without significant Union opposition, during his state of the union address to the Federal Assembly on November 5, 2008.

In depicting EU-Russia mediation over Georgia as a success, Moscow evidently hoped to entice Western Europeans into some special security arrangements with Russia that bypass NATO. The larger EU capitals do not want to isolate Russia through economic or political sanctions because of their expanding energy and business interests with Moscow. Indeed, the EU continues to operate on the status quo paradigm, which lacks any realistic strategic goals toward Russia in terms of its internal transformation, compliance with bilateral agreements, or any "consolidated effort to integrate the new eastern periphery of the Union."[20]

Third, by using military means on the pretext of defending Russian citizens and compatriots, the Kremlin was able to apply pressure and send warning signals to neighboring governments with sizable Russian minorities or confronting internal separatist or territorial disputes. The attack on Georgia sent a powerful message to Ukraine, Moldova, and Azerbaijan that their strategic orientation would not be a sovereign decision. The Georgian crisis was intended as a warning to Ukraine in particular that it should desist from petitioning for NATO entry. Otherwise, Moscow might intervene to protect the allegedly threatened interests of Russian minorities, compatriots, or citizens.

One Russian analyst concluded that Moscow established an important new precedent, through its direct military intervention in Georgia, in which "the legal and political agreements guaranteeing the status quo and the freezing of conflicts no longer works."[21] As a result, even Russia's allies in the CIS and the CSTO were hesitant in giving Moscow unbridled support for the partition of Georgia as many of them have their own separatist skeletons in the closet that the Kremlin could exploit.

Fourth, the Georgian intervention applied pressure on Armenia not to abandon the CSTO, join the GUAM initiative, participate in a Transcaucasian security system with Georgia and Azerbaijan, develop bilateral military ties with the United States, forge closer links with NATO, or allow for the construction of energy transportation routes between Azerbaijan and Turkey that would bypass Russia. Yerevan had indicated its intention to lessen its energy dependence on Russia by intensifying its energy links with Iran.[22] On September 3, 2008, Armenian prime minister Serzh Sarkisian announced that work on the Armenian section of a natural gas pipeline was essentially complete and the pipeline would go on stream by the end of 2008. The projected volume of Iranian gas could cover Armenia's basic needs, provide Yerevan a viable alternative to Russian deliveries, and strengthen its bargaining position in future price negotiations with Gazprom.

And fifth, the Russian armed incursion in Georgia was intended to undermine investor confidence in alternative energy pipeline routes from the Caspian Basin to Europe and thereby enhance Russia's monopolization of energy supplies. The potential breakup of Georgia and the disruption of energy transit from the Caspian into Europe places enormous pressure on Azerbaijan and the Central Asian countries to remain neutral or support Russian policy. Moscow also cajoles

Turkey, which is heavily dependent on Russian natural gas supplies, not to support the U.S. position on Georgia. This is a poignant example of energy blackmail as a major component of Russia's regional strategy.

After its military intervention in August 2008 Moscow evidently concluded that the strategic benefits of recognizing the independence of Abkhazia and South Ossetia in expanding Russia's regional influence outweighed the costs of temporarily unsettled relations with the EU, NATO, and the United States. Moscow is also likely to exploit the specter of recognizing pro-Russian separatists in other nearby states, including Ukraine and Moldova, in order to extract security concessions from the West.[23]

On September 17, 2008, President Medvedev signed treaties of "friendship, co-operation and mutual assistance" with Abkhazia and South Ossetia.[24] The treaties were initialed on behalf of the separatist republics, which Russia recognized on August 26, 2008, by their respective presidents Sergei Bagapsh and Eduard Kokoity. The treaties emphasize cooperation in foreign policy and regional security and economic integration, thus paving the way for the de facto incorporation of the two para-states into Russia's political, defense, and economic domain. Even though a formal annexation of Abkhazia and South Ossetia by the Russian Federation seems unlikely for the time being, the two treaties demonstrate that Moscow is aiming at close practical integration.

From the onset of the armed conflict in Georgia, the EU was effectively duped by the Kremlin. Russia's leaders understood that the Union was fractured and incapable of using any consequential tools to reverse Georgia's de facto partition. Moscow sought to seal the protection of South Ossetia and Abkhazia from any further attempts by Tbilisi to retake its territories. In effect, EU monitors assisted Russian combat troops posing as peacekeepers to consolidate their gains while shielding the two territories from potential Georgian attacks through designated demilitarized buffer zones.

In sum, during the summer of 2008, both the EU and NATO displayed impotence in the face of Russia's strategy to remain a dominant player in the South Caucasus. Potential exclusion from the G-8, stalled progress toward membership in the World Trade Organization, the suspension of high-level meetings of the NATO-Russia Council, and the cancellation of NATO military exercises with Russian forces were viewed by Putin and Medvedev as mere distractions from grand strategy. They seemed convinced that the West needed Russia much more than Russia needed the West. The EU will not formally recognize South Ossetia and Abkhazia, but it will largely go through the motions of censuring Russia, as it is unwilling or incapable of applying any meaningful sanctions.

The Georgian crisis demonstrated the dangers of a security vacuum in regions where NATO has not committed itself to any country's security and where

Russia's empire building could accelerate. The invasion dramatically exposed the strategic confrontation between Russia and the West. The war over Georgia had been brewing for several years. Indeed, Moscow goaded Georgia into outright conflict as international attention was distracted by the Beijing Olympics.[25] The combat readiness of Russia's Fifty-eighth Army had been prepared months in advance of the invasion.

Although he was strongly criticized for his evident gullibility and impetuousness in intervening in South Ossetia and provoking a Russian invasion, Georgian president Saakashvili might actually have done the West a significant favor. Russia's preplanned military invasion starkly exposed the Russian leadership's intentions and left less room for wishful thinking about Russia's ambitions in former Soviet territories.

Following the invasion of Georgia, Ukrainian president Viktor Yushchenko announced that Kyiv was ready to make its missile early warning systems available to European nations.[26] Ukraine's Foreign Ministry stated that Moscow's abrogation of a 1992 accord involving two tracking stations allowed Kyiv to cooperate with other powers. President Yushchenko also sought to implement restrictions on the movement of Russia's Black Sea fleet from the port of Sevastopol, requiring Moscow to obtain Kyiv's approval. The move came after several of the fleet's warships were deployed along the Georgian coastline, thus undermining Ukraine's neutrality. Moscow denounced the restrictions as anti-Russian and asserted that its military commanders would answer only to the Russian president.

In reality, Yushchenko had limited means to defend Ukraine's sovereignty and was unlikely to risk ordering a blockade of the Sevastopol naval base. Officials in Moscow dismissed his statements over Georgia as anti-Russian and ignored his stipulations over the Black Sea fleet. Moreover, Ukraine's political elites remained deeply divided in their response to Russia's assertiveness. While the president sought closer NATO protection and the opposition leader, Viktor Yanukovich declared his understanding for Russia's actions in Georgia and opposed a greater NATO role, Prime Minister Yulia Tymoshenko remained largely silent, cognizant of the fissures in Ukrainian society on the question of relations with the West and with Russia.

The war in Georgia added another weapon to Moscow's neo-imperial arsenal. The use of force against an independent pro-Western state sent shock waves throughout all former Soviet satellites. Russia's leaders were eager to display their revived leadership role along Russia's borders. Simultaneously, the Kremlin calculated that Western capitals would seek to avoid any prolonged confrontations with Russia in its neighborhood. It banked on division and indecisiveness by EU members compounded by a lame duck American presidency and a prolonged transition to a new U.S. administration. By singling out Georgia, Moscow intended to strike against a small U.S. ally to demonstrate American impotence. Without a credible U.S. response, other new allies in CEE might start to doubt America's ability to be a security guarantor, and Moscow could be emboldened to repeat its actions elsewhere.[27]

The Russian-Georgia war has become a test case for EU and NATO unity and effectiveness in dealing with a major European crisis. An inability to pressure Russia to withdraw its troops, to emplace an impartial international peacekeeping mission in Georgia's disputed territories, or to restore Georgia's territorial integrity will send a negative signal to all nearby states threatened by Russia's expansionism. It will also encourage Moscow to more vigorously pursue its broader Eurasian agenda. Through its delays in pulling back forces from Georgian territory outside the separatist zones in line with the EU-brokered cease-fire plan, Russia tested the Western response.

By mounting a major disinformation campaign on its strategy and objectives, Moscow encouraged the accommodationist lobby in the West to defend the Kremlin position. Indeed, the Russia-firsters placed blame on Tbilisi, either for provoking the conflict outright or for grievous miscalculations in its reaction to South Ossetian militia provocations that triggered Russia's military intervention. They tended to play down Russia's responsibility both for the provocation and for the invasion while ignoring or denying Moscow's broader strategy for regional dominance.[28]

The strategic future of the broader Caucasus-Caspian region was placed in the balance by Russia's Georgia intervention. The West relied on Georgia as the center of its energy transit routes from the Caspian Basin to Europe. Threats to pipeline security and questions about the stability of the Georgian government could discourage investment in alternative pipeline routes that pass through Georgia, especially the planned Nabucco gas transmission project, and limit any increase in the carrying capacity of the existing Baku-Tbilisi-Ceyhan gas line.[29]

This strategy also squeezed Azerbaijan, which possesses substantial reserves of oil and gas and is dependent on secure access to the international energy market through neighboring countries. Exploiting this situation, President Medvedev and Gazprom chiefs made an offer to Azeri president Ilham Aliev to buy the entire volume of gas available for export from Azerbaijan at European market rates. The goal was to curtail Azeri supplies for alternative transit routes to Europe, as Moscow viewed energy as an essential component of the strategic struggle with the West. Until the military conflict in Georgia in August 2008, Azerbaijan resisted Russia's overtures, keeping a substantial portion of its gas in reserve for Nabucco.

Moscow's pressures on Baku continued unabated following Vice President Cheney's visit to Azerbaijan in September 2008. Moscow claimed that Washington sought to establish a permanent military presence in the country. In reality, the

Azeri government has not petitioned for NATO entry and does not permit foreign bases on its territory. Fearing potential isolation and loss of energy revenues, as well as a possible South Ossetian and Abkhazian precedent for its own disputed region of Nagorno-Karabakh and several neighboring municipalities occupied by Armenia since the 1991–94 war, Baku may be pressured to accept Russia's offers. Much depends on whether Georgian security is sufficiently stabilized and whether Western investors display long-term confidence in non-Russian energy routes through the South Caucasus.

A full rapprochement between Azerbaijan and Armenia does not serve Russia's interests as it could provide grounds for an alternative energy outlet for Azeri supplies that bypass Russian control. Hence, Moscow seeks to keep alive the territorial disputes between Azerbaijan and Armenia or to interpose as the indispensable mediator. This was evident during a meeting in Moscow, arranged by Medvedev on November 2, 2008, between the Armenian and Azeri presidents, at which they signed an agreement to intensify efforts to resolve the Nagorno-Karabakh conflict.[30] However, the declaration does not commit the signatories to any specific actions within the negotiating process. One major goal of Kremlin involvement was to enable the deployment of Russian "peacekeepers" as guarantors of a future settlement between Armenia and Azerbaijan.

In seeking a dominant position in the Caucasus and excluding U.S. influence, Moscow endeavors to neutralize Turkey by pressuring it not to support the U.S. position on Georgia. Russia is Turkey's main trading partner and second largest tourist market while providing 40 percent of its oil imports, 65 percent of natural gas through the Blue Stream pipeline across the Black Sea, and 56.4 percent of its thermal coal.[31] This is a poignant example of energy and trade blackmail against a NATO member as a major component of Russia's regional strategy.

Moscow may also press Turkey to withdraw its support for the Nabucco pipeline or to include Gazprom in the Turkish component of the project. Ankara is developing an extensive trading relationship with Russia, and Gazprom has been contracted to build an underground gas storage facility in central Turkey.[32] In addition, the sole bidder for constructing Turkey's first nuclear power plant was a joint venture between Russia's state-owned Atomstroyexport and Turkey's Ciner Group.[33]

Turkey remained neutral during the August 2008 war, illustrating its growing dependence on Russia. Moreover, Moscow applied an unofficial trade embargo on Turkish goods during the Georgian war by conducting special inspections on Turkish trucks and ships entering the country, thus costing the Turkish economy approximately $500 million. In a halfhearted response evidently accommodating Russia, Turkish prime minister Recep Tayyip Erdogan proposed a "platform for security and cooperation in the South Caucasus" through a "Caucasus Cooperation and Stability Alliance" to include Russia, Turkey, Georgia, Armenia, and Azerbaijan.[34] The initiative was intended to create a regional security framework by empowering Russia and Turkey to play the lead roles in providing regional security guarantors, while NATO's position would be restricted. The initiative seemed to be more of a genuflection by Ankara toward Moscow than a serious attempt to deal with Caucasian conflicts.

In a glaring example of strategic blackmail, Russia's spokesmen threatened the EU with negative consequences if sanctions were imposed on Moscow for its invasion of Georgia. In September 2008 several states submitted a motion to the Council of Europe Parliamentary Assembly (PACE) to suspend Russia's membership for "serious violations of the basic principles of the CoE [Council of Europe]," in particular for invading, dismembering, and occupying the territory of another CoE member state.[35] In response, Russian spokesmen warned that adoption of the motion would jeopardize Russia's antiterrorism cooperation with Europe, threaten energy deliveries, and entail "heavy costs to the European business community."

In the longer term, the intervention in Georgia may rebound negatively on Russia. In the estimation of Pavel Felgenhauer, a military analyst, hard-liners in Moscow will not have achieved all their targets, as they sought the overthrow of President Saakashvili and the destruction of the Georgian army.[36] The Georgian military withdrew during the Russian advance and avoided serious casualties and matériel losses. Powerful Russian businessmen were also concerned by major losses on financial markets following the invasion and the prospect of Western sanctions denying them access to modern technology. Meanwhile, Georgia could count on large-scale reconstruction assistance and potential U.S. support in rebuilding the Georgian military.

In addition, supporting and recognizing separatist entities in the South Caucasus may impact on Russia itself, which faces a number of internal separatist movements particularly in the North Caucasus.[37] Indeed, periodic reports continued to surface of attacks on Russian troops and police in several North Caucasian republics, including Chechnya, North Ossetia, Ingushetia, and Dagestan, indicating an escalating struggle for independence from Moscow.[38]

In another indication that Russia's regional benefits from the Georgian operation may be limited, other CSTO members were reticent in fully supporting Moscow's position on Georgia despite Kremlin efforts to enlist their solidarity. Although they generally concurred with Russia's explanations about the necessity of the military intervention, no CSTO state recognized the partition of Georgia or the independence of Abkhazia and South Ossetia. They were clearly fearful of establishing a separatist precedent for their own territories that could become disputed by Russia.

Russia's Anti-American Alliances

In its struggle against Western models of democracy and capitalism, Moscow rarely serves as an attractive political alternative. However, Russia's rulers are more intent on developing an international paradigm of sovereign states not tied to NATO, the EU, or the American alliance. This will not simply be an "authoritarian international" alliance because Moscow calculates that such an informal coalition may include states that can be authoritarian or quasi-democratic, capitalist or statist, secularist or clerical, large or small, isolationist or expansive. What provides a semblance of commonality is resistance to U.S. foreign policy by which Washington may challenge the legitimacy or goals of the governments in question.

Moscow's strategy is to stress the concept of separate and distinct global "civilizations," or political and cultural groupings, in which Russia is merely defending itself and other non-Western "civilizations" from the imposition of foreign models, especially the Atlanticist variant in which American homogenization is couched as "globalization." The development of such multipolarity undercuts U.S. unipolarity and Washington's political and economic hegemony. In addition to forging closer political contacts, increasing bilateral trade, and depicting itself as a model of sovereign development that should be globally emulated, Russia has focused on arms sales and energy contracts with non-Western governments in order to boost its reputation as a reliable security provider.[39]

For instance, the Brazil, Russia, India, China (BRIC) initiative is viewed as a useful vehicle for the Russian authorities to curtail U.S. influence among the larger and economically dynamic non-Western states. President Medvedev visited Brazil at the end of November 2008 to enhance trade ties and to gain support for holding the first BRIC summit in Russia in 2009.[40] Moscow is trying to position itself as the informal leader of the world's four major emerging markets even though in the years ahead Russia is likely to be economically weaker than the other three BRIC countries. Medvedev also took the opportunity to blame the United States for the global financial crisis and claimed that the BRIC countries do not have sufficient representation in multinational bodies such as the International Monetary Fund (IMF) and the World Bank.

Russia's rulers are not simply pragmatists or realists devoid of ideology and pursuing their national interests.[41] Autocratic regimes also possess a set of precepts regarding the role of government and specific national ambitions that guide their domestic and foreign policies. This is evident in the case of Putinist Russia, which forges strategic links with other autocracies that value strong government to ensure national unity and a political status quo rather than experimenting with an unpredictable democracy that can grievously weaken the state structure.

The Putinists uphold close relations with states that seek to defend themselves against democratic transformations or popular revolutions where Russia poses as a successful model.[42] Developing close ties with autocratic regimes or defending their allegedly threatened independence is strategically beneficial for Russia. Moscow depicts itself as spearheading opposition to America's alleged hegemonic globalism. It offers diplomatic and other forms of support to regimes criticized by Washington and Brussels and thereby promotes their non-Western orientation, even if the governments in question are not overtly anti-American. In particular, Russian officials pursue strategic links with states that can act as spoilers to undermine U.S. interests in various key regions.

Russia also seeks to estrange countries that adopted authoritarian or paternalistic systems during their post-Soviet transformation from the West in general and the United States in particular. For instance, Moscow offers political support to the Central Asian governments regardless of their record on human rights and democratic governance, calculating that Western criticisms will serve to buttress Central Asian relations with Russia and remove any leverage the West has in these strategically salient states.

Moscow seeks to limit the U.S. presence and reassert its dominance in Central Asia by developing close bilateral and personal ties; by developing multinational institutions directed by Russia, such as the CSTO; and by securing long-term energy contracts in which Russia is the monopsonist partner. Kremlin officials appear to have struck a grand bargain with several Central Asian capitals in which they will not challenge the existing political structures in return for loyalty or acquiescence toward Russia and a minimization of ties with Washington. Nevertheless, key countries such as Uzbekistan and Kazakhstan remain weary of Russian preponderance and may seek to increasingly balance Western and Russian interests while gradually loosening their political structures.

A number of states outside the post-Soviet region exploit deteriorating U.S.-Russia relations to improve their ties with Moscow and benefit from Russia's more assertive anti-American posture. The benefits have included diplomatic protection, favorable trade and investment, and arms sales, including sophisticated weaponry from Russian companies. Washington has been particularly concerned about the sale of Russian-built S-300 antiaircraft missile systems to Iran, which could be used to shoot down American or Israeli planes.

Moscow casts itself as the informal leader or spokesperson for emerging regional and global players from China to Venezuela by advocating national independence and political self-determination as the primary common interest against alleged Western intrusions couched as democracy promotion, regional security, or economic reform. The Kremlin also favors closer contacts with democracies that resist or oppose some aspects of U.S. policy, as evident in the European context. All these approaches demonstrate that the Putin-Medvedev leadership is engaged in limiting and balancing American power by encouraging and embroiling Washington in disputes and conflicts from the Middle East through the Far East to Latin America.

In East Asia, China has carefully resisted manipulation by Moscow in the latter's anti-American machinations. Beijing remains highly suspicious of Russia's motives and its claims to Asian leadership in any bilateral or multilateral formats, including the Shanghai Cooperation Organization (SCO). Moscow promotes the SCO as an exclusively Asian alliance without U.S. involvement. Notably, China did not express support for Russia's military intervention in Georgia in August 2008 that culminated in the partition of Georgian territory.

For the Kremlin, North Korea is the key spoiler of American interests in East Asia. Pyongyang's nuclear weapons program remains a useful foil to keep Washington preoccupied and to maintain Russian influence in the region. Moscow prefers to prop up the Communist dictatorship to prevent reunification of the Korean peninsula that could expand American influence. Russia also endeavors to enlarge its energy interests in East Asia and seeks North Korean support in constructing oil and gas pipelines across the peninsula to the South Korean market.

In the Middle East, Putinist Russia has pursued a more assertive policy to counter U.S. influence especially given America's ongoing conflicts in Iraq and Afghanistan, which may weaken Washington's regional position. Moscow supports Syria and uses Iran to undermine Western interests. Both countries are viewed as useful buffers against U.S. and NATO influence in the Middle East. The Kremlin cultivates Syria as a close regional ally and seeks to secure additional bases for Russia's Black Sea fleet, beyond its current location in Sevastopol. Deployments in Syria also demonstrate Moscow's willingness to defend Damascus against American pressures. Russia has also conferred legitimacy on Hamas and Hizbollah, the two leading armed Islamist and anti-American movements in the Middle East, by not listing them as terrorist organizations and inviting their leaders to Moscow.

Several Russian warships were to be deployed to the Syrian port of Tartus following a meeting in September 2008 between Russian navy commander in chief Admiral Vladimir Vysotskiy and Syrian navy division commander General Taleb Al-Barii.[43] Tartus is the only foreign naval base maintained by Russia since it abandoned Cam Rahn Bay in Vietnam in 2002. Moscow is expanding the Tartus facility and is preparing to defend it with S-300PMU-2 antiair missile systems.[44] Another Syrian port at Latakia is also being expanded in preparation to base Russian ships. These steps demonstrate Moscow's intent to establish a permanent naval presence in the Mediterranean. Although Moscow's deployments to the Mediterranean are not a credible counterweight to NATO in the region, Russia's fleet is becoming a diplomatic irritant and a potential threat to shipping in the eastern Mediterranean.

Following a meeting between President Medvedev and Syria's president Bashar al-Assad in August 2008, Moscow indicated that it was considering selling weapons to Syria, including air defense missile systems, aircraft, tanks, and medium-range ballistic missiles that could target neighboring countries.[45] At the same time, Foreign Minister Lavrov questioned Russia's relations with Israel, charging Tel Aviv with providing military equipment and training programs to Georgia.

Iran views Russia as a valuable counterbalance to the United States and as a secure channel of arms and technology. Russia is the principal source for Iran's nuclear power program, including trainers and technology for uranium enrichment, and the main obstacle to severe international sanctions against the development of nuclear weapons.[46] Moscow has supported only weak economic sanctions against Tehran in the UNSC.

By developing Iran's nuclear reactor at Bushehr, Putin used his ties with Tehran to act as an intermediary between Washington, the EU, and Iran in the controversy over Iran's nuclear plans. However, the intention was not to resolve the crisis but to keep it simmering, especially as civilian-use nuclear technology supplied by Russia can be the basis for a weapons program. Moscow refused to suspend the Bushehr project entirely and sold Iran advanced air defense systems and short-range missiles to protect its nuclear installations. Such moves were designed to make certain that relations between Iran and the West remained strained. In addition, Iran remains the third-largest importer of Russian weapons, including tanks, surface-to-air missiles, and combat aircraft.

Russia has also used the standoff between the United States and Iran to destabilize international oil markets and has thus benefited from the subsequent high prices and Iran's inability to export its large natural gas reserves to Europe. This reinforces Europe's dependence on Russian gas sources and supply routes, while Iran reorients itself eastward toward India and China.[47] In an illustration of its obstructive approach, in September 2008 Russia opposed U.S. moves to impose any new sanctions against Iran and simply agreed to a statement criticizing Tehran's plans for uranium enrichment.

Although the Iranian regime has been dependent on Russia for diplomatic support and military assistance, Tehran itself remains suspicious over Moscow's intentions and views the relationship as a marriage of convenience.[48] It will continue to play on tensions between Russia and the West to gain advantages for itself, including possible membership in the SCO, where it has been included as an observer. Russia for its part calculates that its cordial relations with Iran can shield it from the prospect that Tehran will support Chechen and Muslim insurgents in the North Caucasus. Moreover, a crisis over Iran, including an Israeli or U.S.

strike against its nuclear facilities, could enable Russia to profit from the disrupted energy markets.

In the North African region, Moscow is reviving its Soviet-era relations with Libya. In September 2008 Russian warships visited Libya, while Tripoli was intent on purchasing over $2 billion worth of Russian weapons, including surface-to-air missile systems, fighter aircraft, combat helicopters, and tanks.[49] Russia is also preparing contracts to upgrade Libya's Soviet-era weapons and develop energy ties with the prospect of assistance in building a nuclear power plant.

Even though it has improved its links with Western countries in recent years, the Muammar Gaddafi regime wants to expand ties with Russia as a counter-balance to U.S. influence in the region. At the end of October 2008 Gaddafi visited Moscow to boost energy ties and arms sales.[50] This was his first visit since Soviet times and followed Putin's trip to Libya in April 2008. Gaddafi reportedly offered Russia a naval base in the port of Benghazi. During Putin's visit to Libya, Moscow wrote off billions of dollars of Libyan debt in exchange for multibillion dollar contracts with Russian Railways and Gazprom for oil and gas development.

Russian officials regularly court Muslim countries in the Middle East and depict Russia as an essential counterweight to U.S. hegemony.[51] With observer status in the Organization of the Islamic Conference (OIC), Moscow stresses its commitment to a multipolar world order and nonencroachment on the values, traditions, or sovereignty of Muslim countries. In an effort to promote its influence, in 2006 the Kremlin created the Russia-Islamic World Strategic Vision Group as an advisory body to increase cooperation in all fields between Russia and Islamic countries. The group holds periodic forums in Muslim states, where Russian leaders stress that they see the Islamic world as a distinct pole that undercuts American predominance.

In Latin America, Cuba and Venezuela have become Russia's closest part-ners. Moscow's point man with Latin America appears to be Igor Sechin, a deputy prime minister and one of Putin's closest associates, who is reputed to be vehemently anti-American.[52] Sechin is widely thought to have worked for Soviet intelligence in Africa during the 1980s and has been the most visible face in Russia's expanding contacts with the anti-American president of Venezuela, Hugo Chávez.

Claiming that the United States is interfering and staging provocations in Russia's exclusive neighborhood in the Black Sea, the Kremlin has raised the prospect of a closer strategic alliance with Cuba in the Caribbean Sea, stirring reminders of the Cold War alliance.[53] Russia has intimated that it will reestablish a military presence in Cuba and forge closer economic and intelligence cooperation in retaliation for the U.S. missile defense system and other military advances in CEE and the Black Sea region. This could include a refueling base for its nuclear-capable bombers, the Tupolev Tu-160 Blackjack and the Tupolev Tu-95 Bear, and potentially a Russian naval base. If Moscow earmarks funding for such facilities, they would enable Russia to maintain an almost permanent presence near the U.S. coast. To signal its intent, in December 2008 a Russian navy convoy led by the submarine destroyer *Admiral Chabanenko* visited Cuba for the first time since the Soviet era.

Russia has been assisting the Hugo Chávez regime in Venezuela. In July 2008 Chávez traveled to Moscow to formalize a Venezuelan-Russian strategic alliance. It included an agreement for Venezuela to purchase $3 billion of military equipment, including Sukhoi fighter jets and air-defense systems. Between 2006 and 2008 twelve arms contracts worth a total of $4.4 billion were signed by Russia and Venezuela. Moscow also offered Venezuela a $1 billion credit to buy more arms.

During a meeting in Moscow with President Chávez on September 25, 2008, Putin raised the prospect that Russia would help Venezuela develop a nuclear energy program.[54] A few days later Chávez confirmed that Venezuela planned to develop a nuclear reactor for peaceful purposes, indicating that he felt emboldened by Moscow's offer to challenge Washington. The announcements came only a few days after Russia forced the cancellation of an international meeting to discuss sanctions against Iran over its atomic program. Moscow and Caracas began preparations to sign an energy pact, while Prime Minister Putin announced that the launch of the first Gazprom drilling rig in the Venezuelan gulf was planned for the end of October 2008. On November 27, 2008, Medvedev visited Caracas to sign an agreement with Chávez on building a nuclear energy power plant.[55]

By courting oil-rich Venezuela, Russia is promoting an emerging alliance of oil producers intent on rolling back the liberalizing trends of globalization and thwarting neighboring pro-Western democracies.[56] In a smaller variant of the Russian strategy, Venezuela plans to develop an oil and natural gas monopoly over the natural resources of its neighbors in Latin America, including Bolivia and Ecuador. Russian officials are exploring the prospect of acquiring stakes in projects implemented on the South American shelf, including the Orinoco Delta in Venezuela and the Acero bloc in Bolivia. In addition, Gazprom has expressed interest in participating in the design of the Pan-American gas pipeline that is intended to cross the entire South American continent.[57]

The supply of humanitarian assistance to Georgia by the U.S. Navy in the wake of the August 2008 war was depicted by Moscow as trespassing on Russia's maritime interests. The Russian media also charged Washington with planning to establish a U.S. naval base in one of the Georgian ports.[58] In retaliation, the Kremlin announced that it would deploy significant naval forces to conduct joint exercises with Venezuela, as Russia's first naval mission in Latin America since the end of the Cold War. Russia also sent strategic bomber planes on a trip to Venezuela, their farthest mission since the Cold War.

The Caribbean naval deployment included the guided missile cruiser *Peter the Great*, which carried nuclear cruise missiles and was the largest surface vessel constructed by Russia since the collapse of the USSR. It also included the submarine destroyer *Admiral Chabanenko* and two support vessels. The naval exercises took place in November 2008, evidently to send a strong signal to Washington during the presidential elections. Deputy Prime Minister Igor Sechin asserted that Russia would challenge the United States for influence in Latin America as no nation had "exclusive rights to this zone."[59] According to Putin, Latin America was becoming "a very important link in the chain of the new multi-polar world that is taking shape and we will pay more and more attention to this direction of our economic and foreign policy."

Russia has defended a number of small dictatorships or restrained Western pressures against them. The Robert Mugabe regime in Zimbabwe is a useful example. In Zimbabwe Moscow aims to demonstrate that it is protective of non-Western governments or those regimes that are under pressure of sanctions from the West for their nondemocratic policies or human rights violations. In July 2008 Russia used its veto in the UNSC to block a British-backed resolution to introduce sanctions on Zimbabwe's leaders involved in the fraudulent March 2008 reelection of President Mugabe. U.S. ambassador to the UN Zalmay Khalilzad claimed the veto marked a "U-turn in the Russian position" and "raises questions about its reliability as a G8 partner."[60]

Evidently fearful of setting an example for their own rigged presidential elections, Russian officials asserted that a UN resolution condemning fraudulent elections in Zimbabwe was in violation of the internal affairs of a sovereign nation. Moscow was also anxious that such a resolution could create a precedent for the legalization of "colored revolutions" by the UN. The Kremlin interprets the pro-democracy transformations in Georgia in 2003 and Ukraine in 2004 as anti-Russian, Western-led conspiracies. In addition to displaying its political support or neutrality vis-à-vis Zimbabwe, Russia has increased its arms sales to Harare in recent years, together with personnel training programs.[61]

Russia's seeks to develop various multinational organizations and instruments to rebuild its role as an alternative global leader to the United States and to various Western institutions. Its influence in such groupings as the SCO and the CSTO, which rival the United States and the EU in Central Asia, is likely to increase provided it is able to sustain long-term economic growth under an authoritarian structure. The SCO, established in 2001 by Russia, China, and several Central Asian states, evolved into a forum critical of the American presence, demanding that the United States withdraw from the military bases of all member states.

Russia did not want Washington to develop a permanent military presence in Central Asia in support of its military operations in Afghanistan.

Kremlin officials claim that the Russian model of "managed democracy," national sovereignty, and state centralism has boosted economic growth and global status, not rising energy prices.[62] Such a successful model can then be marketed in various parts of the globe as an alternative to Western democracy. Officials boast that Russia will become the world's fifth-largest economy by 2020.[63] This reinforces their argument that economic growth, political stability, social tranquility, and regional prominence can be ensured outside the Western democratic model and beyond the West's multinational institutions. Such an approach carries some resonance in disparate autocratic states, including Iran and Venezuela, where Russia can pose as an ally or even a protector.

Russia's global projection enables it to rebuild zones of influence and reverse its decline as a premier international player. Strategists calculate that the creation of an effective new pole of power can be accomplished not only by establishing a panregional great power status in Eurasia but also by branching out its global alliances. Russia will then be considered not merely as a junior partner of the United States or the EU, but as a key player increasingly able to balance and counter America's influences.

America's Limited Strategy

U.S. policy toward Russia under the George W. Bush presidency has been ambivalent. Washington has courted Moscow's cooperation in combating common threats such as international jihadist terrorism, restricting WMD proliferation, and keeping pressure on the Iranian and North Korean regimes to dissuade them from developing nuclear weapons capabilities. The overriding assumption has been that Moscow is a factor of stability in various regional crisis points. In reality, Moscow has manipulated the terrorist threat to conduct a brutal anti-independence war in Chechnya away from the international spotlight and to support nondemocratic governments along its borders. Moreover, the Iranian and North Korean standoffs suit the Kremlin's strategic objectives by challenging and undermining American interests in the Middle East and East Asia.

During the second term of the Bush administration, Washington became increasingly critical of Russia in its internal domestic regression and the pressure Moscow has applied on several neighboring states. For their part, America's new allies in CEE have sought a more consistently assertive policy toward Russia from the United States and the NATO alliance as a whole, including a more forthright commitment to bringing Russia's neighbors into the principal Western institutions.

On May 4, 2006, U.S. vice president Dick Cheney's comments at the Vilnius summit, attended by representatives from Europe's newest democracies, refocused the U.S. approach on Russia's shortcomings and potentially destabilizing foreign policy.[64] In a keynote address at the forum titled "Common Vision for a Common Neighborhood," Cheney accused Moscow of restricting human rights and democracy in Russia and of using its energy supplies to manipulate and blackmail its neighbors and undermine their territorial integrity and democratic development.

The Vilnius presidential forum was attended by heads of state from Bulgaria, Estonia, Georgia, Lithuania, Moldova, Poland, Romania, and Ukraine and was designed as a continuation of the "Vilnius 10" process inaugurated in 1997. Cheney's comments elicited condemnation by Russian government spokesmen and parliamentarians but were welcomed by the Central Europeans as indicating a more realistic approach by Washington toward Russia's development.

Although Washington is unlikely to yield to Moscow's objectives to bring Ukraine, Moldova, and Georgia into a Russian security and economic orbit, it may decide to acquiesce to some of Russia's regional policies. At the close of 2008, several CEE officials were apprehensive that the incoming U.S. administration may dilute criticisms of the Kremlin and temper its support for further NATO enlargement eastward. Any perceived U.S. appeasement of Russia's neo-imperialist policies will send negative reverberations throughout Eastern Europe, unsettle America's new allies in Central Europe, and unwittingly encourage Moscow's ambitions.

The election of U.S. president Barack Obama on November 4, 2008, was perceived as an opportunity in Moscow to challenge and test America's asser-tiveness. The Kremlin underscored that Russia was a vital international player whose interests needed to be more assiduously respected than they were under the Bush administration. In his first state of the union address the day after Obama's election, President Medvedev asserted Russia's global interests, threatened to position nuclear weapons along Poland's borders, accused Washington of provoking conflicts in the Caucasus, and claimed that Russia would emerge stronger than before. In effect, Medvedev challenged Obama to make strategic compromises by withdrawing from the planned missile defense system in Poland and the Czech Republic and acquiescing to Moscow's goal to establish more clearly demarcated spheres of influence in Eastern Europe.

Behind the Kremlin's rhetoric lurked a fear that the Obama administration may be a potentially graver threat to Russia's objectives than that of George W. Bush. The new president's popularity could raise America's global stature, reduce anti-Americanism, increase criticisms of Kremlin authoritarianism, enable Washington to rebuild its alliances, strengthen the transatlantic pole, and provide impetus for a more effective Western strategy that could undercut Russia's expansive ambitions.[65]

3

Weakening the Alliance

For Russia's military establishment, its security apparatus, and Kremlin political elites, NATO remains the global all-purpose enemy purportedly controlled by the United States in the pursuit of world dominance and the main institutional threat to Russia's security and national interests.[1] According to ex-president Putin, the enlargement of NATO and moves to emplace U.S. bases and missiles in former Soviet satellite states constitute a form of imperialism designed to impose a Western diktat on Russia.[2] In response to NATO's challenge, the Russian authorities are focused on weakening the North Atlantic alliance and steadily dismantling the transatlantic link. These objectives are pursued through various strategies, including capitalizing on bilateral ties with individual EU states, manipulating anti-Americanism, and discrediting NATO's role in global security. Attacks on NATO, U.S. policy, and related security issues are intended to broaden European disunity concerning the role and scope of the alliance while diluting transatlantic cohesion.

NATO: The Expanding Adversary

NATO has endeavored to engage with Russia in order to reduce Moscow's opposition to alliance enlargement and its "out of area" security operations. A general consensus is evident among NATO members on involving Russia in alliance programs, including inclusion in the Partnership for Peace (PfP) initiative, the Permanent Joint Council (PJC), and the NATO-Russia Council (NRC), a consultation mechanism for security questions. Nevertheless, Russian officials insist that these formats are principally attempts to reduce Russia's opposition to NATO expansion and to disguise U.S. hegemony, without giving Moscow a role in important decision making.

For the Putin regime, NATO's expansion throughout the 1990s and 2000s constituted a blatant exploitation of Russia's military and economic weakness and a betrayal of the alleged mutual agreement to end the Cold War, to withdraw troops from Central Europe, and to refrain from enlarging the alliance to include former Warsaw Pact states' territory.[3] Such an interpretation indicates the Kremlin has not reconciled itself to the fact that the USSR lost the Cold War and had to withdraw its occupying armies from Eastern Europe and that the newly independent states had the sovereign right to ensure their own security against future Russian threats.

In their efforts to compare the voluntary NATO alliance with the Soviet-enforced Warsaw Treaty Organization (WTO), Russian leaders point out that the latter was disbanded in 1990. They fail, however, to acknowledge that subsequently each WTO member state willingly and eagerly petitioned to join NATO. Russian security analysts regularly list the military advantages that NATO possesses and condemn the placement of NATO troops in former East Germany, U.S. deployments in Bulgaria and Romania, NATO missions in the Balkans, and plans to place a U.S. missile defense system in Poland and the Czech Republic.[4]

In its verbal attacks on NATO, Moscow focuses on three major themes. First, it claims that NATO is an instrument of U.S. efforts to dominate the European continent.[5] In this interpretation, Moscow is rightly aggrieved that its support for the United States after the terrorist attacks on September 11, 2001, was not reciprocated with any tangible benefits for Russia. Second, Kremlin spokesmen affirm that NATO is primarily a tool for undercutting Russian influence and enticing or cajoling neighboring states under the alliance umbrella. And third, Moscow asserts that NATO membership actually increases insecurity by sharpening relations between Russia and its immediate neighbors who enter the alliance.

The barrage of attacks against NATO disguises a twofold approach to the alliance. At the domestic and regional levels, the exposure of NATO's purported aggressiveness is intended to mobilize public opinion in support of Kremlin policy, to placate Russia's military and security establishment, and to warn the governments and citizens throughout the "post-Soviet space" that joining the alliance will seriously jeopardize their ties with Russia. Moscow stresses that the West is seeking to capture its neighbors by presenting them with the stark choice of "either with Russia, or with Europe."[6] It also claims that NATO's inclusion of Ukraine, Georgia, or any ex-Soviet republic would result in a serious deterioration in relations between Russia and its post-Soviet neighbors.[7] Some Western analysts parrot Moscow's line by claiming that NATO has "relentlessly" expanded eastward, thus failing to point out that accession to the alliance is the sovereign choice of independent states and that NATO is not a threat to Russia's security but actually helps to stabilize Russia's borders.[8]

Conversely, in Moscow's calculations NATO has become a much-weakened organization, especially as Washington under the Bush administration bypassed the alliance in major combat operations such as Iraq and preferred to deal with smaller "willing coalitions." Hence, Kremlin officials believe that even countries within NATO can be maneuvered into passivity, neutrality, or even outright support for Russian policy. Of course, Russia's leaders prefer to maintain their neighbors outside NATO and thereby diminish the possibilities of expanding U.S. influence. However, membership alone does not fully shield any state from Moscow's political penetration disguised as political pragmatism and economic cooperation.

Officials have periodically raised the prospect of Russia's accession to NATO as a way of demonstrating that the alliance is constructed against Russia rather than positioned to cooperate with it. In reality, there is no realistic prospect of NATO membership for Russia as it does not share the strategic interests or democratic values of alliance members. Furthermore, Moscow does not intend to reform its defense system according to the alliance framework or adjust its civil and military structures to NATO standards, unlike all the CEE states that gained accession in recent years.

The various formats devised to structure and temper NATO-Russia relations are interpreted by Russian officials as primarily a means for pacifying Moscow without giving it any real voice in NATO's development, decision making, and operations. These formats have included the Founding Act on Mutual Relations, Cooperation, and Security, signed in 1997; the Permanent Joint Council, as a forum for regular consultation on security issues; Russia's inclusion in NATO's Partnership for Peace (PfP) program; and the creation of the NATO-Russia Council in May 2002.[9] The NRC replaced the PJC after Moscow suspended its participation in protest of NATO's military campaign against Serbia in March 1999 and allied commitment to NATO enlargement at the Washington summit in June 1999.

It took several years for NATO-Russia relations to thaw. The NRC has focused on specific projects and common goals, such as antiterrorism, nonproliferation, arms control, and civil emergencies, while Moscow established a diplomatic mission at NATO headquarters in Brussels. In the wake of Russia's invasion of Georgia in August 2008 and its swift recognition of South Ossetia and Abkhazia as independent states, the various NATO-Russia formats and joint military exercises were suspended as Moscow's relations with the alliance deteriorated. The NRC sessions were revived in April 2009 as the Obama administration sought to forge more cooperative relations with Russia even though Moscow had failed to withdraw its troops from Georgia's separatists regions. In May 2009 the sharpening of tensions between NATO and Russia over NATO's PfP exercises in

Georgia and the expulsion of two Russian spies from Brussels demonstrated that efforts to establish a genuine partnership remained fraught with difficulties.

Kremlin officials periodically complain that the United States and NATO stand in the way of improved relations between Russia and the EU as the Europeans evidently do not want to alienate the Americans.[10] Moscow initially hoped that the EU's European security and defense policy would weaken NATO and thereby advance Russia's interests.[11] It misunderstood the EU objective of using ESDP as a limited foreign policy tool, combining military and civilian capabilities in areas such as crisis management that would not supplant NATO. Following the alliance intervention over Kosova in 1999, Russian officials realized that ESDP would not constrain U.S. actions and could not evolve into a viable substitute for NATO itself. Nevertheless, they have tried to exert influence over its development through a role in ESDP operations, although the EU does not allow nonmembers to have a role in decision making. In addition to opposing NATO missions, Moscow does not want the EU to have an authoritative role in pan-European security affairs or to exclude Russia from the process.[12]

Russian leaders assert that the inclusion of former Soviet satellites in the alliance has aggravated relations with Russia. They charge that new members such as Poland and the three Baltic states became more aggressive toward Moscow as a result of their inclusion and campaign for anti-Russian policies within the alliance. Russia's military commanders complain that the new members have been the depositories of NATO weaponry and favored provocative NATO air patrols over their territories.[13] Russian officials consistently warn that NATO expansion will lead to a new arms race as Moscow will need to fundamentally revise its military doctrine and bolster its defensive capabilities. In reality, the inclusion of CEE countries in NATO has reduced their vulnerability to Moscow's pressures and augmented their self-confidence to resist Russia's periodic threats.

The Kremlin depicts the Balkan region as a major objective of NATO's expansionist policy cloaked as providing security and humanitarian assistance. NATO's military intervention in Bosnia-Herzegovina in the summer of 1995 was depicted as an American plot in league with Bosnian Muslims and Croatian Catholics to defeat and subjugate the Orthodox Serbs. NATO's direct intervention against Serbia in March 1999 because of Belgrade's attempted genocide against the Albanian majority in Kosova was presented as a primary example of NATO aggression to dismember Russia's principal Balkan ally. Moscow also claims that the inclusion of Albania and Croatia in the alliance, in addition to Bulgaria and Romania, will allow NATO and Washington to expand their direct control over the Balkans.[14]

In a gesture of further confrontation with NATO, in January 2008 Putin issued a decree naming nationalist politician Dmitry Rogozin as ambassador to

NATO.[15] In December 2003 Rogozin was elected to the Duma as leader of the nationalist Rodina Party and regularly lambasted NATO as an aggressive U.S.-dominated organization steadily approaching Russian frontiers. In concurring with Rogozin's warnings, at an annual meeting of Russia's top military officials in November 2007, Putin warned that Moscow "cannot permit itself to remain unaffected by the muscle-flexing of NATO next to the borders of the Russian Federation."[16]

The NATO-Russia Council has been beset with disputes over missile defense, Kosova, and Russia's suspension of the 1990 Conventional Forces in Europe (CFE) Treaty. Moscow has also expressed concern that previously neutral states such as Finland could eventually join NATO. In February 2007 Putin cautioned that positioning NATO's military infrastructure closer to Russia's borders by expanding to Finnish territory would seriously harm relations between Moscow and Helsinki.[17]

Some NATO capitals express concern about Russian intelligence penetration following the entry of new members from CEE, where certain officials have reportedly maintained their Moscow contacts. Evidence from various countries indicates that Russia's foreign intelligence service (SVR) and its military intelligence service (GRU) have significantly increased their operations.[18] They became particularly active among new NATO members to gain access to classified military information and penetrate several NATO committees.

An Estonian Defense Ministry official arrested in September 2008 was suspected of passing on secrets about the U.S. missile shield and cyber-defense to Russian intelligence while working with NATO.[19] In November 2008 Herman Simm was accused of handling all of his country's classified information at NATO, which gave him access to every top-secret graded document from other alliance countries. He was reportedly recruited by Moscow in the late 1980s and was charged in Estonia with supplying highly classified information to a foreign power. In February 2009 Simm pleaded guilty to treason and was sentenced to twelve and a half years imprisonment. Investigators believed that this was potentially the most serious case of espionage against NATO since the end of the Cold War. The spy scandal was expected to result in far-reaching changes in handling classified material in the alliance. A comprehensive probe to seek further leaks among the new NATO allies was also expected.

Apprehensions were voiced in February 2008 about Budapest's decision to name Sándor Laborc from Hungary's National Security Office as head of NATO's special committee dealing with intelligence issues, a post Hungary held as part of a normal rotation.[20] Laborc studied in the 1980s at the KGB's academy in Moscow, and his appointment precipitated discussions in NATO capitals about Russian intelligence penetration that could compromise alliance security. The postcommunist secret service network continues to exert influence and gain intelligence in a number of CEE states that were once comprehensively enmeshed with Russian intelligence. This may convince some NATO capitals to be more wary about sharing sensitive information.

Russian state propaganda stokes anti-Western sentiments at opportune moments. Western hostility and Russia's determination to repel aggressive foreign encroachments was a major theme of Russia's 2007 parliamentary election campaign.[21] Allegedly, the United States intends to encircle Russia militarily and politically; to dominate its traditional spheres of influence in the Black Sea, Caucasus, Caspian, and Central Asian regions; and to control energy transportation routes bypassing Russia, thereby assuring total political, economic, and military preponderance.[22] Liberal parties who criticized the conduct of the Russian elections were denounced by the state media as "jackals" and "enemies" working on the instructions of Western embassies against the interests of the Russian state.

Paradoxically, while it accuses NATO of being expansionist, Moscow also charges the alliance with ineffectiveness, especially in dealing with instability in Afghanistan and the Balkans. Evidently, NATO does not resolve global problems or regional crises but merely fuels them by its heavy-handed interventions.[23] In a report issued by the Moscow-based Council on Foreign and Defense Policy (SVOP) in March 2007, analysts forecast a weakening of the U.S. geopolitical role during the next decade. Russia's Foreign Ministry agreed with the report but added that chaos was not the inevitable outcome of the end of America's supremacy because Russia was prepared to assume a more prominent role in world affairs.[24]

Russia's regime enumerates various plans to either neutralize NATO or to counter its increasing global reach. It underscores the importance of the UN Security Council, where it possesses veto powers, in mandating any multinational military operations. Allegedly, whenever the United States acts outside the framework of the UNSC, it poses "a serious threat to Russia's military and political interests."[25] Moscow also supports alternative security formats to undermine NATO's significance. This includes proposals to transform the OSCE into a multinational security body. Kremlin spokesmen contend that the OSCE has been politicized in the service of Washington's democracy promotion in the "post-Soviet space."[26]

Moscow criticizes NATO for its unwillingness to cooperate with the Russian-dominated Collective Security Treaty Organization and thereby denies it credibility as a co-equal organization. It has proposed dividing Eurasia between NATO and CSTO. Sergei Ivanov, Russia's defense minister, stated in December 2006 that collaboration between NATO and CSTO would be a logical step toward improving international security.[27] The purpose of the proposal was to give credibility to a Russia-dominated military structure that increasingly resembles the Warsaw Pact and prevent further NATO enlargement in the former USSR. Russian analysts admit that the goal of CSTO is to increase Moscow's influence among its post-Soviet allies and counter Western penetration.[28]

The CSTO was established in September 2003 through the institutionalization of the Collective Security Treaty, signed in Tashkent, Uzbekistan, in May 1992, and included Russia, Belarus, Armenia, Kazakhstan, Kyrgyzstan, Tajikistan, and Uzbekistan. The CSTO was designed as a mechanism for the Kremlin to increase its security dominance among member states and limit their NATO contacts. NATO leaders have refused to cooperate with CSTO as an organization; they will work only with individual countries. This has been interpreted in Moscow as part of a broader plan by Washington to dominate the Caucasus and Central Asia.[29]

Nikolai Bordyuzha, the secretary general of CSTO, alleged in May 2007 that NATO is constructing a military infrastructure around the CSTO states that includes U.S. bases, airfields, radar sites, and missile deployments.[30] In addition, NATO airborne early warning and control (AWAC) flights over the Baltic states are allegedly intended as opportunities to collect reconnaissance information about northwestern Russia and its military configurations.[31]

In a sign of increasing militarization of the CSTO, in September 2008 Bordyuzha announced the creation of "a powerful military grouping of five countries in Central Asia." This would reportedly involve the creation of a new armed group and include up to ten thousand personnel tasked with responding to external threats to the region.[32] Currently, the CSTO's military component consists of collective rapid deployment forces, estimated to include ten battalions or four thousand soldiers. Moscow plans for this structure to be subsumed into the new force. With ongoing controversies over troop contributions with several Central Asian states, the new CSTO military will be dominated by Russia, both in leadership and combat personnel. Its main purpose will be to serve as a counterpoint to NATO influence in the region.

The Kremlin aims to enlist Western leaders in its campaign against NATO's eastern expansion. At NATO's foreign ministers' meeting in Brussels in March 2008, German foreign minister Frank-Walter Steinmeier and his French counterpart Bernard Kouchner led Western European efforts against moves by Poland and the Baltic states to offer Ukraine and Georgia membership action plans.[33] Both Russia and opponents of MAPs within NATO conflated the separate issues of awarding MAPs and granting NATO membership. MAPs are stepping stones toward meeting the criteria for NATO entry, but they do not guarantee accession.

Although neither Ukraine nor Georgia received a MAP, NATO's Bucharest summit statement in April 2008 reported that alliance leaders agreed that both states "will become members of NATO."[34] Such a commitment had not been offered before to countries that received MAPs, including Albania and Macedonia.

In response, at the NATO-Russia Council meeting during the Bucharest summit, Putin hinted that Russia might encourage Ukraine's territorial partition if Kyiv advanced toward NATO.[35]

Officials in Berlin and Paris voiced skepticism about whether Ukraine and Georgia met NATO's conditions for obtaining MAPs. In reality both countries were ahead of Albania and Macedonia when the latter two received their first MAPs in 1999. More tellingly, the German and French governments were reluctant to antagonize Moscow and wanted to provide a window of opportunity for incoming president Medvedev to establish more cooperative relations with NATO. Some officials claim that providing MAPs would unnecessarily strain alliance relations with Russia, which were already overburdened by disputes over Kosova's recognition. In effect, Berlin and Paris were prepared to sacrifice their relations with two European states who sought integration into the Continent's institutions and to alienate their CEE allies within NATO and the EU in the hope of improving relations with an authoritarian state that increasingly challenged European interests.

Chancellor Merkel led the opposition to awarding Kyiv and Tbilisi MAPs following her meeting with Putin in Moscow in March 2008. Russia's president also assailed the EU's reservations about a new treaty with Russia and ridiculed the concept of "so-called European solidarity."[36] Merkel played into Moscow's hands by inadvertently discouraging the resolution of the Abkhaz and South Ossetian conflicts by claiming that unresolved conflicts on Georgia's territory disqualify the country from a MAP and eventual NATO membership. Her statement contradicted alliance policy, which stipulates that frozen conflicts are not an obstacle to membership or a MAP as this would give Russia a permanent veto on enlargement.

The NATO ministerial on December 3, 2008, confirmed that Ukraine and Georgia would eventually join the alliance but again failed to offer either country a MAP program. Several NATO members feared Russia's reaction to the MAP process, especially as they were keen to rebuild relations with Moscow following the August war with Georgia. During its sixtieth anniversary summit, held in France and Germany on April 3–4, 2009, NATO did not even consider the awarding of MAPs to Georgia or Ukraine.

Russia selects issues to drive wedges between not only EU members, but also NATO members. Russian officials claimed that offering MAPs to Ukraine and Georgia would be a U.S.-driven initiative that would damage Europe-Russia relations. It dismissed CEE support for these MAPs as devaluing the influence of traditional partners such as Germany and France. The hesitation of Berlin and Paris to provide MAPs to Ukraine and Georgia because of their concerns about Moscow's reaction brings into question alliance unity and highlights an inadequate understanding of Russia's tactics and strategies. Indeed, Russia's military attack on Georgia in August 2008 may have been precipitated by Moscow's calculations that the alliance was divided in supporting Georgia's security.

If relations with Russia override questions of regional security through closer cooperation between NATO members and aspirants, then Moscow has in effect blocked alliance decisions. Moreover, the sacrificing of one security issue in order to pacify Russia and compensate the Kremlin on another security dispute does not form sound policy. It will simply encourage the Kremlin to manufacture new conflicts with the aim of benefiting from further Western concessions. NATO capitals should also avoid personalizing their relations with Moscow by claiming that they need to reach out to Medvedev or any new leader in order to repair ties with Russia. This could precipitate unnecessary near-term concessions and disruptive longer-term disillusionment.

Russia's alleged national interests in maintaining dominance over its neighbors presumes that Moscow must determine the security postures of independent post-Soviet states. In this equation Russia depicts NATO as an aggressive and expansive military organization rather than as an organization that has evolved into a broad security provider both within and outside Europe. In reality, NATO enlargement is not a threat to Russia's security, government structure, or territorial integrity, but a challenge to Russia's expansionism and Moscow's attempts to undermine European security.

Exploiting Arms Control

The Russian authorities focus on several arms control treaties to reassert their role in the international security arena and raise their military stature. Moscow claims that when the United States withdrew from the 1971 Anti-Ballistic Missile (ABM) Treaty in 2002, because Washington considered the accord to be redundant, it freed itself to deploy missile defense systems anywhere in the world and initiated a new arms race.[37] In reality, Washington's move allowed Moscow to test new missile systems, and the Kremlin did not initially register any significant complaints.[38]

In confirming Russia's approval for abrogating or renegotiating various weapons treaties, in June 2006 Putin also proposed the initiation of talks on replacing the Strategic Arms Reduction Treaty (START-1), due to expire in December 2009. However, Russian officials indicated that any new agreement on limiting nuclear weapons would need to be tied to Washington abandoning its plans for the missile defense system in Central Europe.[39]

The Kremlin vehemently criticizes the CFE Treaty for freezing obsolete restrictions on its military while being disregarded or unratified by NATO capitals. In reality, Russia wants to eliminate requirements for international notification and inspection of its military. The CFE Treaty was originally intended to prevent the outbreak of a large-scale conventional war between NATO and the WTO by capping the total number of arms and equipment that either side could station between the Atlantic and the Urals. In 1999 the CFE Treaty signatories met in Istanbul to update the treaty and imposed new arms limits, including Moscow's commitments to withdraw its bases from Georgia and Moldova. NATO agreed to ratify the adapted treaty once Moscow fulfilled those obligations.

Moscow initiated some withdrawals from Georgia but continued to maintain forces and large stockpiles of conventional weaponry in Moldova's disputed territory of Transnistria. Georgia's minister of foreign affairs, Gela Bezhuashvili, welcomed the closure of two Russian bases in Batumi and Akhalkalaki but insisted on the termination of the remaining base in Gudauta. Although the Russian parliament ratified the adapted CFE Treaty in 2004, the Kremlin increasingly attacked it as detrimental to Russia's interests and as imposing unacceptable demands on a Russian state that was no longer weak.

Romanian president Traian Băsescu stated that Romania's signing of the adapted CFE Treaty was conditioned on the withdrawal of Russian troops and weaponry from Moldova and Georgia.[40] The U.S. administration consistently maintained that all NATO members, including Slovenia and the three Baltic states, would ratify the adapted CFE Treaty after Russia evacuated its military units from Georgia and Moldova. Moscow in turn claimed that the United States exerted pressure on several allies not to ratify the treaty in order to threaten Russia.[41]

At the OSCE conference in Vienna in June 2007, Russia endeavored to renegotiate conventional arms control agreements to its unilateral advantage.[42] It demanded new arms limitations for NATO states to compensate Russia for NATO enlargement and the creation of U.S. military installations in Romania and Bulgaria. It also canvassed to remove limits on Russian deployments in the North Caucasus and Russia's northwest region. As no concessions were offered, Moscow withdrew from the CFE Treaty in December 2007 and exempted itself from the treaty's quantitative force ceilings, mutual inspections, and information exchanges.[43] Putin linked this decision to the failure of NATO signatories to ratify the CFE Treaty or respect its provisions, as well as to the proposed missile defense system and NATO's eastward enlargement.[44]

Russia's Duma voted unanimously in November 2007 to suspend implementation of the CFE Treaty because Russia believed it no longer corresponded to its interests.[45] Foreign Minister Lavrov vowed that Russia was planning to "restore strategic stability and the military and political balance on the European continent." He expected the adoption of a new agreement that would "modernize" the CFE Treaty.[46] In reality, the unilateral breach of the CFE Treaty gave Moscow a freer hand to concentrate troops near Georgia, Ukraine, and the three Baltic states and not be subject to monitoring, inspection, or the pre-announcement of military movements.

For the fifth consecutive year, the OSCE's conference in December 2007 failed to adopt a final political declaration on the unresolved conflicts in Moldova and Georgia after Russia threatened to veto. Moldova's minister of foreign affairs, Andrei Stratan, welcomed the U.S. proposal for an international mission to supervise the existing "peacekeeping" operation in Moldova and called for immediate transformation of the operation into a multinational civil mission under an OSCE mandate.[47]

There were indications at NATO's Bucharest summit in April 2008 that the allies could dilute their demands for Russia's compliance with previous CFE stipulations. Summit documents no longer mentioned the withdrawal of Russian troops from Moldova and Georgia as preconditions for Western verification. Instead, they indicated that NATO might tolerate a Russian military presence in order to proceed with ratification so that the Baltic states would join the CFE Treaty.[48]

The German government was at the forefront of efforts to acquiesce to Russia's retention of the base in Gudauta, Georgia, and exempt Russian peace-keepers from an obligation to withdraw from Moldova. Berlin adopted Moscow's position that a political settlement in Transnistria could precede the evacuation of Russian troops. This approach gives the Kremlin an incentive to block a political settlement indefinitely. If Chisinau is pressured by Moscow to accept its military presence in return for political concessions by Transnistria and an increase in Russian influence over Moldova's security, the EU is likely to consent. Several European countries would then be ready to ratify the adapted CFE Treaty, securing a significant strategic victory for Moscow. The Russian regime demonstrated its complete disregard for CFE stipulations on force limits when it staged its invasion of Georgia in August 2008 and emplaced Russian forces in permanent bases in South Ossetia and Abkhazia. Russia plans to use Gudauta as its main base in Abkhazia as well as the ex-Soviet naval base at Ochamchire.

After initially seeking to use the OSCE to replace or weaken NATO, in recent years Russia has sought to emasculate the organization, viewing it as a threat to its national interests because it promotes democratic systems among member states and Russia's neighbors. The Western pursuit of human rights and democratic development is viewed in Moscow as a tool for political intervention.[49] In response, Russian authorities initiated several negative measures, including withholding support for the OSCE budget, increasing veto rights, and engaging in a barrage of propaganda against U.S. influence in the organization. They have also funded various NGOs in several European states to criticize national governments, berate the democracy agenda, and promote Moscow's positions.

The Kremlin's main grievances focus on the OSCE's Office for Democratic Institutions and Human Rights (ODIHR), based in Warsaw, which organizes election-monitoring missions in ex-communist countries. Moscow claims that ODIHR is a politicized institution serving the interests of a narrow group of Western countries that are determined to undermine Russia under the cover of championing democracy. Hence, the Kremlin aims to change the rules by which the OSCE operates.[50] Moscow imposed restrictions on the ODIHR's ability to monitor Russia's December 2007 parliamentary elections, while an emergent bloc of seven post-Soviet states under Russian leadership submitted proposals to terminate the OSCE's democracy-promoting role. With Kazakhstan earmarked to chair the OSCE in 2010, the Russian authorities may try to pressure Astana to weaken the ODIHR or to change its mandate. Moscow can also disable any OSCE operation by blocking the adoption of its budget, as was the case with the Georgia border monitoring mission. In a similar vein, Moscow has endeavored to obstruct any criticism of Russia's domestic and foreign policy in the pan-continental Council of Europe.[51]

Projecting Military Power

Defense Minister Sergei Ivanov has underscored that Russia is committed to rebuilding and modernizing its military capabilities. It operates according to the concept of preemption against looming threats and will counter any attempts to alter "geopolitical reality in a region of Russia's strategic interest."[52] In an indication of Russia's growing militarization, Prime Minister Putin asserted in September 2008 that defense spending would grow 27 percent in 2009, although this evidently did not take account of the growing financial malaise inside Russia.[53]

Having increased their military budget sixfold since 2000, the Russian authorities have flexed their military muscle by engaging in various provocations and threats against neighbors, including airspace violations to test local defenses and displays of prowess vis-à-vis perceived Western adversaries. NATO has generally depicted these as symbolic acts because Russia's strategic forces have shrunk significantly and the technological gap with the West has steadily increased.[54] Nevertheless, Russia's threatening acts serve to put pressure on weaker neighbors and test the alliance's unity in support of NATO newcomers.

In August 2007 Russia's strategic bombers resumed regular long-range flights after a fifteen-year hiatus.[55] Moscow announced that patrols would take place on a regular basis in areas of Russia's interest. During the summer of 2007, Russian patrols flew to the fringes of British airspace and over the Pacific in the direction of the U.S. base in Guam. In August 2007 Oslo reported the largest display of Russian airpower in the Norwegian Sea since the early 1990s. Moscow's decision to resume strategic bomber flights was avowedly in response to the planned U.S.

missile defense program and as a demonstration of resistance to NATO expansion. The high-profile displays paraded Russia's regained power in keeping a fleet of strategic bombers with nuclear missiles permanently airborne.

Russian maneuvers also included unannounced flights of strategic bombers over the Arctic, Pacific, and Atlantic oceans. Russian bombers staged seven exercises in a buffer zone outside U.S. airspace during the summer of 2007.[56] U.S. and Canadian fighter jets were dispatched on each occasion. Russian authorities failed to file flight plans with the United States or Canada, thus raising tensions with NATO. In February 2008 more than forty Russian aircraft participated in exercises over international waters in the Arctic and Atlantic, practicing "reconnaissance tasks, missile and bomb strikes against the enemy's offensive naval groups, and midair combat."[57]

In December 2007 Defense Minister Anatoly Serdyukov claimed that Russia would resume naval exercises in the North Atlantic and Mediterranean in order to ensure a naval presence in "tactically important regions of the world's oceans."[58] In January 2008 a naval task force consisting of four warships, seven support vessels, forty-seven planes, and ten helicopters from the North and Black Sea fleets was assembled in the Mediterranean. The Russian aircraft carrier *Admiral Kuznetsov*, the cruiser *Moskva*, two frigates, and five support ships performed maneuvers in the Mediterranean and sailed to the Atlantic to exercise in waters close to the U.S. coast.

Russian air force spokesman Colonel Aleksandr Drobyshevsky asserted in January 2008 that two Tu-160 strategic bombers made a long-distance flight to the Bay of Biscay off the coast of France, where the Russian navy was holding a large-scale exercise. The two bombers also conducted tactical missile launches. British and Norwegian fighters intercepted and followed the two Tu-160s as they headed for the Bay of Biscay.[59]

In 2006 the U.S. Air Force removed its fighter-interceptors from Iceland's air base in Keflavik, ending a continuous presence since World War II. In May 2008 four French Mirage 2000 interceptors relocated to Iceland with a mission to keep track of Russian bombers that were increasingly penetrating the country's airspace.[60] France is the first country to send combat aircraft to the Iceland Air Policing Area under a rotating NATO plan that will involve the United States, Denmark, Poland, and Spain up to 2010.

In a demonstrative response to NATO's enlargement summit in April 2008, Moscow coordinated a massive air defense system exercise involving eight member states of the CIS Joint Air Defense Force. The exercises included aircraft, helicopters, and missile, air defense, antiaircraft, and electronic warfare units. Additional Russian-directed exercises were expected within the CSTO to exhibit resolve and resistance to NATO expansion.[61]

In July 2008 the commander in chief of the Russian navy, Admiral Vladimir Vysotskiy, revealed that Russia planned to significantly expand its navy.[62] The ultimate aim was to rebuild a blue-water navy that could once again compete with the United States around the globe. Priority was reportedly being given to a new generation of strategic nuclear submarines, but Russia was also planning to construct advanced destroyers and aircraft carriers. The first nuclear submarine armed with new ballistic missiles, Bulava-M, was scheduled to join the Northern Fleet. In September 2008 President Medvedev announced plans to build a "guaranteed nuclear deterrent system" by 2020. The program would include nuclear submarines carrying cruise missiles and an aerospace defense system. Medvedev claimed it was necessary for Russia to "achieve dominance in airspace."[63]

Russia's ambitious military program was treated with a dose of skepticism among Western analysts, given the neglect and dilapidation of military equipment and infrastructure since the Soviet Union's collapse and the prohibitive cost of extensive modernization. Nonetheless, Moscow has a long tradition of living beyond its means in terms of its emphasis on military grandeur to demonstrate Russia's stature as a global power. It was unclear which military projects Russia's leaders were determined and capable of pursuing and which were primarily a propaganda exercise.

Moscow's claim to a vast area of the Arctic as Russian territory is a further means of projecting the country's power. The Kremlin asserts its exclusive rights to potential hydrocarbon resources in this region, even though it is in no position at present to exploit them. It is also strategically challenging the other Arctic states (the United States, Canada, Denmark, and Norway) to acknowledge Russian aspirations, and it has resumed flights of strategic bombers over Arctic waters.[64] Moscow may also be calculating that competing claims to the Arctic by the four NATO members, provoked by Russia's bold assertions, could erode alliance unity.

Missile Maneuvers

Russia's military commanders claim that Washington is engaged in a comprehensive attempt at strategic dominance. This avowedly includes the militarization of space through the development of precision weapons fired from aircraft and spacecraft and the development of new offensive technologies.[65] Further impetus is allegedly given to the U.S. buildup through the planned emplacement of the U.S. missile defense system in Central Europe. Kremlin leaders berate missile defense as an American attempt to dominate Europe and destroy strategic parity with Russia that will ultimately eliminate the nuclear deterrent.

Paradoxically, although the missile defense was envisaged as a defense against potential strikes against European targets by Iran or other states intent on developing nuclear weapons, Moscow's aggressive response effectively transformed it into a mechanism for CEE protection against an increasingly bellicose Russia. Some analysts concluded that the main potential threat of the missile defense shield was that it might contribute to neutralizing Russia's short-range nuclear missiles targeting its CEE neighbors. Russia announced that it was embarking on "retaliatory measures" to develop nuclear capabilities that would outmaneuver the missile defense system.[66] Russia's leaders view their nuclear capabilities as the most effective argument underscoring Moscow's claim for a stronger international role. In August 2008 Russia successfully tested a long-range Topol missile designed to avoid detection by the missile shield.[67] According to Colonel Alexander Vovk of the Russian Strategic Rocket Forces, the launch tested the missile's capability to avoid ground-based detection systems. The RS-12M Topol (or SS-25 Sickle) has a maximum range of 6,125 miles and can carry one 550-kiloton warhead.

On October 11, 2008, Russia test-launched a strategic missile to the equatorial part of the Pacific Ocean for the first time in the history of the Russian navy.[68] The newest missile, the Sineva, was launched by the nuclear-powered submarine *Tula* from an underwater position in the Barents Sea and hit an unspecified target near the equator in the Pacific Ocean. Military leaders describe the Sineva missile as an element of a new generation of Russian strategic weapons capable of surpassing any missile defense system. Medvedev, who watched the launch from the *Admiral Kuznetsov*, claimed that problems caused by global financial turmoil would not hurt Russian plans to revive its armed forces. Prime Minister Putin asserted that the 2009 budget would see a significant growth in defense spending of some 25 percent. These projections were significantly scaled down as the impact of the financial crisis was increasingly felt in Moscow. In February 2009 the Duma's Defense Committee stated that the defense budget would actually be reduced by 15 percent, from $40 to $34 billion.

According to former Russian prime minister and ideologist Yevgeny Primakov, with the end of the Cold War and the redundancy of America's nuclear umbrella to keep the Europeans under control, Washington needed to invent new pretexts for maintaining its hegemony. Hence, the planned deployment of the missile defense system in Central Europe "is being dictated not even by military but political considerations linked to U.S.-EU relations."[69]

Washington's missile defense system became a useful vehicle for Moscow to push an anti-American agenda and create confrontation where none existed. To obstruct the shield's development, Russia stirred tensions between several players, particularly between the United States and its Western European allies. Criticisms of Warsaw and Prague for their willingness to host components of missile defense are also intended to deepen rifts within the EU. Missile defense is depicted as part of an integrated global U.S. missile defense infrastructure directed primarily against Russian interests.

Although the small number of interceptors to be based in Poland would not threaten Russia's offensive capabilities, their total would allegedly be steadily expanded. As a consequence, the Kremlin pledges to upgrade its nuclear missile arsenal, to place more missiles on mobile launchers, and even to move its fleet of nuclear submarines to the North Pole.[70] It also threatens to abandon the 1987 Intermediate-Range Nuclear Forces (INF) Treaty that prevents the deployment of intermediate-range nuclear missiles. All these maneuvers are intended to heighten anxiety throughout the EU.

According to Yuriy Baluyevskiy, chief of staff of the Russian Armed Forces General Staff, the deployment of U.S. missile defense components in CEE will launch a new, uncontrollable arms race challenging European security.[71] To give credence to such statements, Moscow announced a buildup in its nuclear and aviation deployments along the border with NATO states, including in Kaliningrad, Belarus, and Russia proper.[72] It also launched propaganda attacks against Warsaw and Prague, claiming that their acceptance of the missile defense system was contrary to the position of WE neighbors and against public opinion in both states.

Russia's spokesmen assert that the missile interceptors in Poland can be easily replaced by long-range or intermediate-range nuclear missiles targeting Russia. In February 2007 General Nikolai Solovtsov, commander of Russia's strategic forces, threatened to neutralize the danger by targeting missile defense installations in Poland and the Czech Republic, if the two countries agreed to their construction.[73] In response, the Czech Foreign Ministry accused Moscow of blackmail. Russian pressure on the Central European states to reject the missile defense program actually served to stiffen government resolve in both Prague and Warsaw. Czech officials became more outspoken in favor of the system in the face of Russia's attempts to interfere in Prague's security arrangements with the United States and pressed ahead with a status of forces agreement with Washington.[74]

The Kremlin manipulates the missile defense question to gain influence in EU decision making and to replicate its role during the Cold War, when it could decide on the security configurations of at least half of Europe. It appeals to a wider EU audience to apply pressure on Warsaw and Prague not to allow for the construction of the missile defense systems, claiming that they undermine the development of a common EU defense and security policy.[75]

Some senior Russian advisers also assert that the CEE capitals have little say in U.S. decisions on militarizing the region but are becoming involved in a dangerous strategy directed from Washington.[76] The Kremlin's goal is to appeal to pacifists throughout Europe by making comparisons to the deployment of Pershing II missiles in Germany in the 1970s, which provoked a wave of Soviet-sponsored anti-Americanism.[77] By threatening Poland with a nuclear strike for hosting the missile shield, Russia's leaders wanted to demonstrate that Washington was avowedly engaged in a military buildup close to Russia's borders and had embarked on a new arms race.

In response to Moscow's propaganda offensive, the Polish authorities under-scored that Warsaw possesses the same rights as the UK or Denmark or any other EU or NATO member in constructing a missile defense structure with the United States.[78] Indeed, Warsaw pushed for a U.S. commitment to invest in modernizing Poland's air defense system with Patriot-type missiles and to provide more concrete bilateral security guarantees as part of a package for basing the American interceptors. The U.S.-Polish missile defense agreement was signed in August 2008 soon after the Russian military intervened in Georgia, indicating Warsaw's growing concerns about Moscow's aggressive policies.

Even countries that are not on the American radar screen to receive elements of missile defense have supported the system if it strengthens CEE and NATO security. In May 2007 the Lithuanian defense minister, Juozas Olekas, stated that the placement of the missile defense system in Poland and the Czech Republic would reinforce Lithuania's security.[79] He dismissed Kremlin assertions that missile defense deployments target Russia and even suggested that Vilnius may be interested in hosting some components of missile defense within a NATO setting.

In a sign of solidarity with Poland and underscoring aspirations toward NATO entry, in March 2007 Ukraine's president Viktor Yushchenko voiced support for the U.S. system.[80] He called on European countries to close ranks behind Washington in its military plans. Pro-Kremlin politicians in Kyiv inter-preted the move as anti-Russian and warned that Ukraine could be pressured to accept elements of the defense shield. Foreign Minister Lavrov speculated in September 2007 that the real reason the United States wanted a missile defense system in CEE was not to defend Europe from Iranian missiles but to spy on Russia.[81] Hence, the reason U.S. officials rejected Moscow's offer of a Russian-operated radar station in Azerbaijan was that the Azeri site could not be used for monitoring Russia.

In June 2007 Defense Minister Ivanov cautioned that the missile defense system would amount to "a new Berlin Wall" across Europe. In response, Russia was prepared to target the missile defense sites with medium-range missiles stationed in Kaliningrad. Putin informed a meeting of military and intelligence officers in July 2007 that Russia must strengthen its military and espionage capacities in response to the missile defense system and any deployment of U.S. troops in CEE.[82] Moscow charged that the American system was not intended to defend against attacks from rogue states, but to monitor Russia's modernization of its strategic arsenals, to eliminate the deterrence factor, and to alter the balance of power in Washington's favor.[83]

One key Kremlin objective in announcing the suspension of the CFE Treaty was to fracture the West, particularly in respect to missile defense. Its ploy paid some dividends. For instance, Ruprecht Polenz, head of the German parliament's Foreign Affairs Committee, criticized German foreign minister Frank-Walter Steinmeier for suggesting that the West should compromise with Putin on missile defense. Polenz charged that Putin was using missile defense to split the West and to divert attention from Russia's own failures in observing the CFE pact.[84] In an illustrative example of conceding one security issue in return for Moscow's cooperation in another dispute, one U.S. senator suggested abandoning missile defense plans in CEE and recognizing Russia's dominant role in the Caspian Basin to obtain Kremlin support for stiffer economic sanctions against Iran.[85]

Polish foreign minister Anna Fotyga complained in August 2007 that Germany and some other EU states were not treating Poland as a full-fledged NATO or EU member when they questioned Poland's right to host a missile defense system while several countries already had missile defense agreements with the United States.[86] In March 2007 Czech prime minister Mirek Topolánek added that it was not up to the eighteen EU member states that host U.S. military bases to comment on the existence of a similar presence in the Czech Republic. He was responding to comments by German Social Democratic leader Kurt Beck that his party would not agree to the missile defense sites in CEE without Russia's approval.

In June 2007 NATO Secretary General Jaap de Hoop Scheffer stated that because the proposed U.S. missile shield would not cover all NATO states, the alliance would assess the possibility of complementing it with its own defense systems.[87] These will provide "short- and medium-range theater missile defense, a system which can be 'bolted onto' the general missile defense" to cover Romania, Bulgaria, Greece, and Turkey, which are not shielded by the proposed U.S. sites.

Following Scheffer's announcement Russia's threats continued unabated with plans to place missiles within a few miles of the Polish border, a move that would be in direct breach of the INF Treaty, which mandated limitations on missile ranges.[88] The underlying asymmetry resided in the offensive purpose of Russian missiles versus the defensive nature of the proposed U.S. antimissile elements. Moscow was testing the West's response to a direct threat, and if effective, such challenges could be repeated or escalated. The Lithuanian authorities underscored that Russia's assertiveness made it imperative to demilitarize the Russian-controlled Kaliningrad region on the Baltic coast between Poland and Lithuania, but there was little response from the major WE countries.

U.S. Secretary of State Condoleezza Rice and Defense Secretary Robert Gates's visit to Moscow in October 2007 enabled Putin to issue a series of ultimatums and potential reprisals if the United States did not abandon its missile defense program.[89] Putin also announced that the INF Treaty must be turned into a global agreement and that all countries needed to eliminate their intermediate-range missiles or else Russia would abandon the treaty altogether. Before Rice and Gates arrived in Moscow, some Russian experts stated that U.S. interceptors in Poland would actually be nuclear intermediate-range missiles that could hit the Kremlin within two minutes, killing Russia's leaders before they could respond.

Major General Vladimir Zaritsky, commander of artillery and missile forces for Russia's ground troops, warned in November 2007 that Russia might deploy an unspecified number of short-range missiles in Belarus if the United States went ahead with its missile defense program. Zaritsky was referring to missiles with a range of five hundred kilometers, which could be modernized if Russia renounced the INF Treaty.[90] In July 2007 Defense Minister Ivanov engaged in nuclear blackmail by asserting that Russia would desist from deploying new weapons in Kaliningrad or Belarus only if Washington either abandoned its missile defense or agreed with Moscow's proposals for a joint system.[91]

The Polish authorities expressed outrage when General Baluyevskiy warned in December 2007 that "firing an antimissile rocket from Poland could be seen by Russia's automated system as the launch of a ballistic missile, which could provoke an answering strike" and all-out nuclear war. Polish prime minister Donald Tusk responded that "this kind of declaration is unacceptable. No declaration of this kind will influence Polish-American negotiations" on missile defense.[92] The Russian navy also issued a statement claiming it had successfully conducted a test launch of a new intercontinental ballistic missile from the nuclear-powered submarine *Tula* in the Barents Sea. General Solovtsov boasted that Russia's new weaponry would outperform any missile defense system.[93]

Foreign Affairs Committee chairman Kosachyov cautioned in February 2008 that Moscow could target components of the U.S. missile defense system in Poland and the Czech Republic.[94] This threat came shortly after Polish foreign minister Radek Sikorski met with Secretary Rice and announced that Warsaw agreed in principle to deploy elements of the missile defense system after receiving assurances that Washington would help Poland strengthen its security by modernizing its air defenses. Russia's military spokesman warned about the deployment of its own "missile systems of a new type," presumably referring to the RS-24 intercontinental ballistic missile, armed with six warheads.[95]

Foreign Minister Lavrov demanded a permanent Russian presence at U.S. missile defense sites in Poland and the Czech Republic.[96] Under a proposal brought to Moscow by Secretary of State Rice and Defense Secretary Gates in March 2008, Russia would be able to benefit from monitoring equipment and periodic official visits. But neither Warsaw nor Prague would permit a permanent Russian military presence on their territories, and both proposed reciprocal access to Russian military installations. This could include the A-135 missile defense system covering Moscow, considered a top-secret installation.[97] Warsaw has also sought the right to inspect Russian military facilities in Kaliningrad, a region of special concern for Poland and the Baltic states since Moscow suspended the CFE Treaty on military deployments.[98]

Moscow realizes that it cannot ultimately block missile defense and may instead push for face-saving concessions from Washington. In return for greater accommodation, Russia could aim to benefit from American antimissile technology while modernizing its own nuclear arsenal. Rumors also surfaced that Washington and Moscow might arrange a compromise whereby the United States agrees to joint control over a U.S.-Russian integrated radar framework and Moscow accepts joint development and use of strategic and tactical missile defense systems and integrates its southern radars into them.[99]

Despite Moscow's opposition, the NATO summit in Bucharest in April 2008 confirmed allied support for the missile defense system in Central Europe.[100] Secretary General Scheffer stated that the allies "recognized the substantial contribution" that the system will provide and "decided to task NATO to develop options for comprehensive missile-defense architecture to extend coverage to all allied territory and populations not otherwise covered by the U.S. system." In July 2008 U.S. and Czech officials signed an agreement on stationing a missile defense radar site in the Czech Republic pending parliamentary ratification. The accord with Warsaw on stationing a battery of U.S. interceptors was initialed in August 2008 but required parliamentary approval.

Washington and Warsaw agreed on August 14, 2008, to sign an accord on placing parts of the missile defense system in Poland. A former military base near the Baltic Sea would host ten interceptor missiles. The United States concurred with Warsaw's requirements, including assistance in modernizing Poland's military, particularly its air defenses. It planned to locate Patriot missiles and a garrison of U.S. servicemen in Poland for added security. The two countries also signed a declaration on strategic cooperation, designed to deepen their military and political partnership. It includes a mutual commitment to come to each other's assistance immediately if one is under attack, thus enhancing existing NATO obligations. The agreement indicated that the applicability and effectiveness of NATO's article 5 guarantee was increasingly treated with skepticism in CEE, given the accommodating approach toward Moscow in several WE capitals.

At a press conference in Moscow shortly after the missile defense announcement in Warsaw, Russia's deputy chief of general staff, General Anatoly Nogovitsyn, charged that the U.S. move "cannot go unpunished" and Russia will redirect its missiles at Poland.[101] A few weeks later, in September 2008, Russia test-fired a new-generation Bulava strategic missile from a submarine, the latest launch of a multiple-warhead weapon designed to breach antimissile shields.[102] The Bulava can be equipped with up to ten individually targeted nuclear warheads. Analysts believe that Russia has upgraded its missile systems to counter the U.S. shield, which Moscow claims is an attempt to undermine its nuclear deterrent. The test came three weeks after Russia test-fired an intercontinental RS-12M Topol missile, also designed to avoid detection by missile defense systems.

Realizing that Moscow could not reverse Poland's decision over missile defense, Moscow adopted a new tactic by seeking to bribe Warsaw into making concessions in other arenas in return for Russia's acquiescence to the missile defense system.[103] During a visit to Warsaw in the aftermath of the Georgian crisis on September 11, 2008, Foreign Minister Lavrov asserted that the Polish authorities should accept Russia's predominance in the "post-Soviet space" and support the construction of the Nord Stream pipeline under the Baltic Sea. In return, Poland would benefit from lucrative business contracts with Russia, and Moscow's threats to target the missile defense system on Polish territory would be suspended. Lavrov's offer underscored that despite all the propaganda posturing, the missile defense system was not viewed in the Kremlin as a threat to Russia but as a valuable bargaining chip in Moscow's strategy of security chess.

In an evident challenge to the incoming U.S. administration, on November 5, 2008, the day after Barack Obama was elected U.S. president, Medvedev announced that Russia would deploy short-range Iskander missiles in Kaliningrad to "neutralize" the planned missile defense shield. He also stated that Moscow would deploy the Russian navy against the shield and aim to jam the U.S. antimissile system electronically. Medvedev claimed that the conflict in the Caucasus was used as a pretext for sending NATO warships to the Black Sea and for "foisting America's anti-missile systems on Europe."[104] Moscow subsequently softened its approach when President Obama indicated that the missile defense system would not be constructed unless it was proved to be effective.

Basing Controversies

Russia protested vigorously over the building of U.S. military staging positions in Romania and Bulgaria and demanded discussions on the development of U.S. bases in any new NATO country. Washington and the two host countries rejected such proposals.[105] The U.S. administration made it clear that it would make only periodic deployments with limited military infrastructure to Bulgaria and Romania for training purposes, while Russia insisted that the United States planned to create the conditions for a rapid troop buildup on Russia's doorstep.

Budapest also hosts some NATO infrastructure. Papa airport in western Hungary was transformed into a base for NATO's strategic air transport fleet to carry troops and military cargo to Iraq and Afghanistan.[106] The Papa Air Base, established in July 2001 as a component of Hungary's national commitments in the NATO Infrastructural Development Program, became the main operating base for three or four Boeing C-17 Globemaster III transport planes. It also hosts Hungarian Air Force Search and Rescue helicopters.

According to Russia's military experts, the United States is gradually leaving behind Western Europe and moving its military resources and capabilities eastward, despite commitments made in the Founding Act on Mutual Relations, Cooperation, and Security signed between NATO and Russia in May 1997. They also allege that the U.S. bases in Romania and Bulgaria are not intended for dealing with the "arc of instability" across the Middle East, as Washington already possesses facilities in Turkey, Afghanistan, Israel, Kuwait, and Iraq. Instead, the new bases will become military footholds for establishing domination over Eastern Europe, the Black Sea region, and Transcaucasia.[107]

Moscow also charges that Washington will aim to convert the port of Savastopol in Crimea into a NATO base once Ukraine joins the alliance and the Russian fleet is pressured to vacate the facilities. When missile defense installations in CEE are added to this strategic equation, Moscow postulates that the grand plan is to surround Russia by bringing mobile U.S. battle groups closer to its borders. Romanian, Bulgarian, and Ukrainian bases will thereby make it easier to conduct air strikes against Russia, sealift ground troops on Russian territory, and neutralize Russia's Black Sea fleet.

While it opposes U.S. or NATO basing anywhere near its borders, Russia continues to maintain military bases in several neighboring states, including Belarus, Georgia, Ukraine, and Moldova. Government spokesmen claim that alliance enlargement has necessitated closer military integration between Russia and Belarus. Belarus is integrated in Russia's air defense system, and Moscow owns two military installations on Belarusian territory: a rocket early warning station and radar center and a navy command and control post.

Moscow has also reportedly established four S-300 missile bases close to the Belarusian-Polish border as an evident countermeasure to Poland's deployment of forty-eight F-16 fighter planes in its air force.[108] Although Belarusian president Alyaksandr Lukashenka has resisted forming a political union with Russia in which Belarus would simply become another Russian province, he fully supports Russia's military presence, a unified regional air defense system, and a common defense of the country against alleged "NATO encroachment" and "U.S. expansionism."[109] For Lukashenka, the missile defense system was avowedly part of a grand plan to destabilize Russia's deterrence potential, necessitating that Moscow and Minsk create a Russian-Belarusian Joint Regional Defense System.[110]

The bases issue has also been raised in the context of Russia's nonimplementation of the CFE Treaty. In May 2007 Defense Minister Ivanov warned that Russia would suspend its fulfillment of the CFE Treaty's mutual obligations for onsite inspections of forces and prenotification of military movements. He emphasized that U.S. deployments in Romania and Bulgaria violated CFE agreements.[111] This was a vivid example of how Moscow manufactures a dispute, pushes for advantageous concessions from the West, and acts unilaterally in another security arena, for example by abandoning the CFE Treaty, claiming it is simply seeking strategic parity.

4

Dominating Europe: Former Empire

Russia's Putinist foreign policy focuses on establishing several zones of enduring and expanding influence among immediate neighbors and former satellite states. The post-Soviet republics and CEE satellites are viewed among Russia's policy-makers as pawns in a broader struggle between Russia and the West in which their sovereignty is provisional and conditional. This chapter outlines two broad categories of relations that Moscow is developing: political dominance over the post-USSR republics and preeminence among the CEE states that were part of the Soviet bloc. By examining these international spheres and specifying the major foreign policy tools at the disposal of the Russian government—ranging from diplomatic offensives and informational warfare to energy blackmail and the purchase of political influence—one can assess Europe's position in Moscow's grander strategic ambitions.

Controlling Post-Soviet Republics

Putinism as a state strategy is intent on limiting Western institutional enlarge-ment while expanding the spheres of Russia's political influence. Reintegrating the "post-Soviet space" under Moscow's dominance became a priority under Putin as it gave credence to Russia's aspirations as an important global player and as a stabilizing factor in Eurasia. The Kremlin opposes any significant foreign military presence in the Commonwealth of Independent States and dissuades its neighbors from inviting U.S. forces or petitioning for NATO entry. It obstructs the creation of regional alliances or initiatives that may inhibit Russian inroads, and it pursues integration of its neighbors in Moscow-controlled institutions. Russian officials also oppose EU entry for CIS countries, viewing such a process as weakening their own multinational institutions and damaging their political and economic interests. The "Putin doctrine," seeking the restoration of Russian domination over the former Soviet Union, leaves targeted countries with a stark choice: either to accept a status as a Russian dominion, effectively abandoning ambitions to function as truly independent states, or to push ahead with genuine sovereignty in foreign policy, thus risking a fate similar to Georgia's or at the very least strong aggressive measure on Russia's part.[1]

The development of close relations between the West and Moscow's "near abroad" is depicted as Russia's "strategic defeat."[2] Russia claims special or privileged interests in this region while asserting the right to provide "comprehen-sive protection of rights and legitimate interests of Russian citizens and compatriots abroad."[3] Kremlin leaders assert that only Russia is capable of and entitled to "stabilize the post-Soviet territory" and to "prevent any unwelcome developments in this part of the continent and the adjacent territories."[4] According to Leonard and Popescu, Russia's fundamental challenge to the EU and NATO is not merely a question of energy security, diplomatic and political obstruction, or a host of international disputes. Buoyed by its soaring energy revenues, Russia did not aspire to join the West, but instead "it is setting itself up as an ideological alternative to the EU, with a different approach to sovereignty, power, and world order. Where the European project is founded on the rule of law, Moscow believes that laws are mere expressions of power—and that when the balance of power changes, laws should be changed to reflect it."[5]

The key battlegrounds with Western institutions and individual governments are Ukraine, Georgia, and Moldova, which are perceived as swing states in Moscow because of their governments' potential pro-Western orientation. Kremlin strategists believe that all three countries should have limited sovereignty under Russia's stewardship and that their national interests should be subordinate to those of Russia. The Kremlin offers incentives and threatens sanctions in order to develop closer asymmetrical ties.[6] The inducements include cheap energy, a growing market, employment for guest workers, visa-free travel, diplomatic support, and assistance in developing the security sector. The disincentives and pressures on neighboring governments include the exploitation of Russian minority populations through the alleged defense of their unique and endangered interests, support for oppositionist parties and pro-Russian movements, periodic energy embargoes, sudden and massive price hikes for gas and oil, trade sanctions, political demands, security threats, and even military actions as demonstrated in Georgia in August 2008.

Another intrusive mechanism was inaugurated in May 2008 with the creation of the Federal Agency for CIS Affairs.[7] It was attached to the Foreign Ministry and was mandated to deal with soft security questions in Moscow's relations with neighbors, especially in assisting Russian citizens resident in the post-Soviet countries, whose conditions serve as one of the primary justifications for Moscow's intervention.

The Russian regime enlists local elites in CIS capitals by enticing them with lucrative business contracts and assurances of political support in return for their political loyalty and the weakening of pro-Western orientations.[8] The urgency of this strategy was highlighted in the aftermath of the "colored revolutions" in Ukraine (2004) and Georgia (2003), which moved both countries closer to Western institutions. The Kremlin perceived those democratic breakthroughs as all-out confrontations with the West, and it condemned alleged interference in the internal politics of Ukraine and Georgia while fearing similar revolutions in other CIS countries and even in Russia itself.

Russian ambassadors play a key role in articulating Moscow's threats against neighboring governments and interfering in local politics. For example, Ambassador Viktor Chernomyrdin has frequently decried Ukraine's moves toward NATO and endorsed candidates in Ukraine's general elections.[9] In 2003 Russia's ambassador to Azerbaijan, Andrei Ryabov, in response to U.S. secretary of defense Donald Rumsfeld's offer of military assistance, declared, "There has not been and there will not be any kind of American presence in the Caspian. We will not allow it as they have nothing to guard here."[10]

One fundamental objective of Russia's policy is to keep aspirants from the CIS outside NATO. Moscow lobbies intensively against membership for Ukraine and Georgia and meddles directly in their internal affairs to disqualify them from NATO accession and turn public opinion against the alliance.[11] In the case of Ukraine, Russia exploits various pressure points to keep Kyiv off balance. It encourages the Russian population in Crimea to actively demonstrate against NATO, to prevent the holding of joint Ukrainian-NATO exercises, and to claim that the alliance is intent on destroying "Slavic unity."[12] The long-term uncertainty over the presence of Russia's Black Sea fleet in Sevastopol may also prove an obstacle to Kyiv's NATO aspirations, as it indicates that the country may not be fully independent because part of its territory is occupied by Russian forces.[13]

When the Ukrainian government indicated that it would seek a NATO membership action plan, Russian foreign minister Sergei Lavrov warned that "future cooperation between Russia and Ukraine depends to a large extent on how Ukraine's movement towards NATO membership develops."[14] Kremlin propaganda claimed that Ukraine's NATO entry would damage its political, economic, and social ties with Russia and even fracture the state by precipitating the secession of Crimea and eastern Ukraine. Such threats were most evident in the wake of the NATO summit in April 2008, following the alliance's declaration that Ukraine and Georgia would eventually become NATO members even though they had not received membership action plans.[15]

Moscow emphasizes the construction of an alternative alliance to NATO that would embrace all former Soviet republics. In October 2007 Russia's Nikolai

Bordyuzha, secretary general of the Collective Security Treaty Organization, announced that the CSTO was establishing its own peacekeeping forces without a United Nations mandate.[16] The force could evidently be deployed not only among member states (Russia, Belarus, Armenia, Kazakhstan, Kyrgyzstan, Tajikistan, and Uzbekistan) but also in the territories of neighboring countries.

Russia has steadily built up its military presence in Central Asia by reinforcing its bases in Tajikistan and Kyrgyzstan under the cover of CSTO agreements and remains by far the strongest military power in the CIS. There is little doubt that if any of the nondemocratic governments in the CIS were threatened by a "colored revolution" or popular upheaval, Moscow would come to their rescue, even by providing direct military assistance.

Moscow has also included the two secessionist regions of Abkhazia and South Ossetia inside Georgia as part of an exclusive zone of Russian responsibility and as potential future units of the Russian Federation. Moscow may adopt a similar position toward Moldova's separatist Transnistrian enclave, in which Russian peacekeepers are stationed without a UN mandate. Offers to internationalize these military contingents under the CSTO are designed as a countermove to Georgian and Moldovan proposals for a genuine multinational force under the auspices of the EU or the Organization for Security and Cooperation in Europe. In case of outright secession, article 65 of the Russian constitution legitimizes the admission of new territories to the Russian Federation and the creation of new federal subjects, thus enabling Moscow to manipulate the lever of annexation against neighboring states.[17]

The Kremlin's promotion of the Single Economic Space and a broader Eurasian Economic Community is designed to tie immediate neighbors into a Russian-dominated economic system and energy network and prevent any progress toward EU membership. The SES plan, involving Russia, Belarus, Ukraine, Kazakhstan, and Uzbekistan, envisages a customs union; a free trade zone; a common energy, agriculture, and transportation market; and eventual coordination of investment and tax policies with a common currency. Kyiv in particular is reluctant to integrate too closely within the SES lest it limit the country's prospects for meeting the criteria for a free trade agreement with the EU and eventual EU accession. It opposes most of the EAEC objectives, resists signing a single economic constitution, and refuses to coordinate its entry into the WTO with Russia.

The more expansive EEC initiative includes Russia, Belarus, Kazakhstan, Kyrgyzstan, Tajikistan, and Uzbekistan, with Armenia, Moldova, and Ukraine afforded observer status. The EEC was established in October 2000, when the founding states adopted a plan for "Eurasian economic integration." Members committed themselves to adopting common policies on trade, migration, currency exchange, and infrastructure development. The EEC developed an institutional framework with an administrative secretariat and an interparliamentary assembly designed to coordinate legislation. The members initialed several agreements designed to coordinate labor, monetary, customs, employment, tax, and investment policies. Moscow maintains a 40 percent share in EEC voting; Kazakhstan, Uzbekistan, and Belarus are afforded 15 percent each; while Kyrgyzstan and Tajikistan are allowed 7.5 percent each.

Such regional economic groupings dominated by the largest partner are not a viable substitute for multilateral trade agreements and could hinder access to global markets. Indeed, most CIS countries are reluctant to sign or implement any accords that bind them too closely to Moscow and preclude their integration with other multinational organizations. In November 2008 Uzbekistan suspended its membership in EEC, seemingly dissatisfied with its role in the organization as a primary commodities producer and its increasing economic subordination to Russia. In a response that reaffirmed Uzbekistan's well-grounded fears of Moscow's dominance, Foreign Minister Lavrov declared on November 17, 2008, that Tashkent's decision was not in Russia's best interests.[18]

Russia's authorities oppose the creation of alternative pan-national bodies in the territory of the former Soviet Union. They have condemned GUAM as a Western-inspired plot to undermine Russia's national interests. Several post-Soviet states seek to protect themselves from Moscow's interference and eventually to join Western organizations. With these long-term objectives, GUAM was founded in 1997 as a counterpart to the Russia-sponsored CIS. Although it initially achieved little in terms of regional economic and security cooperation, the initiative enabled the four countries to pool their efforts within various multinational formats.

A GUAM-U.S. program was established to promote trade and coordinate counterterrorist and anticrime operations. However, for several years GUAM languished as Uzbekistan withdrew its support in 2003 and the remaining countries found it difficult to implement an effective common agenda. In efforts to revive GUAM, in May 2006 leaders of the four member states met at a summit in Kyiv and renamed GUAM as the Organization for Democracy and Economic Development (ODED-GUAM).[19] They stressed the importance of ODED-GUAM in accelerating their integration into NATO and the EU and promoting democracy in the wider region. Participants adopted a GUAM statute as an international organization open to other states. Members also signed a free trade agreement, and work was scheduled to unify border and customs services between the four countries. In addition, members pledged to intensify cooperation in the energy sector, especially through diversification and construction of new delivery routes for Caspian resources. President Viktor Yushchenko of Ukraine asserted that one of ODED's main goals was to challenge Moscow's energy-export dominance.

Despite the momentum following the May 2006 summit, GUAM began to lose its impact after Ukraine's parliamentary elections in March 2006, in which NATO-neutral forces gained a majority of government posts. The Moldovan government also became more susceptible to Moscow's overtures to settle the Transnistrian dispute on Russia's terms. At GUAM's parliamentary assembly session in Chisinau, Moldova, in October 2006 representatives failed to issue a statement in support of Georgia in its escalating conflict with Moscow.[20] Furthermore, little was accomplished in formulating proposals to resolve the frozen conflicts in either Georgia or Moldova. The Ukrainian delegation's opposition was viewed as one of the main reasons for GUAM's paralysis in adopting a unified position.

The GUAM summit in Batumi in July 2008 exposed further fractures in the initiative that Moscow was determined to widen. Moldova's authorities appeared to snub the gathering as President Vladimir Voronin was again conspicuous by his absence. Voronin evidently calculated that his neutrality toward NATO would convince Moscow to resolve the Transnistrian conflict.[21] Moldova's potential withdrawal from GUAM would significantly weaken the organization and even lead to Azerbaijan's departure.[22] Baku itself is anxious not to antagonize Russia as its major concern is the capability to export energy. It views Russia's assertiveness in the Caucasus as a threat to its energy-export diversification and may succumb to Moscow's pressures to sell the bulk of its supplies to Russia; the alternative would be potential isolation as Moscow intends to undermine independent outlets of energy to Europe.

Another regional initiative, the Community of Democratic Choice, was launched by Kyiv and Tbilisi to promote democratic transformation and economic links among post-Soviet states. In August 2005 Ukrainian president Yushchenko and Georgian president Mikheil Saakashvili signed the Borjomi Declaration to establish a community of democratic countries in the Baltic–Black–Caspian Sea region. The presidents of Poland and Lithuania joined them when the CDC was formally launched at an inaugural summit in December 2005.[23] The CDC initiative was subject to criticism in addition to Moscow's condemnation because it appeared to divide states according to their democratic development, even though all of Moscow's neighbors were equally under threat from a resurgent Russia. According to Stephen Blank,

> Russian actions toward Georgia and Ukraine—threats to dismember them or occupy their territory, threats of targeting them with missiles, economic and energy boycotts, the deportation of Georgians residing in Russia, attempts to overthrow their governments or sabotage their elections—are not accidents or one-off policies. They are logical extensions of Russia's belief that it, as the only true "sovereign" state in the post-Soviet region, has the right

to demand fealty from CIS members and to undermine their stability if its interests are not sufficiently respected.[24]

Russian officials threatened to fracture Moldova and Georgia and absorb their separatist regions into Russia. According to the foreign minister of Moldova's Transnistria entity, the region will integrate into the Russian Federation in several stages over a five- to seven-year period.[25] This will include accession to the ruble zone, integration of educational systems, and the harmonization of laws. Similar statements have been made with regard to the two separatist enclaves in Georgia. In effect, Moscow imposes a state protectorate over the secessionist regions of Georgia and Moldova by providing Russian passports to the local population and economically subsidizing its political supporters. Russian and local businesses also benefit from the unsettled status of separatist regions, which allows for substantial profits to accrue from unaccounted economic activities, re-exporting, and illicit smuggling.

Moscow's ideal solution would have been to federalize or confederalize both Moldova and Georgia. In such an arrangement, the autonomous entities would maintain veto powers over the foreign and security policies of the central governments and effectively keep both countries outside NATO. The Kremlin has adopted various measures to stymie Chisinau's attempts to regain Transnistria. These have included a coercive energy policy through the manipulation of supplies, prices, and debt management, as Moldova is almost fully dependent on Russian supplies, as well as periodic embargoes on Moldovan wine and other vital agricultural exports.[26]

In a meeting with Moldovan president Vladimir Voronin in January 2008, Putin proposed a settlement that would ensure Moldova's permanent neutrality under international guarantees.[27] This would entail transforming Moldova into a federation with Transnistria while prolonging the presence of Russian troops until a final settlement was agreed on. Although Chisinau rejected the proposals, Voronin succumbed to Kremlin pressure by failing to ratify the GUAM charter, thus undercutting GUAM's recognition as a full-fledged regional organization.

Moscow is also wary of closer ties between Moldova and the EU and has undermined Union initiatives in Transnistria. It complained vigorously against the EU border mission between Transnistria and Ukraine designed to enforce Moldovan customs regulations. Moscow condemned the operation as a trade embargo, and Russian officials pressured Kyiv to suspend Ukrainian customs regulations that required goods exported from Transnistria to be registered with Moldova's customs authorities.[28]

The Kremlin has consistently supported pro-Russian separatist movements in Abkhazia and South Ossetia inside Georgian territory. The purpose was to exert pressure on Tbilisi and prevent the country from moving into the Western security orbit. Since the secessionist entities broke from Georgia in the early 1990s, Moscow has conducted a gradual annexation without formalizing its policies. It has stationed its troops on the territories without Georgian approval and expanded their numbers unilaterally, armed the local security forces, participated in the appointment of the local leadership, distributed Russian passports to the majority of residents, claimed its right to protect Russian citizens, and established official relations between Russian government bodies and the secessionist authorities.

Disputes with Georgia were intensified in May 2008, when Russia sent additional troops to Abkhazia without informing the Georgian government or any international organization.[29] It also heated up the prospect of South Ossetia's merger with North Ossetia prior to absorption in the Russian Federation. Moscow thereby demonstrated its disregard for the Georgian-Russian border and for Georgian sovereignty. Russia's "collective peacekeeping" operation lacked a legal basis either bilaterally or internationally, as no organization mandated Russia to conduct such a mission. Moscow's maneuvers also underscored the EU and NATO's weak response to unilateral Russian military deployments in former Soviet territories.

Russia's authorities engaged in political blackmail, asserting that Georgia's territories would be truncated if it joined NATO, but that it could regain Abkhazia and South Ossetia if it remained "neutral." With Tbilisi committed to NATO entry but denied a MAP by the alliance at the April 2008 NATO summit, Moscow's South Ossetian proxies felt more emboldened to provoke Georgia into military action in August 2008 by shelling Georgian villages. As frustration increased in Tbilisi over losing its territories, the Georgian military began an assault on the South Ossetian capital of Tsinkhvali.

The subsequent large-scale Russian military intervention destroyed much of the country's infrastructure and gave a pretext for Russia's recognition of the independence of South Ossetia and Abkhazia. It also enabled Russia to increase its troop presence in both secessionist republics and to control the new borders. Moscow's principal objectives were to undermine the Saakashvili government while discrediting and weakening Georgia as a NATO candidate. Critics of the Russian invasion asserted that Georgia's membership in the alliance would have deterred the military intervention, whereas divisions in NATO over Georgia's accession allowed Moscow to reassert its regional dominance.

Throughout the post-Soviet era Armenia has remained Russia's closest ally in the South Caucasus. The alliance is based on close historical ties and Moscow's defense of Armenia against Turkish and Azeri interests in the region. The Russian authorities have openly supported Armenian leaders who favor tight relations with Moscow, including the current president Serzh Sargsyan.[30] Russia has voiced confidence that Armenia, unlike neighboring Georgia and Azerbaijan, will not petition for NATO membership or pursue close military ties with the United States. In June 2008 President Medvedev criticized Sargsyan for seeking to improve links with both the EU and NATO, thus stepping outside his restricted international mandate.[31] Trade between the two countries has also steadily increased each year, and Russian investment and purchases in the Armenian economy have accompanied it.

Acknowledging its vulnerability and potential isolation in the Caucasus, Azerbaijan has tried to enhance its ties with the West but without fully estranging Russia. This was especially evident in the wake of the Russian invasion of Georgia in August 2008, when Baku supported its ally Georgia but refrained from condemning and potentially provoking Russia. Moscow has applied various pressures and incentives toward the Azeri government to prevent the construction of a U.S. base in Azerbaijan, forestall Baku's potential bid for NATO membership, and preempt Azerbaijan from supplying the Western-sponsored Nabucco pipeline. It has offered to buy all of Baku's natural gas exports at market prices having further undermined the reliability of transit through Georgia.

Undermining NATO and EU Aspirants

The muted EU and U.S. responses to Russian government campaigns against Ukraine, Moldova, and Georgia have convinced Moscow that it has a relatively free hand to intimidate pro-Western governments in all three states. For example, in October 2006 Georgia lobbied for the UN Security Council to help introduce an international contingent of peacekeepers in Abkhazia. Washington buckled to Russian pressure to provide only for CIS troops after Moscow agreed to back the United States in its policy toward North Korea. This was a valuable example of how the Kremlin balances various outstanding international disputes to gain strategic advantages vis-à-vis the West.

Russia has employed a litany of subversive strategies toward EU and NATO aspirants in order to disqualify them from both organizations. Kremlin officials, including Defense Minister Sergei Ivanov, have consistently threatened that Russia's relations with Kyiv and Tbilisi will deteriorate sharply if either were to join NATO.[32] President Medvedev told his Ukrainian counterpart in June 2008 that Ukraine could be in breach of the 1997 bilateral friendship treaty if it entered NATO.[33] President Yushchenko's administration also accused Russia of using energy disputes to influence Ukrainian politics and foreign policy after the September 2007 elections, during the process of forming a new government.[34] In October 2007 Gazprom declared that Ukraine owed more than $1.3 billion for gas supplies and threatened to cut back stocks if the debt was not paid promptly.

Russia's elites have an imperialistic and patronizing posture toward Ukraine, denying the existence of a separate and distinct Ukrainian history and national identity. Indeed, Ukraine is depicted as Russia's "younger brother," destined to remain in a close union dominated by Moscow.[35] When Kyiv misbehaves by petitioning for NATO, officials in Moscow employ a range of weapons to bring Ukraine into line. For instance, they exacerbate the Crimea question by raising the specter of a potential fracturing of Ukraine and the creation of a new frozen conflict that could destabilize the government in Kyiv. Russian organizations sponsored by the Kremlin have periodically stoked tensions in Crimea. For instance, in the summer of 2006 rallies were organized in Crimea against the annual NATO-Ukrainian emergency response and peacekeeping exercises. Moscow has also supported politicians who are hesitant about Ukraine's NATO membership, including the current opposition leader and former prime minister, Viktor Yanukovich.

In July 2008 Ukrainian president Yushchenko raised the necessity of starting talks with Russia on the removal of the Russian Black Sea fleet from Sevastopol in 2017, when the twenty-year lease in the Ukrainian port officially expires. His statement came amid louder calls from some Russian politicians to break Crimea away from Ukraine.[36] In July 2008 Moscow mayor Yuriy Luzhkov urged the Duma not to prolong the 1997 Russian-Ukrainian Treaty of Friendship, Cooperation, and Partnership, which was due to expire in December 2008. The document recognizes the current borders of Ukraine, effectively legalizing the handover of Crimea by Russian leader Nikita Khrushchev to Ukraine in 1954. If the treaty was not renewed, Russian politicians could intensify their demands to return Crimea to Russia, as they did during the treaty ratification process in 1998.[37]

The "Statement of the Russian Ministry of Foreign Affairs on Russian-Ukrainian Relations," issued on September 11, 2008, called into question the 1997 treaty by linking its renewal to Kyiv's willingness to extend basing agreements for the Russian Black Sea fleet beyond December 2017. Otherwise, Russia would evidently be within its rights to reconsider the 1997 treaty, in which Moscow recognized Ukraine's sovereignty and territorial integrity. As neither Russia nor Ukraine took action to block the treaty's renewal, it was automatically renewed for a period of ten years on October 1, 2008. Nonetheless, fears persisted that Crimean separatism remained a potent weapon in Russia's anti-Ukrainian arsenal. Indeed, the prospect of partition is a useful method for pressuring Kyiv to prolong the presence of Russia's Black Sea fleet in Sevastopol beyond 2017.

In this context, Mayor Luzhkov, who is closely connected with the Kremlin, is accused of channeling funds to Russian separatists in Crimea, including the unregistered National Front Sevastopol-Crimea-Russia. The National Front was created in August 2005 and includes twelve pro-Russian public associations.

In 2007 it declared the beginning of a campaign bearing the slogan "Ukraine without the Crimea." The majority of Crimea's population is Russian, and a large percentage of Crimeans have reportedly been issued Russian passports. Thus Moscow could intervene on the peninsula on the pretext of defending the interests of its citizens following the Abkhaz and Ossetian model applied against Georgia.

Russia's authorities endeavor to fracture GUAM by playing different capitals against each other, punishing pro-Western administrations, and bribing governments with lucrative economic benefits.[38] During 2003 Moldova turned westward under President Voronin, as it felt ostracized by Russia with the persistent lack of progress on resolving the Transnistrian standoff. Voronin also outraged the Kremlin by moving closer to Ukrainian president Yushchenko and Georgian president Saakashvili within the GUAM framework and was placed on Moscow's blacklist of unfriendly leaders. This was accompanied by trade embargos on Moldovan products, including wine, a key export industry. Moscow's boycott demonstrated that politics took precedence over profits, given that Russian businesses own an important section of Moldova's largest wineries.[39]

Moscow has kept the Moldovan government off balance in its European aspirations by maintaining the frozen conflict in Transnistria and opposing the EU Border Assistance Mission (EUBAM) launched in December 2005 to curb smuggling along the Transnistrian-Ukrainian frontier. Russia actively supports the Transnistrian regime through economic assistance and diplomatic backing, by affirming the region's right to secession and by refusing to withdraw its troops from the breakaway territory. Transnistria's leader, Igor Smirnov, has little incentive to compromise with Chisinau in his drive toward independence.[40] In an indication that Moscow's intimidation was having an impact on Moldova, in June 2007 President Voronin did not attend the GUAM summit in Kyiv to avoid exacerbating disputes with the Kremlin.

Following the invasion and partition of Georgia, the Kremlin intensified its pressure on Chisinau in brokering a settlement with Transnistria on terms favorable to Moscow and Tiraspol, the capital of Transnistria. Following Moldova's contentious parliamentary elections in March 2009 and with President Voronin intent on leaving a legacy of reunification after serving his final term in office, Moscow had several options in pushing for a final settlement in which Transnistria would become either a co-equal federal unit or an autonomous territory with guaranteed government representation. Both options could disable Moldova from moving closer to Western institutions and place the country more firmly within Moscow's orbit.

In September 2008 Russian authorities pushed Moldova toward a bilateral settlement to reunify the state under Moscow's oversight and to demonstrate that countries such as Moldova that do not seek NATO entry will be treated leniently.[41] Under the planned agreement, Russia would become the guarantor of a final settlement and retain a military presence in Moldova. Meanwhile, Tiraspol would obtain blocking powers over Chisinau's policies through amendments in Moldova's constitution and the introduction of numerical overrepresentation of Transnistrian deputies in a reunified Moldovan parliament. This would enable Tiraspol to prevent Moldova from harmonizing its legislation and policies with those of the EU. Russian officials have informed Chisinau that both NATO and the EU were political-military blocs and that accession to either would be incompatible with Moldova's neutrality.

The Russian authorities adopted a policy of destabilization toward Georgia after Saakashvili was elected president in January 2004. The primary aim was to prevent the country from completing a successful bid for NATO membership. Kremlin attempts to destabilize the government in Tbilisi have included political subversion, a planned coup d'etat, and the exacerbation of ethnic division and conflict in various regions of Georgia. In September 2006 the Georgian government arrested four Russian GRU officers on suspicion of planning a coup in Tbilisi. In response, Moscow recalled its ambassador from Tbilisi; cut postal, phone, and banking links with Georgia; warned that it would double the price of gas; imposed an extensive embargo on key Georgian exports such as wine and mineral water; threatened the status of Georgian citizens working in Russia, whose remittances are important for the Georgian economy; closed the only legal land-border crossing between the two countries; and regularly violated Georgian airspace.

The purpose of Russia's tactics was threefold. First, it sought to undermine popular support for the Saakashvili government while holding out the prospect that a new Russia-friendly administration that rejected NATO accession would restore normal relations and boost economic prospects.[42] Second, Moscow posed as the sole protector of the populations of Abkhazia and South Ossetia against alleged Georgian aggression. And third, the Kremlin tested the resolve of the EU and NATO in supporting Tbilisi when confronted with an escalating conflict with Russia. The EU's lukewarm responses to such provocations reassured the Kremlin that it need not fear Western reactions.[43]

Moscow prefers to turn Georgia into a neutral state so that it does not become a bridgehead for the "deployment of strategic elements of a military machine."[44] Defense Minister Ivanov claimed that Georgia would automatically become an adversary of Russia if it joined the NATO alliance and sought to squash contentions that NATO entry would enable Georgia to regain its breakaway territories.[45] General Yuriy Baluyevskiy, chief of the General Staff of Russia's armed forces, declared that NATO's readiness to launch an "intensive dialogue" with Tbilisi increased tensions between Georgia and Russia and led to Georgia's "militarization."[46] In the longer term, the Kremlin is intent on repositioning Georgia under

Russia's sphere of influence and freezing its Western aspirations. This objective was starkly exposed following the military invasion in August 2008.

The Kremlin supported the separatist conflicts in Abkhazia and South Ossetia to disqualify Georgia from NATO, as Tbilisi did not control the entire country and was in direct conflict with Russia. Kremlin officials asserted that they were defending their own citizens and military peacekeepers in both breakaway regions against "Georgian aggression." Several Muscovite politicians and government leaders threatened to recognize the two quasi-republics.[47] Meanwhile, the two entities were steadily integrated into the Russian state through financial, economic, and administrative instruments, including the provision of passports and pensions to the inhabitants.[48] Following the Russian invasion in August 2008, Kremlin leaders declared that Abkhazia and South Ossetia would not return under Georgian control and raised the prospect of full separation. On August 26, 2008, President Medvedev declared Russia's formal recognition of the independence of South Ossetia and Abkhazia.[49]

Belarus, under the autocratic rule of President Alyaksandr Lukashenka, is not an EU or NATO aspirant, and Moscow is determined to maintain that position and not replace Lukashenka with a less predictable or pro-Western leader. Although progress on the Union State of Russia and Belarus has stalled in recent years—largely because Minsk resisted proposals for full incorporation in the Russian Federation—Moscow favors Belarus as an anti-Western outpost with which it maintains close security ties.[50] Signs of a more assertive Russian policy were visible at the end of May 2008, when Putin was also named as prime minister of the Russia-Belarus Union State.

Lukashenka himself is engaged in a balancing act between full Belarusian independence and a union with Russia. He seeks to preserve Moscow's energy subsidization, which keeps the economy afloat, and is weary of Western support for the democratic opposition. But he is also unwilling to fully expose the economy to Russian capital, as this could break his political stranglehold.

Following Russia's invasion of Georgia in August 2008, Lukashenka gave indications that he wanted to end his isolation from the West in facing an assertive Russia that could seek to incorporate Belarus within the Russian Federation. Lukashenka sought to improve ties with the EU in particular, and by freeing political prisoners on September 28, 2008, the eve of general elections, Minsk wanted the EU and Washington to lift the travel ban on forty Belarusian officials. EU officials stated that they would consider easing or lifting sanctions against Belarus if the elections were freer and fairer than the previous national ballot.[51]

Some Kremlin advisers have also floated the idea of an Eastern European Union that could reportedly include all the post-Soviet states as well as Turkey and Russia itself.[52] The objective of Russia's officials is to create an alternative pole of attraction to the EU and to counterbalance Union influence and especially that of the newest EU members, who seek to bring countries such as Ukraine and Georgia into the EU and NATO. Such ambitions, with Moscow posing as the counterpart to Brussels, not only envisions a multipolar world but also a bipolar Europe.

Reorbiting Former Satellites

Putin and Medvedev understand that Russia cannot prevent NATO enlargement in the former Soviet bloc countries of Central and Eastern Europe. Instead, they aim to minimize the impact of NATO's growth by building a firewall around the former USSR republics and gaining a role in alliance decision making to weaken NATO's effectiveness. Simultaneously, the Kremlin endeavors to keep the EU at a measured distance from its immediate neighbors, realizing that any fast progress toward Union accession could weaken Russia's political, economic, and security leverage with subordinate CIS capitals. In pursuit of these strategic goals, Russia's policy toward former CEE satellites is regionalized into three main zones: the Baltic republics, the Central European states, and the southeast European, or Balkan, countries.

The Central European and the Baltic states are viewed in Moscow as buffer zones against further Western encroachment on former Soviet territories. They are also perceived as a potentially negative source of influence over their CIS neighbors and therefore in need of neutralization, marginalization, and containment. The Kremlin's goal is to weaken and isolate their influence within the EU and NATO and to transform them into peripheral international players.

In its propaganda attacks, Moscow claims that CEE capitals, especially Warsaw, Vilnius, Riga, and Tallinn, are injecting Russophobic positions into the EU and NATO. To counteract such trends, the Kremlin pursues closer bilateral relations with Western European states so as to convince them to marginalize the troublesome CEE newcomers in the EU's decision-making process. Central Europe also provides opportunities for Russian inroads to the pan-European and transatlantic institutions through economic, political, and intelligence penetration. Russian officials focus on influencing political decisions in these capitals through a combination of diplomatic pressure, personal and professional contacts, economic enticements, and energy blackmail. They also promote political, ethnic, and social turbulence in targeted states to unsettle adversarial governments.

Russian intelligence services seek to influence public opinion among new EU and NATO members through their financially generated access to politicians, the media, and opinion leaders. In September 2008 the Czech counterintelligence agency, the Security Information Service (BIS), disclosed that Russian agents had become extremely active in the Czech Republic in stirring public sentiment against the planned U.S. missile defense radar base. According to the BIS report, Russian intelligence services "have attempted to contact, infiltrate and influence people and organizations that have influence on public opinion." The BIS annual report concluded that Moscow's "active measures" were intended to weaken the integrity of NATO and the EU, isolate the United States, and "renew control over the lost Soviet security perimeter in Europe."[53]

Moscow realizes that direct political and military control over CEE is no longer feasible. Instead, it seeks to capture preeminent influence over the foreign policy orientations and security postures of the most vulnerable states, to obstruct forms of regional cooperation that counter its own objectives, and to isolate uncooperative governments. Russia's success rate has varied. In some cases it has exerted leverage over a country's international priorities; in other instances its influences are limited or divisive; and on occasion its policies backfire, as suspicions about its motives in part propel several capitals in a more determined westward direction. But Kremlin strategists calculate that temporary setbacks can be reversed given the appropriate mixture of incentive, pressure, and subterfuge.

Russia exploits differences between EU and NATO newcomers, as CEE is not a unified bloc of states. Instead, general differences have emerged between the Baltic and Central Europe. The Baltic group of "frontline states" (Poland, Latvia, Lithuania, Estonia) feels especially vulnerable to pressure from Russia, is assertive in focusing EU policy on the "Eastern Question" by embracing former Soviet republics, and views the transatlantic relationship as paramount.

In contrast, a group of Central European countries, or the "safe states" (Slovenia, Hungary, Czech Republic, Slovakia), are more circumspect in their policy toward Russia and other post-Soviet states and focus on deepening EU integration and economic development. Romania fortifies the Baltic group, while Bulgaria is a more neutral actor. Capitals that perceive more immediate security threats in their neighborhood and calculate that older EU members will not resolutely defend their interests exhibit a stronger Atlanticist orientation and view Washington as more capable than Brussels in providing political and security assistance.

Targeted foreign investments and strategic infrastructural buyouts in CEE equip Moscow with stronger leverage over any government's economic, financial, trade, and investment policies. Russia has also conducted trade wars with its immediate western neighbors through a series of economic blockades designed to undermine their economies. For instance, Russia has periodically banned fish imports from the three Baltic states and meat and vegetable imports from Poland.[54] In the energy sector the Kremlin is determined to become a regional monopolist. It aims to convert CEE's overwhelming dependence on importing energy supplies into long-term intergovernmental influence by mobilizing Russian enterprises to subvert officials, parties, and media outlets in the CEE states. According to Mitchell, in the longer term, "by subverting the national political and business elites of CEE countries [Russia] is steadily eroding the foundations of Atlanticism that make possible the region's security link with the United States."[55]

Several cases of direct political subversion have been reported in which Russian businessmen tied to the Kremlin's intelligence services have purchased influence. Such ploys unseated President Rolandas Paksas in Lithuania in 2003 through an impeachment process and placed other officials under suspicion of collaboration and corruption. This included the leader of the Labor Party in Lithuania, the Russian-born Viktoras Uspaskich, who was granted political asylum in Russia in 2006 but returned to Lithuania eighteen months later. Reports surfaced that the Labor Party had received payments from Russian secret services. The Lithuanian parliament is also investigating the subversive role of Gazprom's intermediaries in recruiting senior Lithuanian intelligence officers. Both Paksas and Uspaskich remained politically active in their respective parties and were widely deemed to be susceptible to Russian influence.

On October 12, 2008, the eve of Lithuanian parliamentary elections, analysts believed that the country's factionalized political spectrum provided inroads for outside influence. For instance, members of the Lithuanian Social Democratic Party (LSDP), among other politicians, have reportedly benefited from campaign contributions from donors linked with the Russian-Lithuanian gas trade. Vytautas Landsbergis, a former Lithuanian president (1990–92) and a leader of the conservative Homeland Union-Christian Democrats (TS-LKD), stated, "Russia works with Lithuanian politicians, distinguishing between the more pro-Russian and pro-western parties. Such an approach creates the conditions for confrontation. What Russia wishes is not just to disseminate ideas but, rather, to have an impact on decision-making and hence on individual politicians. It wants to influence parliament and, ideally, install 'its' people in governing positions. Even the presidency seems an attainable target."[56]

Reports regularly surface in Slovakia, Hungary, Bulgaria, and other CEE states that old comrade networks continue to operate, based on financial and friendship connections rather than ideological or political convictions. Nonetheless, socialist and social democrat parties, to which many of the ex-Communists have gravitated, appear to provide the most beneficial opportunities for Russian penetration. Lucrative business contracts, donations to political campaigns, and the purchase of media outlets enable Moscow to exert political influence and convince key politicians to favor Russian investments and strategic interests.

In Latvia, Kremlin-sponsored penetration of governmental bodies precipitated wide-ranging investigations of official corruption and resulted in the resignation of the entire administration in December 2007.[57] As Blank points out, Russia's strategy "utilizes the connections of Russian energy companies, intelligence agents, and businesses tied to or subsidizing local politicians and which have the potential to subvert governments."[58] Moscow has also been active in sponsoring nongovernmental organizations (NGOs) in Latvia and the other Baltic countries to campaign against government policy and promote the interests of Russian minorities in such areas as education and language use.

If influence cannot be readily purchased or induced, Moscow fosters suspicion and distrust within and among neighboring countries and brings into question their stability and reliability as EU members or NATO allies. By planting disinformation about official connections with Russian intelligence services or with organized crime in a region where distrust of officialdom is widespread, the Kremlin can undermine incumbent governments or blackmail individuals to promote its interests.

Moscow also practices a policy of differentiation in the Baltic and Central Europe. For instance, while Lithuania appeared to be favored in the late 1990s, Latvia was depicted as a major anti-Russian offender, and intensive political and economic pressures were applied against Riga. Anti-Estonian campaigns have been more consistent and predictable. Russia conducts a similar policy of discrimination between Warsaw and nearby CEE capitals that are less outspoken about Moscow's strategy. The objective is to weaken CEE solidarity, isolate particular capitals, and undercut arguments that the Baltic and CEE states generate regional stability through their membership in NATO and the EU.

Since the early 1990s Moscow has viewed the southeastern European or Balkan region as an important zone of interest where competition with NATO and the United States was pronounced, where armed conflicts and interstate tensions could be manipulated to Moscow's advantage, where potential new allies could be found, and where economic opportunities, especially in the energy sector, could be exploited to Russia's benefit. Moscow is seeking a string of weak or divided states across the Balkan Peninsula through which it can exert influence and counter the American presence.

At the Organization of the Black Sea Economic Cooperation (BSEC) summit in Istanbul in June 2007, President Putin confirmed that Russia was purposively returning to the Balkan and Black Sea regions.[59] Through its control of oil and gas supplies and energy networks, Moscow was intent on restoring its preeminence and checking NATO and U.S. expansion. In this context, the international dispute over recognizing Kosova as an independent state served Kremlin policy by injecting Russia as a major player, through its veto powers in the UN Security Council, in support of Serbia's position against Kosova's statehood.

Russia has offered lucrative energy contracts to several Balkan states, including Bulgaria, Serbia, and Greece, to eliminate prospects for alternative energy supplies into Europe. Romania has proved a tougher proposition for the Kremlin in penetrating political networks and gaining Bucharest's support in Russia's pan-European energy strategy. Putin snubbed Romanian president Traian Băsescu at the energy summit in Croatia in June 2007, when he stated that Russia's link with the EU would be assured by Bulgaria.[60] The Romanian president responded by lobbying for a Union-wide energy policy, criticizing the blackmail practiced by the Kremlin toward the EU and calling for free competition, transparency, and nondiscrimination on the energy market.

Marginalizing New Alliance Members

Moscow employs a legion of policy instruments to weaken the impact of new members from CEE within both NATO and the EU.[61] These range from propaganda attacks, discrediting campaigns, and institutional penetration to energy blackmail, political corruption, and attempts to destabilize neighboring governments. Russia's authorities regularly attack the Polish and Baltic administrations for injecting destructive anti-Russian influences into the EU and pro-American influences into the CIS. They refer specifically to CEE criticisms of Russian policy and efforts to bring Ukraine, Moldova, and Georgia into the EU and NATO.

Russian officials claim that CEE governments are acting at Washington's behest to drive a wedge between Russia and Western Europe—by, for example, promoting an energy strategy aimed at reducing European dependence on Russia.[62] The Kremlin focuses much of its fire on the three Baltic capitals partly to marginalize their influence in the EU and NATO and partly to discourage other states from aspiring to NATO membership. Russia's officials allege that the three suffer from a "victim syndrome" and that they continue to equate the Russian Federation with the Soviet Union.[63]

Moscow insists that, contrary to conventional wisdom, the entry of the Baltic countries into NATO worsened their relations with Russia because the governments in Tallinn, Riga, and Vilnius felt more emboldened to discriminate against Russian and other non-Baltic minorities and to "glorify fascism."[64] By escalating conflicts with Estonia, Latvia, and Lithuania, the Kremlin sought to discourage Ukraine and Georgia from petitioning for NATO entry, as their membership would avowedly jeopardize their relations with Moscow and create more problems for NATO with respect to Russia. Provocative acts against the Baltic capitals are also designed to test NATO and EU responses and to demonstrate that Russia remained the dominant regional player even though Moscow's direct military incursion against a NATO member seemed unlikely.

To punish the Baltic capitals, Moscow has applied discriminatory rail tariffs and export duties on various products contrary to its agreements with the EU during the WTO accession process. However, the most egregious example of

Russia's economic pressure was the full-scale trade sanctions imposed against Georgia during 2006–7 that included transportation and travel blockades between the two countries after four Russian spies were arrested in Georgia in September 2006.

Moscow has also expressed opposition to EU membership for Bulgaria and Romania and complained that it was not "consulted" on their incorporation.[65] Hence, it threatened to include both countries in its ban on meat imports and other restrictions because of alleged health and safety concerns. EU Commissioner Olli Rehn called the move a "political game" and a "disproportionate threat," as hygiene norms in all member states met EU standards.

At the EU-Russia summit in Samara, Russia, in May 2007, the Union partially stood up to Moscow's bullying of its small EU neighbors.[66] In a mark of solidarity with Poland and the Baltic states, European Commission president José Manuel Barroso warned Russia not to drive wedges between EU countries by banning Polish meat imports or accusing Estonia of fascism. However, Warsaw and its neighbors remain distrustful that EU assertiveness toward Russia will evolve beyond the issuing of occasional critical statements.

The May 9 anniversary of the end of World War II has served as a useful date for Moscow to stir up domestic hostility against the Baltic states and isolate these EU newcomers. Kremlin spokesmen condemn historically accurate assertions by Estonian, Latvian, and Lithuanian officials that the Red Army occupied these formerly independent states at the close of the war and that the period of Soviet rule resulted in mass repression and economic retardation.

In May 2007 Tallinn accused Moscow of launching a concerted anti-Estonian campaign after the government decided to move a Red Army statue from the center of the capital to a military cemetery. The statue represented Soviet conquest and occupation of Estonia and was an affront to the majority of Estonian citizens.[67] Subsequently, Russia's secret services and the Russian embassy in Tallinn were accused of organizing various provocations, including violent demonstrations in the Estonian capital and a sustained cyberattack on Estonian government websites and critical communications infrastructure. Eventually, both the European Commission and NATO expressed solidarity with Estonia over the confrontation. Perversely, Russian foreign minister Lavrov claimed that their backing for Tallinn "contradicts European values and culture."[68]

In November 2007 Russia's deputy defense minister, General Vladimir Isakov, claimed the government was taking "additional measures" to prevent acts of "vandalism" at Russian military cemeteries abroad in the wake of Estonia's removal of the Red Army memorial from the center of Tallinn.[69] Although it was unclear how Russia meant to prevent such developments outside its borders, the warning was intended to undermine the sovereignty and security of several neighboring states.

In the wake of the cyberattacks on Estonia, NATO decided to send cyber-security staff to Tallinn to investigate how government websites could be better secured. Among the sites affected were those of the Estonian president's office, the government, the official press service, parliament, several ministries, and other government agencies.[70] Urmas Paet, Estonia's foreign minister, claimed that some of the attacks originated from addresses registered in the name of Russia's presidential administration. In response, Russia's spokesmen claimed that the cybersabotage was actually staged by Tallinn to fuel tensions between Russia and the EU. As a consequence of the Estonian episode, NATO reaffirmed its position that cyberterrorism constituted a serious threat to national security and supported the creation of a cyberdefense center in Tallinn.

Moscow launches air patrols over the territories of new NATO members to which it has objected. This is particularly the case in the Baltic states. In an indication of Russia's refusal to accept its reduced status in the region, all three Baltic capitals have reported periodic violations of their airspace by Russian military jets.[71] Russian forces have also staged military exercises near the Estonian and Latvian borders simulating the reconquest of the Baltic states and the prevention of NATO assistance. Moscow argues that the Balts are a source of regional instability and a security threat to Russia because they are not signatories of the Conventional Forces in Europe Treaty and could be recipients of large amounts of NATO weaponry.[72]

Periodic expulsions of diplomats are also a feature of bilateral relations with Moscow. For instance, in January 2008 Riga expelled a Russian diplomat, assert-ing that his presence posed a threat to national security. Reportedly, the official was involved in espionage involving sensitive government facilities.[73]

In maintaining a state of siege against its democratic neighbors, Moscow regularly attacks the Baltic governments for alleged repression against Russian-speaking minorities despite all evidence to the contrary. In October 2007 Putin engaged in blatant disinformation when he informed members of the European Jewish Congress that Estonia and Latvia glorified Nazism while the EU remains silent.[74] He also complained that the Ukrainian government allowed veterans of partisan groups that fought both the Nazis and the Soviet occupation forces to hold war remembrances. Russian NGOs persistently lobby against the Baltic capitals in the European Parliament and the European Court of Human Rights.

Riina Kionka, personal representative on human rights to Javier Solana, the EU's high representative for common foreign and security policy, stated that Russian charges of "crimes against humanity" against former Latvian president Vaira Vike-Freiberga and former Estonian president Arnold Rüütel were an attempt to ward off criticisms of Russia by taking the offense against two small neighbors.[75] Kionka's charges were confirmed by the activities of the youth group

Nashi (Ours), which was closely tied to the Kremlin and engaged in an "antifascist marathon" protest outside the offices of the European Commission in Brussels. Kionka pointed out that the Baltic states would not have been admitted into the EU if Moscow's accusations were accurate.

In another example of Moscow-inspired provocations, shortly after the Russian invasion of Georgia, a number of Russian news agencies reported that several minority-populated villages in Estonia were seeking independence.[76] The claims proved to be fabrications, but the purpose may have been to keep Tallinn preoccupied, to stoke domestic tensions, and to create the impression that Estonia was unstable. Russian activists have also established the Night Guard Movement in Tallinn to allegedly defend the minority population and to petition for establishing a Russian autonomous region within Estonia.

The Kremlin has consistently complained about the destructive influence of EU newcomers on EU-Russia relations and on perceptions in Western Europe of Russia's policy.[77] It stresses Poland's and Lithuania's blockage of the renewal of the Partnership and Cooperation Agreement despite strong support for its speedy renewal by Germany and France.[78] According to Russian officials, some CEE capitals engage in political intrigues against Moscow and hold the EU hostage to particularistic interests. Moscow was clearly encouraged by the fact that despite its invasion and annexation of Georgian territory in August 2008, the majority of Western European states pushed for a speedy renewal of the PCA and did not succumb to the alleged "anti-Russian" caucus inside the EU. In November 2008 EU foreign ministers decided to resume partnership talks with Russia, despite failing to reach unanimous agreement because of opposition from Lithuania and Poland.

Dividing Europe: European Union

Moscow capitalizes on unresolved international disputes or manufactures regional or bilateral conflicts to drive wedges between EU countries and between Europe and the United States. The objects of these disputes have included the planned U.S. missile defense shield in Central Europe, the parameters of energy security, and the validity of various arms control treaties. Aggressive diplomacy, negative propaganda, and the promotion of pan-European altercations also amplify the Kremlin's drive to marginalize troublesome new EU and NATO members that are critical of Moscow while undermining the aspirations of potential candidates to both organizations. Furthermore, Moscow courts particular European capitals and estranges others, so that it can more easily divide and dominate by weakening EU and NATO consensus while developing interest groups and political supporters who will favor elements of Russia's foreign and security policy.

Russia's Divisive EU Policy

In seeking to fracture EU-U.S. relations, Moscow follows three approaches. First, it develops problem areas to create rifts in the North Atlantic Alliance and the European Union. Second, it capitalizes on existing policy differences between the United States and the larger EU countries to establish informal coalitions in opposition to American policy. And third, it focuses on bilateral ties with individual EU states to undermine Union institutions and preclude a common policy while distancing the targeted capitals from Washington. In applying these strategies, Moscow operates on the notion that "it is in Europe's interest to dissociate itself from U.S. policy, which is impossible without cooperation with Russia."[1]

Russia seeks direct relations with EU institutions, but not ties as a candidate or member state, in which its influence would be diluted. It refuses to surrender any elements of its sovereignty to EU institutions but prefers a strategic partnership, which would expand its international interests and restrict criticisms of its policies. Moscow is focused on raising its economic importance and security profile vis-à-vis Europe while constructing its own Eurasian economic and military organizations.

The points of dispute between Russia and the EU and several member states have expanded precipitously over recent years. By the close of the Putin presidency in May 2008, they included such questions as missile defense; the status of Kosova; the future of the Organization for Security and Cooperation in Europe as a democracy-promoting organization; the Conventional Forces in Europe Treaty and arms control arrangements more broadly; NATO enlargement; claims to the Arctic region; NATO air patrols in the Baltic states; the frozen conflicts in Moldova and Georgia; the future security orientations of Ukraine, Georgia, and Moldova; Russian military overflights of NATO members' airspace; Russia's increasingly aggressive naval exercises; and bilateral disputes with specific capitals, including London, Warsaw, Tallinn, Riga, and Vilnius.

In countering "NATO-centrism," "American dominance," and "pro-Atlanticism," Moscow sides with selected Western European governments against specific U.S. policies. It favored the Moscow-Berlin-Paris "axis" during U.S. preparations for the invasion of Iraq in the spring of 2003 in a ploy designed to decouple "core Europe" from America. The axis proved a temporary arrangement, however, because of changing EU priorities, the softening of Washington's criticisms of its European allies, and the replacement of governments through new elections in both Germany and France. On a more consistent basis, Moscow furthers its ties with individual states to forestall the emergence of a common EU policy and diminish the role of member states applying a more forthright agenda toward Russia.

A struggle has unfolded inside the EU regarding the most effective approach toward Russia, with Warsaw and Vilnius at the forefront of capitals advocating a more assertive policy. Polish and Lithuanian officials believe that the Union should show greater concern about antidemocratic tendencies in Russian politics and neo-imperial trends in Moscow's foreign policy. Central and Eastern European capitals also highlight that Russia fractures the EU by favoring differing approaches toward the WE and the CEE countries and using its ties with the former to undermine the impact of the latter.[2]

One major arena in which several CEE capitals attempt to limit Russian dominance and divisiveness is energy policy. They strongly support a common EU energy strategy focused on alternative gas and oil supplies from the Caspian Basin to reduce dependence on Russian transit routes. Poland and the Baltic states vehemently oppose the construction of a new trans-Baltic pipeline in a deal between Germany and Russia that would bypass Poland, Ukraine, and the Baltic countries. Warsaw asserts that such projects need to be decided within the Union and not on a bilateral basis with Moscow.

The projected Nord Stream pipeline under the Baltic Sea, contracted between Berlin and Moscow without EU consensus and despite staunch CEE opposition, epitomizes Russia's divisive approach. Nord Stream serves four major objectives: to limit Russia's reliance on transit across Central Europe; to deepen Western European dependence on Russia; to generate disputes between WE beneficiaries such as Germany and the CEE capitals; and to marginalize the Poles and Balts within the EU by depicting them as incorrigible Russophobes and nonpragmatic Union members.

The Kremlin not only manipulates divisions between older and newer members; it also aims to undermine common policies between EU newcomers. Among former Soviet satellites, Hungary, Slovakia, and Bulgaria are the primary targets for lucrative energy deals and other business contracts. Moscow capitalizes on long-standing personal connections with socialist government officials to forge long-term supply contracts and to construct pipelines and distribution points that will preempt Europe's attempts at energy consensus and supply diversification.

In the winter of 2007–8 the Socialist Party governments in Bulgaria and Hungary decided to support the construction of Gazprom's South Stream gas pipeline under the Black Sea to the Balkans. The initiative was designed to bypass Ukraine, Romania, and Turkey and supply Caspian gas under Russia's control to the EU. If implemented, the project may scuttle the EU's planned Nabucco pipeline from the Caspian, which is viewed as essential in avoiding overdependence on Russian-controlled gas transmission. The prospect of financial windfalls lured Budapest and Sofia, as Moscow promised to transform both Hungary and Bulgaria into European hubs for Russian-transported gas. Greece and Italy were also tied into South Stream in a move intended to severely undercut Western efforts at ensuring supply diversification.

Lithuanian prime minister Gediminas Kirkilas stated in May 2007 that Russia was fixated on dividing EU member states by concluding bilateral energy deals with individual countries rather than ratifying the EU's Energy Charter.[3] According to Sergei Yastrzhembsky, Putin's special envoy to the EU, the Union is divided between "consensus" countries, which want a "strategic partnership" with Moscow, and "countries infected with an anti-Russian virus," which need to be "cured." He argued that self-conscious elites infected with an "anti-Russian virus" have gained power in several CEE states and that "curing them" will take time.[4] In a revealing comment pinpointing Moscow's approach, Yastrzhembsky also criticized the EU's principle of presenting a united front, as this allegedly impairs relations with Russia: "Because of so-called European solidarity, bilateral problems are pushed to the level of European-Russian relations. And that is something that we generally cannot agree with."[5]

The EU-Russia summit in Samara in May 2007, involving President Putin, German chancellor Angela Merkel, and EU Commission president José Manuel Barroso, was downgraded because of persistent disputes.[6] Moscow placed the blame on Poland, Estonia, and Lithuania, and the deputy chairman of the Federation Council's Committee for Foreign Affairs, Vasily Likhachyov, asserted that Russian diplomacy should adopt a more differentiated approach in contacts with EU members and cooperate with only those capitals that view Russia as a strategic partner. Jonathan Eyal dismisses arguments that the EU has no alternative to engagement with Russia and that a substance-free summit is preferable to no talks and a possible confrontation, because "Europe is not facing a new Cold War. Instead, it is being targeted by a Russian policy that seeks to undermine the essential foundations of stability in Central Europe. Until the EU reaches a consensus on how to respond to this challenge, holding summits with Putin can only deepen the current security predicament."[7]

Decisions regarding the final status of the territory of Kosova provided an additional opportunity for Moscow to accentuate splits within the EU and across the Atlantic. While Washington and several EU capitals were eager to resolve the untenable status quo in Kosova by the time of the NATO summit in April 2008, Russian officials interjected in the dispute to block Kosova's recognition by the UN Security Council. Moscow encouraged Serbia to resist Kosova's sovereignty by questioning the competence of the UN special envoy for the territory, and it appealed to EU countries such as Spain, Romania, and Slovakia by raising the specter of separatist precedents on their territories.

Russia's delaying tactics over Kosova's final status served two purposes. First, it enabled the Kremlin to interject as a major player in Europe's trouble spots, even though it had contributed little to regional security, political reform, or economic growth. Second, Moscow benefited from international disputes over Kosova's status as this deflected attention from Russia's own regional ambitions and contributed to hindering the emergence of a Western consensus on expanding the transatlantic and pan-European projects throughout the Black Sea and Caspian regions.

CEE governments observe with increasing concern as Moscow pursues a neo-imperialist policy toward neighboring countries.[8] Poland, Romania, and the three Baltic states consider themselves frontline states facing persistent security challenges to their east. They calculate that even NATO and EU membership is not a sufficient barrier against "coercive policy measures" applied by the Kremlin.[9] CEE governments are not supportive of Russia's membership in either the EU or NATO, and some express unease over close organizational partnerships with Moscow as such arrangements could turn both the Union and the NATO alliance into weak political organizations devoid of any meaningful security capabilities.

CEE capitals calculate that Russia's negative influences in the region can be curtailed by pursuing a realistic prospect of international institutional integration for Ukraine, Belarus, Moldova, Georgia, and other states aspiring to join Western structures. They voice dissatisfaction with the EU's European Neighborhood Policy that places these countries in the same category as the North African ENP partners, who have virtually no prospect of EU accession. Poland and its neighbors raised the notion of an Eastern European Union for the European ENP countries as a variant of the Mediterranean Union promoted by France, with a focus on energy, security, migration, democratic development, and human rights.[10]

New members urge both the EU and NATO to respond in unison to a concerted Kremlin-directed strategy to redivide Europe and forestall further Euro-Atlantic enlargement. Several CEE capitals maintain contentious issues on the NATO and EU agendas, wary of Western compromises with Moscow that could weaken the U.S. role in European affairs and endanger their own security interests. They view Washington as the most credible protector against growing Russian penetration in European affairs, regardless of American-Russian collaboration in other arenas.

There are three especially troubling EU positions that Moscow can exploit.[11] First, if Russia seriously escalates one or several disputes with the EU, Brussels may seek to compromise on certain issues to avoid a comprehensive breakdown in relations. Hence, Moscow directly benefits from manufacturing or escalating a particular confrontation with the Union.

Second, if Russia were to promote a crisis in a country such as Belarus by replacing its leadership, the EU is unlikely to intervene. Officials in Brussels contend that the EU may directly engage only if a democratic transition is threatened, whereas Moscow can claim that it is acting against an authoritarian and ostracized regime in Minsk, similar to the U.S. intervention in Iraq or elsewhere, and thereby further curtail Belarusian independence.

Third, Russian officials argue that there are international precedents for its intervention in Georgia, claiming that its military invasion in August 2008 prevented a Georgian "genocide" against the South Ossetians and followed a precedent established by NATO in the Balkans. In reality, Russia set its own precedent when the USSR collapsed in 1991 by supporting and arming separatist movements in Georgia, Moldova, and Azerbaijan and conducting a creeping annexation of Georgian territory. Russia's Georgia precedent could be applied to other wayward republics and internationally justified with similar humanitarian and preemptive explanations. Moscow will assume that the EU will not take a tougher stance than it did during Russia's invasion of Georgia in August 2008.

In applying its divisive diplomacy, Moscow has questioned the purpose of various Western-sponsored organizations, such as the OSCE, that promote democratic governance. Instead, it wants the OSCE in particular to focus primarily on confidence building in the security arena. Similarly, it prefers that the Council of Europe concentrate on issues such as migration and culture rather than human and minority rights, which evidently exposes Russia to "interference" in its internal affairs through CoE monitoring. The Kremlin has also attempted to weaken the European Court of Human Rights by blocking reforms that would enable a faster submission and processing of complaints by Russian citizens against state abuses.

In another maneuver to undermine Western involvement in democratization programs in the "Russian space," in October 2007 at the EU-Russia summit in Mafra, Portugal, Putin called for establishing a joint "Russian-European institute for freedom and democracy" based in Brussels. The purpose of the institute was to enable Russia to monitor human rights and the condition of democracy within the EU as a counterpoint to EU monitoring within Russia and the former Soviet states. Several Western human rights organizations dismissed Putin's offer, and Amnesty International's European branch claimed that the proposed initiative would be subject to Moscow's political controls.[12] In a related move to purportedly monitor democratic shortcomings in the United States, the Moscow-based Institute of Democracy and Cooperation registered its New York branch in December 2007 after opening an office in Paris.

Russia's officials contest any significant EU involvement in resolving the "frozen conflicts" in Moldova or Georgia, as that could undermine their own influence and spur those states toward integration with Western institutions. They also resist any moves by the EU or its member states to forge institutional links with regional organizations that exclude Russia, such as GUAM or the CDC. Moscow banks on the fact that a number of EU and NATO members are reluctant to offer Ukraine, Georgia, Moldova, and other pro-Western governments anything beyond the EU's European Neighborhood Policy and NATO's Partnership for Peace. Neither format involves steps toward accession. Key EU capitals such as Berlin and Paris contend that the EU is not institutionally prepared to assimilate the Eastern European aspirants and that the latter are not structurally ready to become absorbed. Underlying these positions is a persistent apprehension in the EU of antagonizing Russia over what Moscow considers its predominant zone of influence.

CEE governments argue that without a realistic prospect for EU and NATO accession, Ukraine, Moldova, and Georgia may confront aspirant fatigue and even become sources of domestic and regional instability. Such developments will have damaging security implications for CEE, which remains susceptible to the Kremlin's economic blackmail and political pressure. The EU treats the post-Soviet countries differently from the western Balkan states, which were offered the prospect of EU accession through stabilization and association agreements (SAAs) provided that they fulfilled the required criteria. By contrast, the ENP does not envisage EU membership but instead provides action plans to gradually engage these countries in EU programs. Without more effective incentives, especially the achievement of EU entry, the ENP is in danger of lacking sufficient momentum and incentive to promote structural reform or reinforce commitments to Western integration.

At an EU foreign ministers meeting in May 2008, Poland and Sweden proposed an Eastern Partnership Program (EPP) to strengthen the EU's ties with Ukraine, Moldova, Georgia, Azerbaijan, Armenia, and Belarus.[13] The proposal was supported by the Visegrad group in CEE, consisting of Hungary, Slovakia, and the Czech Republic in addition to Poland. However, resistance was evident from the EU's external relations commissioner, Benita Ferrero-Waldner, while France and Germany were also reluctant to move beyond the ENP program and the EU's Black Sea Synergy (BSS) project, designed to increase cooperation between the littoral states. While ENP was widely viewed as a substitute for membership, the BSS has been restricted to developing civil societies.[14]

The EPP called for deepening bilateral relations between the EU and individual ENP states, specifically in migration, visa facilitation, free trade, and exchange programs, and for creating a "permanent formula for multilateral cooperation" in such areas as security, rule of law, transborder questions, economic integration, and environmental protection. The proposal, officially released at the EU Council of Foreign Ministers meeting in June 2008, did not mention a membership perspective but offered "more profound integration" with the EU. The EPP was inaugurated in Prague on May 7, 2009, with the intention of expanding aid and trade and creating closer political ties, while avoiding the controversial question of EU accession. Moreover, the Union remains politically divided on the scope of the EPP and faces serious financial constraints on its operations.

NATO may be willing to enlarge eastward, but two factors will need to be considered before decisions are finalized on including the remaining Eastern European countries. First, the commitment of the candidate states, including their political elites and citizens, to NATO membership needs to be assured. Second, a commitment by the alliance that such inclusion is in NATO allies' strategic interests needs to be affirmed. Decisions at the NATO summit in Bucharest in April 2008, where Ukraine and Georgia were not afforded membership action plans, indicated that Berlin and Paris were not prepared to undermine their relations with Moscow at a time when a new Russian president was assuming office.

Czech foreign minister Karel Schwarzenberg has asserted that Russia wants to regain the superpower status the Soviet Union once had in determining Europe's future. Moscow's aim is to "achieve the same status [vis-à-vis America] that the former Soviet Union had. Then the two of them, Washington and Moscow, would be the two to decide European issues."[15] In this sense, Russia's leaders view the

EU as a weak and divided institution and claim that the multinational organization is in decline following repeated failures to adopt a Union constitution. According to Foreign Minister Lavrov, "Russia is on the rise, Western Europe lacks ideological unity, and the United States finds itself in a blind alley." He even warned that Russia could "bring down" the international system based on NATO, the OSCE, and the CFE. This would avowedly herald the creation of a "new system" of international relations.[16]

Manipulating Selected States

Russia has adopted a dual-track approach toward the EU as a whole and toward the WE members in particular. First, it capitalizes on Europe's major institutions to reduce U.S. influence on the Continent, whether by creating or expanding transatlantic divisions or by developing the EU's trans-Eurasian links with Moscow, which exclude Washington.

Second, Moscow pursues the nationalization or bilateralization of relations with individual EU capitals to prevent the Union as a whole from acting against Russia's national interests or uniformly supporting U.S. policy. Such a ploy promotes and exploits fissures within the EU as well as ruptures with Washington. Some analysts believe that Moscow views the EU itself as a temporary phenomenon that will disintegrate when the interests of sovereign states eventually prevail to determine Europe's future.[17] The Kremlin seeks to hasten this process and undermine the effectiveness of EU institutions, if its most reliable Western European partners prove unable to determine Union policy as a whole.

Additionally, Moscow endeavors in several CEE states to favor and support specific parties, factions, and politicians who will adopt policies favorable to Russia and detrimental to the Atlantic alliance or who can obstruct a more assertive approach toward Russia. This method is replicated in other parts of the EU and has also been pursued toward selected members of the European parliament. The financial and political subversion of targeted countries and leaders, as was evident with Germany's former chancellor Gerhard Schroeder, could even signal potential dangers for governmental accountability, transparency, and democratic procedures in parts of the Union.

The Kremlin has singled out the three largest continental EU states—Germany, France, and Italy—as the core of a deeper Russia partnership that can bypass Brussels and Washington. Moscow has therefore invested in developing close relations with these countries through intensive diplomatic contacts, lucrative energy contracts, expanding trade ties, and favorable investment opportunities, as well as by nurturing personal friendships with their political leaderships. Failure to negotiate a new accord to supplant the Partnership and Cooperation Agreement before it expired in December 2007 actually enabled Russia to intensify its bilateral ties with specific EU members.

A selective approach empowers Moscow to capitalize on existing divisions between EU countries, whether between older and newer members or between the more and less Atlanticist-oriented states. Even within the CEE region, it has deliberately promoted differentiation to undercut the emergence of a broader common front by favoring center-left governments in Budapest, Bratislava, Belgrade, and Sofia in energy contracts while omitting Warsaw, Prague, and the three Baltic capitals.

In encouraging differentiation, the Kremlin provokes disputes with particular governments while favoring others to preclude the emergence of a unified Russia strategy by the EU. Kremlin policymakers demonize many of the EU newcomers as spoilers of good EU-Russia relations by allegedly injecting Russophobia and a Cold War mentality into the EU decision-making process. In WE, Moscow has singled out the United Kingdom as an unreliable partner and criticizes those political leaders in other capitals who support a more assertive approach toward Russia.

The Kremlin capitalizes on various international permutations to puncture the transatlantic alliance. During the U.S. intervention in Iraq in 2003, Moscow pursued a "troika" format with Germany and France in opposition to Washington's policy. It thereby positioned itself as one of the key decision makers in a broader Europe dealing with critical security threats.[18] This was also envisaged as the nucleus of a non-American bloc in Europe. Although the troika was a temporary arrangement conditioned by specific political leaders in Paris and Berlin who vehemently disagreed with the Bush White House, it allowed Moscow to pose as a defender of pan-European interests and an opponent of American hegemony.

By intensifying its political involvement in the European arena, Moscow intends to curtail the Europe-America link. The long-term objective is to strengthen the Europe-Russia, or Eurasian, strategic pole vis-à-vis the United States and to establish a Russia-EU system of international security for the Old Continent in which the EU becomes Moscow's junior partner. Russia's growing international status and its involvement in numerous regional crises that remain important for allied interests, from Iran to North Korea, also help protect Moscow from foreign pressures. European leaders are less likely to confront the Kremlin on questions of democratic regression or its imperial approach toward neighbors when Russia is viewed as an indispensable partner in a broader security framework and when economic and energy dependence on Russia have been intensifying.

Cultivating Germany and France

The Russian authorities pride themselves on their close relations with Germany, view Berlin as their chief advocate in the West, and do not consider Germany to be a geopolitical rival in the "post-Soviet space."[19] The Kremlin has enumerated a number of areas where the two sides are avowedly united, whether in counter-terrorism, regional security, multilateralism, international law, or arms control.[20] Russian politicians and analysts routinely manipulate several themes to tie Germany more closely to Moscow. This includes the studious cultivation of a German guilt complex over Nazi policy during World War II, the mythical notion of a deep historical friendship between the two peoples, the allegedly critical Russian role in the reunification of Germany, the dismissal of the CEE states as peripheral troublemakers who seek to weaken German power and the German-Russian alliance, and the pursuit of "pragmatic" economic relations that will benefit the German economy.[21]

Moscow also strives to build up German self-confidence that it is the leading European power by asserting that a strong Germany with an independent foreign policy that is no longer submissive to U.S. strategy is pivotal to the development of Eastern-Western European relations. This would consolidate Germany's position as Russia's closest European partner and distance Berlin from Washington.[22]

Tight political relations between Moscow and Berlin were consummated during the chancellorship of Gerhard Schroeder through personal ties, common business interests, and opposition to U.S. policy.[23] Annual German-Russian summits, together with regular bilateral consultations at different levels of government, were inaugurated, and the so-called Petersburg Dialogue was initiated as a forum of discussion on issues of common interest. Schroeder asserted that Russia was the EU's main priority and that Germany was the main initiator and motor of the EU's policy toward Russia.[24] Berlin has also initiated regular German-French-Russian summits since 1997, excluding other EU states from the proceedings.

Since the collapse of the USSR, Germany has become Russia's largest trading and financial partner, with a record €52.8 billion in bilateral trade in 2007, and accounts for about 32 percent of accumulated foreign investment in Russia.[25] Berlin's primary imports consist of oil and natural gas, which cover more than three-quarters of Germany's needs. Moscow plans to substantially increase this supply through the construction of the Nord Stream gas pipeline, claiming that Germany will become a major center for distributing gas to other European countries. Germany's share in Russia's foreign trade reached 13 percent in 2006; it mostly exported machinery, cars, chemical products, and spare parts. In a clear demonstration of how business enticements influence political decisions, German MEPs (members of the European Parliament) closely linked with German energy companies have been engaged in intensive lobbying in favor of Gazprom's pipeline policy.[26]

German capital investment in Russia amounted to $10 billion by 2006 and was projected to rise significantly.[27] In 2007 alone, German firms invested $3.4 billion in Russian industry, with major investments in the energy sector. The

August 2008 Georgian war precipitated a drop in foreign investment in Russia, but the Kremlin calculated that capital would continue to flow into the country as European companies have invested heavily in Russian industries and will need to raise their stakes to ensure continuing growth and profitability.[28]

The German connection demonstrates how Moscow establishes bilateral pacts with the largest EU capitals while avoiding the need for a full-scale EU-Russia agreement.[29] The newest EU members frequently criticized Chancellor Schroeder for his close relationship with President Putin and his acquiescence to Russia's expansionism. German politicians welcomed the stronger role of the Russian state, as it would allegedly decrease corruption and criminality and provide greater predictability for business.

Statements by Putin claiming that close cooperation between Russia and Germany had "always had a stabilizing influence and opened up the road to peace and stability on the European continent" have understandably been treated with incredulity by countries who have traditionally suffered from pacts between Moscow and Berlin.[30] In reality, the German economy was becoming increasingly dependent on Russian energy imports, while the Russian market presented substantial opportunities for German exports and investments.

Even Germany's traditional center-right seemed to be enamored of Putin's Russia. Edmund Stoiber, head of Bavaria's government and chairman of Germany's conservative Christian Social Union (CSU, the Bavarian wing of the governing Christian Democratic Union, or CDU) visited the Kremlin in July 2007 and endorsed Russia's opposition to the U.S. antimissile defense system in Poland and the Czech Republic.[31] He repeated Putin's proposal that the missile defense initiative should be resolved within the framework of the NATO-Russia Council and placed under joint NATO-Russia command.[32]

Stoiber was not authorized to speak on behalf of the German government, but Moscow benefited from conflicts within the governing party, between Stoiber and Chancellor Angela Merkel, as well as between the CDU/CSU and its junior coalition partner, the Social Democratic Party (SDP). Chancellor Merkel has endeavored to place German-Russian relations on a more balanced footing and to establish better relations with CEE states that fear Russian expansion. Merkel and the Social Democratic foreign minister Frank-Walter Steinmeier clashed repeatedly over Berlin's policy toward Moscow. While Steinmeier maintains former chancellor Schroeder's line that Russia must be courted as an indispensable partner in resolving security threats and ensuring energy supplies, Merkel has been more critical. Nevertheless, she had to compromise with two powerful interest groups, the Social Democratic left and important elements of the German business lobby, which benefits from close ties with Moscow.

Germany's CDU-SDP coalition disappointed Russia's vulnerable neighbors by supporting the Nord Stream pipeline, failing to effectively push for EU peacekeeping missions in the secessionist regions in Georgia, and blocking MAPs for Georgia and Ukraine at the NATO summit in April 2008. Steinmeier has continued Schroeder's accommodating policy toward Moscow. He supports Russia's integration in the EU's economic system, calculating that this would transform Russia into a law-abiding European state. Some concerns were also voiced in Berlin that a more concerted Anglo-French policy toward Russia, following the election of President Nicolas Sarkozy, would undermine Germany's leading position in relations with Moscow.

During 2007 and 2008 the German government backed Russia's proposal for an alternative to a U.S. missile defense deployment in Central Europe. In March 2007 Germany's defense minister, Franz Josef Jung, asserted that missile defense is an issue that should be handled between NATO and Russia. Conversely, the EU's foreign and security policy chief, Javier Solana, stated that Russia could not impose a decision on the Poles and Czechs with regard to missile defense by threatening to target missiles at the proposed U.S. bases.[33]

After Medvedev's inauguration as president in May 2008, Steinmeier paid a weeklong visit to Russia as Medvedev's first prominent foreign guest. The two politicians had developed a close relationship since holding posts in the previous German and Russian governments. Steinmeier headed the chancellor's office under Schroeder, a post with similar duties to Medvedev's position as head of Russia's presidential administration.

Merkel also traveled to Moscow in March 2008 as the first foreign leader to meet Medvedev after he was awarded the presidency. Steinmeier offered a "modernization partnership" with Russia comprising wide-ranging cooperation in legal matters, administration, and health care. Traveling with Steinmeier was a delegation of German deputies and business leaders. In a further indication of Berlin's warming relations with Moscow, Steinmeier rejected calls by Georgian president Saakashvili to replace Russian peacekeepers in the breakaway regions of Georgia with NATO troops.[34]

Medvedev paid his first EU visit to Germany in June 2008 and proposed a comprehensive European security pact that would replace all existing treaties, eliminate NATO, and reduce U.S. influence on the Continent.[35] He told a gathering of leading German politicians and business figures that the regional agreement should be based on the UN charter and would clarify Russia's relations within the Euro-Atlantic community. Medvedev suggested holding a European summit to launch preparations for the treaty. The objective was to lure European powers such as Germany away from the transatlantic alliance by offering them more predictable and nonconfrontational relations with Russia. Medvedev also combined enticements with threats, warning that if NATO expands any further eastward "relations with Russia will be spoilt once and for all" and "the price of this will be high."[36]

Only a few weeks after Russia's invasion of Georgia, normality was evidently restored in Russian-German relations at their bilateral summit in St. Petersburg on October 3, 2008.[37] Medvedev and Merkel presided over meetings between key ministers and business leaders. With the German economy sliding into recession, Berlin underscored that business interests took precedence over political irritants such as the invasion of Georgia. To remove any political obstacles to trade and investment, Merkel stated that the "time was not ripe" for granting Georgia and Ukraine NATO MAPs. Russia also sought a return of EU investors following dramatic downturns on its stock market at the outset of the international credit crunch. The key agreement involved Germany's E.ON, which acquired a 25 percent share in the Yuzhno-Russkoye gas field.

For former French president Jacques Chirac, Russia was a vital strategic partner in building a multilateral and multipolar world, and Paris endeavored to steer the EU in that direction.[38] Through trade, investment, and increasing energy dependence, Moscow has sought to intensify its influence in Paris, with which it maintained cordial relations throughout Putin's presidency. By 2004 France was the ninth-largest exporter to and the eighth-largest direct investor in Russia.

President Chirac was effusively accommodating toward Putin, partly because he viewed Moscow as a useful counterweight to President Bush's unilateralism. Conversely, the French approach was useful to Moscow in distancing "core Europe" from Washington. The Kremlin was also content that French foreign policy focused on the Mediterranean and did not impinge on Russia's "near abroad." Chirac frequently obliged in criticizing U.S. policy by, for example, warning that the missile defense system risked "returning Europe to the tensions of the Cold War."[39]

The new French president, Nicolas Sarkozy, elected in May 2007, pledged to create a more equitable balance in French-Russian relations by speaking out against human rights abuses and violations of democratic norms inside Russia.[40] While still a presidential candidate, Sarkozy publicly disagreed with Putin on numerous issues, including NATO's policy toward Georgia and Ukraine, and his advisers claimed Paris's new Russian policy would "avoid indulgence without lapsing into confrontation" to distinguish it from the Chirac era. Reportedly, Putin waited two days after the May 2007 French elections before congratulating Sarkozy on his triumph, while Kremlin commentators voiced suspicion about an Atlanticist French president of Hungarian extraction.

In December 2007, however, Sarkozy stepped outside a common EU position that was critical of Russia's parliamentary elections by telephoning to congratulate Putin, again indicating a more accommodating stance toward Moscow. In May 2008 French foreign minister Bernard Kouchner met with Medvedev in the Kremlin and offered the new Russian leader an invitation from Sarkozy to visit

Paris. In addition, Medvedev held one-on-one talks with Sarkozy during the G-8 summit in Japan in July 2008, and relations were expected to deepen following the Russia-EU summit in France in November 2008.[41] After Kouchner's visit to Moscow, Paris signaled that it was intent on improving EU-Russia relations during its six-month EU presidency in the second half of 2008. The studious avoidance of confrontation helps to explain Sarkozy's acceptance of a vaguely worded cease-fire during the Russian-Georgian conflict in August 2008 that allowed Moscow to expand its area of control inside Georgia.

Medvedev's statements before his inauguration as president, favoring liberalization, the rule of law, and the renovation of EU-Russia ties, convinced some EU governments that relations with Moscow could markedly improve. Nevertheless, the Union remained divided as to whether Medvedev's policy would signal a mere change in tone rather than a perceptible shift in substance. Suppositions blossomed about a "renewal of leadership" in Moscow whereby "Russia might seek practical inclusion in modern Europe, with a more attractive re-branding of its foreign policy image."[42] Despite the wishful thinking of some Western leaders that Medvedev was a closet liberal without a KGB background, a major theme of the new president's election campaign had been a pledge of policy continuity following his predecessor. Moreover, Putin himself remained the decisive figure in the role of Russia's new prime minister. The military intervention in Georgia and the fracturing of Georgian territory indicated how Moscow was re-branding its foreign policy image as a confident and aggressive power.

President Sarkozy fell into several Russian traps during France's EU presidency. Moscow outmaneuvered him in Georgia, where Russia effectively separated South Ossetia and Abkhazia while Sarkozy believed he had reversed the Russian invasion and restored the status quo ante. The French president also inadvertently promoted Russia's divisive transatlantic policy at the EU-Russia summit in Nice on November 14, 2008, by supporting Moscow's proposal to hold an OSCE summit in mid-2009 on a proposed new European security framework while urging a freeze on any new missile deployments by both Russia and the United States.[43] Sarkozy's remarks were disputed by the Czech Republic, which was due to take over the EU presidency in January 2009. Officials in Prague asserted that Sarkozy had no mandate for his remarks.

Isolating Britain

British-Russian disputes during the Putin era date back to 2003, with the granting of political asylum by London to Russian oligarch Boris Berezovsky and Chechen leader Akhmed Zakaev. What was once a strategic partnership was transformed into a strategic conflict as Moscow purposively escalated its disputes with Britain and sought to isolate London from the major continental powers. Relations deteriorated further after Russia's refusal to extradite Andrei Lugovoi, the prime suspect in the 2007 radioactive polonium-210 poisoning in London of former Russian security officer Aleksander Litvinenko, who had defected to Britain. To add further strain on bilateral relations, in October 2008 Russian authorities asked London to extradite former oil tycoon Mikhail Gutseriyev, the former president of Russneft oil company, who fled the country alleging harassment by the Russian state.

Kremlin leaders claimed that Britain wanted Russia to change its constitution because it sought Lugovoi's extradition. Putin declared in July 2007 that the UK was acting like a colonial power, although Russia had never been Britain's colony.[44] In the wake of the controversy, both London and Moscow expelled four diplomats, and relations reached their lowest point since the end of the Cold War. Although there may not have been an initial grand plan to single out Britain, the Kremlin intended to send a strong signal that sheltering major opposition figures would precipitate a bilateral dispute with any European state.

Although Chancellor Merkel expressed understanding for Britain's position, officials at the German Foreign Ministry, controlled by former chancellor Schroeder's Social Democrats, asserted that London "overreacted" in expelling four Russian diplomats.[45] In sum, Britain did not obtain the concerted response it may have expected from other EU members, including the Portuguese, who held the EU presidency at that time, as there was no consensus among members. Portuguese foreign minister Luis Amado simply emphasized that the matter was a bilateral issue between the UK and Russia.

Threats and security pressures by Moscow against London increased during 2007. In July two Royal Air Force Tornado fighter jets scrambled to intercept two Russian Tu-95 "Bear" intercontinental bombers apparently headed for Scotland from Russia's Kola Peninsula.[46] The Bears were shadowed by two F-16 fighter jets of the Royal Norwegian Air Force and turned back for home before reaching British airspace. Colonel General Aleksandr Zelin, who headed the Russian air force, claimed that the two Bears were on a normal training mission and not heading for British airspace, but added that Russian long-range aviation was recovering after several years of decline.

In November 2007 MI5 Director General Jonathan Evans, Britain's chief domestic intelligence official, revealed that his agency had to divert critical resources from antiterrorism to defend against rising Russian espionage activities intended to steal sensitive technology on civilian and military projects.[47] Evans asserted that since the end of the Cold War, there had been no decrease in the number of undeclared Russian intelligence officers in the UK. In July 2008 the UK's security services reclassified Russia as the third-largest security threat after al Qaeda terrorism and Iranian nuclear proliferation.[48] British and U.S. intelligence officials have noted that Russian spying has reached levels not seen since the end of the Cold War. For instance, in November 2007 British authorities arrested a former soldier in the Royal Armoured Corps on suspicion of spying for Russia.[49] He was allegedly planning to hand over unspecified military secrets to Russian intelligence.

To counter British charges, Nikolai Patrushev, head of Russia's Federal Security Service, asserted in the October 10, 2007, issue of the Moscow weekly *Argumenty i Fakty* that Washington and London were spearheading an espionage campaign against Russia in which the intelligence services of Poland, Georgia, and the Baltic states were also active. Patrushev added that the UK's MI6 foreign intelligence service was also intent on disturbing domestic developments in Russia.[50]

In a further illustration of pressure against London, in December 2007 Foreign Minister Lavrov asserted that the British Council had to close its offices outside Moscow because it was in violation of Russian law.[51] Lavrov claimed that the British government had embarked on a "systematic deterioration of bilateral relations" by expelling Russian diplomats, ceasing counterterrorism cooperation with the FSB, and freezing work on an agreement to ease visa requirements for Russian citizens. Shortly after, Britain's ambassador to Russia, Tony Brenton, announced that a European arrest warrant had been issued for suspected Russian assassin Andrei Lugovoi. Meanwhile, the murdered Litvinenko's associate, Andrei Sidelnikov, fled to London in search of political asylum.

London eventually succumbed to Moscow's pressure and closed the British Council offices in St. Petersburg and Yekaterinburg. Britain's foreign minister David Miliband charged that Russia's actions raised serious questions about Moscow's commitments to international law.[52] Some British analysts suggested that the British Council feud was engineered as part of a wider political strategy by Moscow to pressure the UK and the EU into giving way on other unrelated issues.

Moscow has also exerted pressure on British energy companies investing in Russia as part of its political offensive. For instance, in July 2008 Robert Dudley, the chief executive of BP's Russian joint venture TNK-BP, left Russia because of "sustained harassment." TNK-BP has faced lawsuits, visa rows, industrial spying claims, disputes over investments, and administrative investigations. BP owns 50 percent of TNK-BP while the Russian share consists of a consortium of billionaires, styled as Alfa Access-Renova (AAR) with close ties to the Kremlin. These include Mikhail Fridman, the TNK-BP chairman. BP executives expressed outrage at this "orchestrated campaign of harassment."[53]

Moscow's representatives have also sought to curry support among the Conservative Party opposition in Britain against Labour Party policy toward Russia.

For instance, the United Russia Party formed a coalition in the Council of Europe, whereby in return for Conservative support of Russia's chairmanship of the council and backing for the Kremlin's foreign policy toward the Balkans, missile defense, and other questions at odds with EU policy, the Tories were promised prominent positions in the CoE's governing bodies.[54]

Assorted Continental Connections

In addition to Germany and France, Moscow has cultivated strong bilateral connections with a number of Western European states to forestall the emergence of a united front challenging its strategic objectives. In the case of Italy, Putin and Prime Minister Silvano Berlusconi developed a close personal relationship during their terms in office, indicative of an underlying economic or business interest. Berlusconi openly contradicted official EU criticisms of Russia's policy in Chechnya and became widely viewed as a staunch defender of the Kremlin within the Union. When Berlusconi was reelected as premier in April 2008, Putin was his first foreign visitor. The Italian leader confirmed that "the Russian Federation is very important for us [because] we get 30 percent of our oil and gas from them." Their talks reportedly focused on energy transactions, as Gazprom was interested in exchanging assets in Libya with Italy's ENI energy conglomerate, as well as on Russian-EU relations and the possibility of Russia's Aeroflot buying an interest in Italy's Alitalia airline.[55]

By 2007 Italy was Russia's fourth-ranked trade partner and its second-placed importer.[56] In April 2008 President Putin sought to recruit outgoing Italian prime minister Romano Prodi as chairman of the planned South Stream gas pipeline project.[57] Although Prodi turned down the offer, the overture indicated that the Kremlin was eager to engage a senior European figure who would reassure the EU about Russia's intentions. Schroeder's chairmanship of the Nord Stream project had evidently established a valuable political precedent.

As are Italy, France, and Germany, Greece and Cyprus are widely perceived as being accommodating to Russia's interests within the EU on issues ranging from the EU's "Eastern dimension" (in dealing with the post-Soviet states) to the regulation of energy markets. Both countries have periodically backed Moscow's position by opposing a more assertive and inclusive European approach toward the Black Sea region, Belarus, and the South Caucasus.[58] In the energy sector, Greece and Cyprus have generally opposed European Commission proposals to unbundle the large energy companies and to create a more competitive European energy market that would undercut the position of Russian corporations.

Moscow also exploits lingering grievances in Athens over the EU and NATO's failure to acknowledge Greece's economic and military predominance in the Balkans. The South Stream agreement that tied Greece into a new Russian-controlled gas pipeline for Europe was heralded in Athens as potentially elevating Greece's strategic position in the Balkans as an important hub for energy resources.[59]

Spain has also been a persistent target of Russian overtures. Kremlin spokesmen stress the similarity of the Russian and Spanish federal models and the commitment of both capitals to combating "localism, separatism, and attempts to forcibly change the territorial-administrative organization."[60] The Kremlin plays adroitly on Spain's fears of a Kosova precedent in Catalonia and the Basque country. Moscow also appreciates that Madrid, similar to Paris and Rome, focuses on the EU's Mediterranean neighborhood rather than on the Union's eastern states and does not interfere in Russia's neighborhood.

Russian leaders frequently underscore their good ties with Finland and consider "Finlandization," or the country's neutrality during the Cold War, as a model to be emulated among Russia's other neighbors.[61] Much stressed are the well-developed trading ties between the two countries, which include plans to develop special economic zones, cross-border regions, and business incubators. In a further indication that Russia is wooing Finland, in August 2008 spokesmen for Russia's controversial Nord Stream pipeline, designed to bypass CEE and increase WE dependence on Russian gas, announced the hiring of former Finnish prime minister Paavo Lipponen to its board of directors.

During a visit to Prague, Finnish foreign minister Alexander Stubb claimed that democracy in Russia will develop under Medvedev as the country's transition allegedly follows three stages: the Yeltsin breakthrough, the Putin stabilization, and the Medvedev era. In stark contrast, Foreign Minister Stubb's host, Czech prime minister Mirek Topolánek, dismissed any prospects for substantive changes in Russia's foreign policy.[62] Swedish foreign minister Carl Bildt also proved circumspect about Russia's evolution, acknowledging that some of Medvedev's comments were well received but stressing that it remained to be seen how those words would be translated into action.[63]

Periodic disputes have marred relations between Moscow and some of the other continental states. This has been the case with three Scandinavian countries: Norway, Denmark, and Sweden. Moscow's claims to large tracts of the Arctic as an extension of Russian territory have soured relations with Oslo and Copenhagen. The geopolitical and economic importance of the Arctic as a source of energy and mineral wealth has been recognized and acted upon by Moscow through the projection of military power, by the planting of the Russian flag on the Arctic seabed in August 2007, and by submitting a claim to the UN Convention on the Law of the Sea to an area of some 460,000 square miles.[64]

On September 17, 2008, a meeting of the Russian Security Council chaired by President Medvedev was devoted to Russia's expanding interests in the Arctic.

The council declared that the Arctic was a region of strategic importance for Russia and that delimiting the external border of Russia's continental shelf in the Arctic zone was a national priority.[65] International recognition of Russia's claims in this area has become an important objective of Moscow's foreign policy and could cause increasing disputes with the other Arctic states in Europe and North America.

The Norwegian authorities also criticize Russia's more aggressive military posture, its absence from joint military exercises under NATO's PfP framework in northern Norway, its expansion of mining activities on the Spitsbergen archipelago (which is under Norwegian sovereignty), and persistent disagreement on the delineation of the continental shelf and economic zones in the Barents Sea, which has prevented oil and gas exploration.[66]

Stockholm's support of a stronger EU "Eastern dimension" to encompass Ukraine and Georgia and its joint initiative with Poland for an Eastern Partnership with former Soviet republics has angered and estranged Moscow. Sweden has also obstructed preparations for the construction of the Nord Stream underwater gas pipeline on the grounds of potential environmental damage and maritime safety in the Baltic Sea.

Energy as Strategy

The manipulation of energy resources has become Russia's predominant form of soft power toward Europe. Energy is Moscow's primary tool of foreign policy influence and attempted dominance, and the Kremlin has systematically undertaken to become the leading energy superpower in Eurasia.[1] Russia's officials contend that a "new economic order" needs to be established that is not dominated by the West but, rather, reflects the role of rapidly developing emerging nations.[2] In such a system, Russia would play a major role not only as an energy superstate but also as an international financial center that would break the monopoly of the U.S. dollar and the Euro currency and establish an allegedly more stable multipolar world.

In this context, Russia offers Europe a privileged relationship as the Continent's primary energy supplier and threatens the EU with Moscow's reorientation eastward toward China and India if political relations seriously deteriorate. Europe's energy dependence and close bilateral ties between some Western European capitals and Moscow have constrained a united and effective EU policy that would challenge Russia's reimperialization. Nonetheless, at the close of 2008 the deepening global economic recession that precipitated a fall in demand for energy and a dramatic reduction in energy prices provided the EU with an opportunity to diversify its sources and limit its dependence on Russia.

Russia's Energy Strategy

With its substantial energy wealth and a steady annual economic growth rate of some 7 percent during the past decade, the Russian state has focused on monopolizing supplies of crude oil and natural gas for the European market, eliminating private Russian competitors such as Yukos, increasing the number and volume of pipelines to Western Europe, and steadily purchasing major stakes in Europe's energy infrastructure.[3] Moscow has embarked on a strategy to increase Europe's dependence, especially in gas, by controlling supplies, pipelines, and prices and diversifying its transmission routes to preclude bilateral dependence. As there is no global market for gas, the construction of specific pipelines binds consumer countries into lengthy contracts with producers and suppliers. Europe possesses some energy alternatives to restrict its dependence on Russia, but they will require commitment to new North African gas pipelines, greater reliance on Norwegian gas, and more focus on domestic production.

Russia's major energy companies are not simply motivated by profit. In line with state policy, they may temporarily trade profit maximization for political and strategic gain. They are willing to incur losses by suspending gas deliveries to paying customers in order to exert political pressure on targeted countries at the Kremlin's behest. One of Putin's primary goals as president was to reacquire for the state former government energy companies so that these "national champions" could serve Kremlin interests.[4] Putin appointed his close aides to high positions in several energy giants, including Dmitry Medvedev to Gazprom, Vladislav Surkov to Transnefteprodukt, Igor Sechin to Rosneft, and Viktor Khristenko to Transneft. By the close of Putin's second presidential term, direct state ownership of the largest energy, metal, and manufacturing companies exceeded 50 percent. The authorities also maintain full control over energy distribution and export through Gazprom for natural gas and Transneft for crude oil.

Russian companies invest significantly less in domestic extraction and development than in purchasing energy infrastructure in European states and ensuring control of transit routes from the Caspian Basin. For strategic reasons, they focus on expensive Europe-wide pipeline projects such as Nord Stream rather than on cheaper land alternatives in order to increase Moscow's leverage over states that will lose their significance as transit points and supply destinations. Simultaneously, the planned South Stream gas pipeline through the Balkans is not merely intended to preempt alternative supply sources to Europe but is designed to foster competition between potential beneficiaries and widen divisions within the EU.

While energy has always been a strategic resource, it now occupies a central place in regional politics and the national strategy of global aspirants. There are several reasons for this prominence. Demand for energy has been steadily rising as populations increase and economies grow. Alternative energy sources have not significantly affected the demand for hydrocarbon fuels, especially crude oil and natural gas, even though the EU is investing in alternatives and the economic recession that set in at the close of 2008 served to flatten demand.

In effect when demand for energy grows in Europe, dependence on foreign suppliers increases. The major sources of energy are scarce, in geopolitical terms, as the locations of significant gas and oil reserves are limited; their extraction, transportation, and price are costly; and their supply has become a source of regional tension, global competition, and great power politics. Regional disparities have pushed many countries into dependency relationships with specific energy suppliers, thus exposing them to political pressures and destabilizing economic vulnerabilities. Such vulnerability has been faced by a broader Europe as the Continent becomes increasingly dependent on supplies from or through Russia.

Devoid of significant military might, ideological messianic fervor, or direct political control, Moscow sees energy as its central tool for expansion and influence, one that can be used for developing monopolies, promoting economic dependence, and ensuring political subservience. Locking in supply recipients and ensuring extensive infrastructural acquisitions are the two prongs of Moscow's energy strategy. For this purpose, Russian business and intelligence services have been mobilized to expand control over foreign energy infrastructure and to neutralize any common EU approach to diversify and liberalize Europe's gas markets.[5]

Russian companies maintain a stranglehold over most energy transit routes from Central Asia and resist opening up pipelines to Western competition. Gazprom is the biggest extractor of natural gas in the world, accounting for approximately 93 percent of Russian natural gas production and controlling more than 19 percent of the world's gas reserves.[6] During Putin's presidency, Gazprom became the third-largest company in the world according to market capitalization. By maintaining a relative scarcity of gas production and underdeveloping new gas fields, Moscow can foster competition among European consumers for vital supplies. As the market price for gas is administratively decided, not fixed, Gazprom is able to manipulate costs as a political device, claiming that it is subsidizing certain neighboring economies or raising prices to "normal levels."

Although Russia needs foreign investors to develop its untapped resources and modernize its decrepit infrastructure, it places restrictions on foreign participation in strategic industries such as the energy sector in contravention of the EU's Energy Charter. In several instances, Western companies have been warned of investment problems if they seek to undercut the control of Russian state companies, as was the case with Shell's investments in the Sakhalin II project. Moreover, foreign companies can obtain access to Russia's natural resources only if Russian companies can purchase distribution, refinery, and transportation assets in Europe.[7]

Russia signed the EU Energy Charter in 1998, but it has not ratified the treaty and has failed to conclude a transit protocol with the EU that would necessitate Gazprom surrendering its gas transportation monopoly from the Caspian Basin to Europe. The charter envisages opening up Russia's energy sector to fair competition. In violation of charter principles, in June 2006 the Russian authorities approved Gazprom's exclusive right to export natural gas while limiting the participation of foreign companies in Russia's oil and gas extraction.[8]

Gazprom remains the largest and most important Kremlin-controlled company and has become the symbol and substance of neo-imperial Russia. It does not operate as a standard corporation that respects the laws of the market. Gazprom is a Russian state monopoly and not a private company and is staffed by loyalist ex-KGB officials.[9] It operates largely through intermediary companies with unclear ownership structures, and extensive revenues are reportedly diverted to unregistered beneficiaries.

Russia has aggressively used its primary resources to elevate its global power by steadily strengthening its position on Europe's energy market. At present, about half of Russia's energy exports are earmarked for EU countries, including 53 percent of its oil and 36 percent of its natural gas.[10] The CEE states have a much higher level of dependence on Russia for oil and gas supplies than the WE countries. Simultaneously, their demand for energy continues to grow. By 2030 Poland expects an increase in energy consumption of some 60 percent compared to 2007, and Romania's projected increase is close to 85 percent. CEE dependence on gas imports averages 72 percent, with some countries almost fully dependent on Russian sources, as compared to 41 percent in WE countries. In the case of oil imports, the figures are 87 percent in CEE and 76 percent in WE. However, the bulk of CEE oil supplies are from Russia, while the WE has more diversified sources.

The level of WE dependence on a single source for energy does not currently exceed 30 percent, while in CEE dependence on Russian hydrocarbons ranges from 50 to 100 percent. Nonetheless, trends have indicated that the EU as a whole is becoming increasingly reliant on Russian energy, especially as, according to several projections, the Union will need to increase its imports of both gas and oil over the coming years from about 50 percent from all external sources at present to over 70 percent by 2030.[11] If the Russian-directed Nord Stream and South Stream gas pipelines are completed and other routes are finalized, it is projected that by 2030 the EU's external energy dependency will reach 70 percent, with the figure for gas exceeding 80 percent.

Some capitals are highly cognizant of their vulnerability to Russia's energy strategy. Because of their overwhelming dependence, each CEE country is susceptible to unpredictable disruptions, whether because of sabotage, environmental or climatic emergencies, decreasing extraction capabilities, infrastructural breakdowns, or deliberate cutoffs engineered by the Russian authorities to exert political pressure on targeted states. Energy dependence is heightening as the CEE economies expand, demand for energy increases, and alternative sources to Russian supplies remain costly.

Some EU representatives stress that Europe and Russia are interdependent in their energy relations. In reality, Russia's hand is stronger.[12] The energy sword can be double-edged, as was evident in the protests of EU countries whose gas supplies suffered when Gazprom engaged in a "gas war" with Ukraine in early 2006 and dented Russia's reputation as a reliable source. As a result, Moscow decided to lessen its dependence on specific transit countries for its supplies to reach the West. Through the diversification of transportation routes and contracts with individual EU states, Moscow can selectively embargo and damage specific European economies without incurring major revenue losses.

The Russian-Ukrainian gas war and the severing of Russian gas supplies to Moldova in early 2006 were not isolated commercial disputes but part of a broader Kremlin strategy to dominate its neighbors. In the fall of 2005 Foreign Minister Lavrov openly talked about using energy to punish recalcitrant former Soviet states.[13] Energy can activate a number of pressure instruments, including threats of supply interruptions, discriminatory pricing, the creation and usage of debts, coercive negotiations, and even acts of sabotage.[14] Moscow also focuses on acquiring energy infrastructure such as pipelines, ports, refineries, storage sites, and other related facilities.

Pronounced energy dependence on a single source has several negative consequences. Economic dependence can lead to growing political oversight. It can increase official corruption and corrode the rule of law. It can obstruct a country from meeting EU and NATO standards of governance. And it can accelerate Moscow's political and strategic leverage by drawing Europe more firmly under Russia's energy umbrella. An additional looming threat for the EU is Russia's inability to meet its supply contracts because of falling domestic extraction capacity. Shortfalls are expected in Russian-supplied gas by 2010, largely because of stagnant output, even if Central Asian gas is included in the mix. Growing dependence on specific supplies and routes combined with decreasing deliveries could prove catastrophic for several European economies.

Gazprom's ambitious plans for supply contracts, pipelines, and other infrastructure demonstrate that it seeks untrammeled control over Europe's gas market. This would enable the company to foster competition among European customers for potentially scarce resources and to engage in various forms of political blackmail. Moscow has underscored that a stable energy supply to European customers is partly dependent on Russia's ability to gain interests in key European energy companies. A similar scenario is evident in the oil sector, where Russia absorbs almost all of the crude that Central Asia channels through its ports into Europe. The planned oil pipeline across Bulgaria and Greece will enable Russia to bypass the Bosphorus, preempt any alternative non-Russian supplies from the Caspian Basin, and greatly increase EU dependence on Russian routes.

While the EU contemplates the diversification of supplies, Russia actively diversifies its interdependence. Moscow calculates that it may not always be economically advantageous to sever supplies and more profitable politically to control the national infrastructure and energy transportation routes into Europe. Hence, the planned Nord Stream and South Stream pipeline systems are designed to control gas distribution into Europe from Russia, the Caspian Basin, and eventually the Middle East. Moscow is also planning to tighten its stranglehold over Europe's gas supplies by gaining greater control over gas supplies from North Africa to European customers. Moscow seeks shares in the Algerian state company Sonatrach, the second-largest gas exporter to Europe, which provides 10 percent of the Continent's consumption.

Although Moscow has used energy as a weapon since the early 1990s, especially against the three Baltic states, under the Putin regime Russia's energy diplomacy became more emboldened and systematic. Europeans, particularly those in the eastern part of the continent who are most vulnerable to Russian pressures, are attempting to focus their attention on alternative energy sources. Even though the financial costs will be burdensome, the long-term political costs of dependence on a Russian energy spigot could be graver.

Moscow employs financial and supply pressures to purchase industries and infrastructure in targeted countries, especially where neighbors cannot pay the full price for energy supplies or are indebted to Moscow. For instance, the January 2006 Russian-Ukrainian gas delivery agreement guarantees Russia's monopoly on transport and marketing of Central Asian gas to Europe. Some analysts have described this as a "middleman monopoly" that will lock Ukraine into a monopolistic gas transport system across Eurasia. Kyiv received a discounted price on gas supplies but in return will experience increasing dependence on Moscow and lessened chances of diversification, as it will have no direct access to Central Asia.

Russia seeks control of downstream energy infrastructure and distribution networks in Europe, allowing it to gain middlemen's profits and to control supply options. This strategy is more lucrative and politically profitable than investing in developing new fields or in its own domestic market, which generates little income because of regulated low prices. Russian-Ukrainian gas deals deliver Ukraine's energy infrastructure, including transport pipelines, into the hands of Russian companies tied to Gazprom. Gazprom is the leading partner in RosUkrEnergo, the Russian-Ukrainian joint venture to market gas within Ukraine, and three-quarters of Ukraine's oil-refining capacity is already owned by Russian companies.

Supplies and prices are manipulated by Moscow to acquire energy assets or controlling positions on company boards throughout the ex-Soviet region. Energy companies suddenly increase the price for gas in order to build up sizeable debts among targeted countries, which are unable to pay the debt and are forced to cede control over their infrastructure. Russia's price demands on dependent neighbors can force local energy industries into debt and increase opportunities for debt-for-asset deals in favor of Russian companies.

In the EU market, Gazprom is acquiring controlling shares in new pipelines and steadily purchasing major infrastructure and utilities. In April 2007 U.S. Assistant Deputy Secretary of State Matthew Bryza accused Gazprom of buying up European utilities "like a player of the board game Monopoly swooping on key properties."[15] His comments reflected growing concern in Washington about Russia's commercial expansion in Europe's energy market and the slow pace of EU diversification. In February 2008 Michael McConnell, U.S. director of national intelligence, concluded the following: "Aggressive Russian efforts to control, restrict, or block the transit of hydrocarbons from the Caspian to the West—and to ensure that East-West energy corridors remain subject to Russian control—underscore the potential power and influence of Russia's energy policy."[16]

Russia's oil companies are also expanding their reach abroad, in both sales and acquisitions. Lukoil is systematically purchasing oil refineries and petrol stations, and it is estimated that half of Lukoil's business will be outside Russia in the next few years. Lukoil has the second-largest foreign assets of any non-financial company in the CIS and in southeastern Europe, behind only Gazprom.[17] It has established numerous joint stock companies in the Balkans, and plans are under way to construct oil pipelines across the region, including the Burgas-Alexandroupolis pipeline, which will bypass the Bosphorus.

As an indication of Russia's own energy diversification within Europe, the government is seeking to enter the CEE's nuclear power business by buying out companies in Hungary and the Czech Republic. This was evident during Putin's March 2006 visit to Budapest and Prague. Russian energy giants are also pushing into other sectors, such as electricity and liquefied natural gas (LNG), in order expand their portfolios with ambitions to become the world's dominant energy companies.

In the longer term, with Russia's oil production capabilities likely to decline over the next five years, Moscow is focused on monopolizing the purchase and transit of crude oil from the Caspian Basin to Europe, by tying both producers and consumers into a Russian-controlled pipeline system. In April 2008 Leonid Fedun, vice president of Lukoil, conceded that Russia's oil production has peaked and may never return to current levels.[18] In the first three months of 2008 Russian production averaged about 10 million barrels a day, a 1 percent drop from the first quarter of 2007. Rising domestic demand and a failure to develop new technology or exploit new fields with Western technology has hindered Moscow's ability to export oil. However, Moscow is increasingly focused on monopolizing the supply of natural gas, a resource that is growing in importance on the European market.

In October 2003, in an ominous development for Russia's neighbors, Defense Minister Sergei Ivanov outlined situations in which Moscow might carry out preemptive military strikes.[19] Russia reserved the right to conduct such operations if there was a distinct, clear, and inevitable military threat to the country or if Moscow felt threatened by reduced access to regions where it possessed crucial economic or financial interests. The flexibility of such a doctrine is becoming a major cause of concern as Russia acquires control over its neighbors' energy infrastructure and seeks to stifle any credible competition.

One of the intended consequences of Russia's military intervention in Georgia in August 2008 was to threaten energy transportation routes across the South Caucasus that bypassed Russia and to undermine investor confidence in constructing the non-Russian Nabucco gas pipeline from the Caspian to Europe. Only about a third of the natural gas capacity for Nabucco had been secured from Azerbaijan by mid-2008, and progress on construction of the pipeline proved slow even before the Russian invasion. In March 2009 Gazprom and the State Oil Company of Azerbaijan signed a memorandum of understanding for long-term supplies of Azeri gas to Russia, further undermining Baku's commitment to the Nabucco project.

The Supply Weapon

Moscow is intent on entrapping and encircling Europe in its expanding energy web. By mobilizing its major energy companies, Russia's regime has applied direct pressure on selected governments to alter their policies and allow for the penetration of Russian economic interests. Gas in particular is a "dependency-inducing fuel" that is difficult to replace because of its broad industrial and consumer use.[20] Some analysts believe that a natural gas cartel led by Russia is emerging, similar to the Organization of the Petroleum Exporting Countries (OPEC) in the oil sector. This would enable Moscow to increase its economic and political leverage vis-à-vis European consumers.[21]

Actual cutoffs and threatened disruptions to gas and oil supplies have been favored methods employed by Moscow against the CEE states. Between 1992 and 2006 at least fifty-five cases were reported to achieve specific economic or political objectives, including purchasing energy infrastructure and influencing foreign policy.[22] The Baltic states have experienced periodic cutoffs in oil deliveries either as demonstrations of Moscow's displeasure with government policies or to force the sale of energy infrastructure to Russian corporations. During 2003 the state-owned oil pipeline monopoly, Transneft, terminated shipments of crude through the Latvian port of Ventspils, citing "technical reasons." In reality, Transneft sought to acquire the port facilities at a reduced price, while the Latvian government was seeking to divest itself of a 42 percent stake.

In Lithuania, Lukoil halted oil supplies during 1999–2001, when it tried to bankrupt and purchase the Mazeikiai refinery. Transneft emulated that behavior by halting all supplies to Lithuania through a spur of the Druzhba pipeline as punishment for the resale of Mazeikiai to a Polish company. When Mazeikiai was sold to the U.S. company Williams International, Lukoil disrupted oil supplies to the refinery, thus temporarily putting it out of operation and causing substantial financial losses. Russia terminated deliveries of oil to Lithuania in July 2006, using a minor accident as an excuse to permanently close the sole pipeline. Moscow has refused ever since to answer Lithuanian and EU queries about the nature of that mishap and plans to repair the line. Observers noted that the "accident" was Moscow's retaliation against the purchase of Lithuania's Mazeikiai refinery by the Polish PKN Orlen, which had been in competition with Russian companies for the contract.[23]

Belarus has experienced energy blackmail on several occasions. Gas supplies were severed in 2004 when Minsk refused to sell a 51 percent stake in BelTransGaz or to pay a substantially higher price for Russian gas deliveries. In January 2007 German refineries experienced oil supply shortfalls for three days as Transneft stopped all deliveries to Europe through the Druzhba pipeline during a dispute with Belarus over the terms of Russian oil deliveries. A number of downstream countries in the EU were affected by the stoppage, which Chancellor Merkel described as undermining trust in Russia's reliability as an energy supplier.[24]

In January 2006 Gazprom cut all gas supplies to Ukraine during a pricing dispute after it doubled the cost of supplies at short notice. The purpose of the price rise and subsequent cutoff was to punish Kyiv for staging the Orange Revolution and electing a pro-Western president. The policy backfired, as it disrupted supplies to EU states and tarnished Russia's image as a reliable supplier. The Ukrainian authorities have consistently criticized energy deals with Russia involving nontransparent dealings by overseas firms. Under the complex January 2006 agreement between Russia and Ukraine, all Gazprom gas supplies to Ukraine were funneled via Swiss-registered RosUkrEnergo. Gazprom held a 50 percent stake in RosUkrEnergo, while Ukrainian businessman Dmitry Firtash owned 45 percent. UkrGazEnergo, a joint venture between RosUkrEnergo and Ukraine's Naftohaz, acted as the sole gas importer into Ukraine and was suspected of corrupting local politicians.

In October 2007 Gazprom had warned Ukraine that it would reduce gas deliveries unless Kyiv paid $1.3 billion worth of debt arrears. The timing of Gazprom's announcement was designed to apply pressure after the September parliamentary elections and to emphasize Russia's designs to control Ukraine's gas-transit network. Both President Yushchenko and Prime Minister Yulia Tymoshenko have called for Russian gas supplies to Ukraine to become more transparent. The creation of RosUkrEnergo was not Kyiv's initiative, and the Ukrainian authorities preferred to maintain direct relations with Gazprom without intermediaries.

In a recent demonstration of Russia's use of the supply weapon, shortly after the signing of an agreement between Prague and Washington in July 2008 on building a missile defense radar facility on Czech territory, Transneft announced that oil deliveries to the Czech Republic would be cut through the Druzhba pipeline from the contracted volume of 500,000 tons down to 300,000 tons for the month of July.[25] Transneft officials did not explain the reasons for this disruption and failed to specify whether supplies would fully resume. Given Moscow's record in manipulating energy supplies to gain political advantage, the timing of the oil reduction appeared intended to intimidate and punish Prague for its security decisions.

Gazprom exploits accrued debts to blackmail neighboring states and has engaged intermediary companies to bankrupt Ukraine's state company, Naftohaz. If successful, this policy would enable joint Russian-Ukrainian control of the gas transit system in lieu of debt repayments.[26] To discredit Kyiv among EU members, Moscow also accuses Ukraine of illegally siphoning gas intended for WE. As Russian companies control the metering system, they can inflate the amount of pilfered gas when submitting a bill to the government in Kyiv. In addition, local companies linked with the major Russian companies actually benefit from the diversion of gas supplies for which the Ukrainian state then has to pay.

In disguising its political components, Gazprom depicts its debt-collection claims as market-driven. However, Russia's ambassador to Ukraine and former Gazprom chief Viktor Chernomyrdin has been more explicit. In September 2007 he warned that talks on gas prices would depend on the results of Ukraine's elections. Chernomyrdin also claimed that joint control of Ukraine's gas transit system was in Ukraine's national interest, and if Kyiv refused to settle its debts by sharing control of transit pipelines, Russia would switch its gas export routes to seabed pipelines.[27]

Ukraine's prime minister Tymoshenko was seen as a threat to Russia's expansive interests because she underscored Kyiv's intent to remove intermediaries from the gas supply process. President Yushchenko alleged that Gazprom's threat to cut off supplies was a response to his government's announcements that it would exclude RosUkrEnergo from the gas-delivery scheme and revise prices for transportation across Ukraine's territory.[28] In response to Russia's persistent threats, in January 2008 Tymoshenko proposed that the EU and Ukraine initiate a gas pipeline from Turkmenistan via the Caspian Sea, the South Caucasus, and the Black Sea to Ukraine.[29] She called for direct EU involvement in constructing energy corridors via the Caspian and Black seas directly to Europe.

Energy prices have also been manipulated vis-à-vis Moldova when Moscow sought to place pressure on Chisinau for aligning itself with postrevolution Ukraine and Georgia. In June 2006 Gazprom demanded a large increase in the price of gas to pressure Chisinau away from the Western orbit. A provisional deal was eventually struck during 2007, which included a lesser price rise to $170 per thousand cubic meters.[30] Moscow also signaled it would lift the embargo on Moldovan wine exports, while President Voronin pledged that Moldova would not petition to join NATO.

In addition to pressuring Moldova to sell its energy infrastructure, Russian companies transformed the debts of the separatist Transnistrian authorities into energy assets. For example, Gazprom planned to acquire the Transnistrian stake in the Moldovgaz joint venture as payment for gas deliveries to the breakaway province.[31] By mid-2007 Gazprom already controlled a 50 percent stake in Moldovgaz; Transnistria's share in the company stood at 13.44 percent.

Russia's supplies have also been manipulated vis-à-vis Western Europe, where energy companies have sought higher prices or valuable assets in strategically situated states. In one glaring example, Lukoil's oil deliveries to Germany through the Druzhba pipeline that traverses Poland and Ukraine abruptly decreased by some 30 percent in August 2007 and halted altogether in February 2008.[32] Lukoil was reportedly pressuring Western firms into selling refineries, including Germany's Wilhelmshaven complex.[33] Germany remains heavily dependent on Russian-delivered oil, to the tune of 45 percent of its imports, and receives some 22 million tons of Russian oil annually through the Druzhba pipeline, with Lukoil supplying almost a quarter. Two German refineries, in Schwedt and Leuna, are connected to the Druzhba system.

Lukoil was evidently trying to accomplish several objectives by cutting deliveries: to push out an intermediary, the Sunimex company, from the oil trade; to increase the price of supplies for the next contract period; and to intimidate German owners into ceding shares in refineries as a guarantee of steady Russian supplies. Moscow may also be manufacturing scarcity to demonstrate that it will favor the most "cooperative" European partners.

Energy Infrastructure: Northern Routes

Russia aims to diversify its energy export routes and destinations in order to reduce its dependence on any specific transit state with whom it may be embroiled in a political dispute. Simultaneously, it seeks to eliminate its energy transit fees across CEE. The most glaring example of this process has been the planned Nord Stream pipeline along the Baltic seabed from Russia to Germany. Its main owner will be Gazprom, and its smaller shareholders include Germany's biggest energy companies, E.ON Ruhrgas and Wintershall, a section of BASF.[34]

Moscow intends to counter perceptions that Nord Stream is a purely Russo-German venture. It calculates that a broader consortium would convince Brussels to ignore opposition to the project from several CEE capitals. Gazprom is luring various Western companies into the project to discredit the protests of CEE states. These have included the Dutch company Gasunie, which bought a 9 percent stake in Nord Stream in November 2007 and in return offered Gazprom a 9 percent share in the undersea Balgzand-Bacton Line (BBL) pipeline to the UK.[35] Russian gas will reach Holland overland, and from there Gazprom plans to target the UK market through BBL, delivering supplies to the British company Centrica in return for shared ownership of Centrica's gas distribution network and electrical power plants.

A primary purpose for building Nord Stream is to bypass Poland, Ukraine, and the three Baltic states, undercut their importance as energy transit countries, diminish their transit revenues, and deepen their isolation from EU energy markets. The Kremlin would then be in a position to exert political pressure on those states without fear that its gas supplies to WE would also be ruptured. Lithuania, Latvia, and Estonia also face electricity shortfalls owing to the planned closure of Lithuania's Ignalina nuclear power plant in 2009 as ordered by the EU because of estimated safety risks. Ignalina's decommissioning combined with the lack of pipeline connections to the rest of the EU could force the Balts to import electricity from Russia and thereby substantially increase their economic dependence.

Nord Stream will enable Russia to have a significant voice in Germany's domestic energy policy and the gas market in the broader Central European region. Germany's dependence on Russian-transported gas could rise from about 44 percent in 2007 to 80 percent when all phases of the pipeline are completed.[36] By the close of 2007 Gazprom estimated the cost of the Russo-German gas pipeline to be €6 billion—a 50 percent increase over the initial €4 billion figure in October 2005.[37] The pipeline's proposed route also became a subject of controversy. Finland asked the Nord Stream company to shift the route farther from its coast. Poland demanded that the route around the island of Bornholm be moved northward. Sweden requested that the Nord Stream company abandon the idea of building a compressor station near the Swedish island of Gotland.

Persistent opposition to the Nord Stream route necessitated new planning and additional costs at a time when Russia's revenues and reserves were shrinking, at the close of 2008. Baltic littoral countries are also anxious about Russian legislation authorizing Gazprom, Transneft, and other state monopolies to establish quasi-military units to protect their assets and infrastructure. The legislation was adopted in July 2007, and President Putin signed it the following month. Following protests from the Nordic states that they would block Nord Stream, Moscow seemed to backtrack on its threats or at least played down their impact.

To gain a stake in Nord Stream, Gazprom's two German partners, E.ON Ruhrgas and Wintershall, had to provide Gazprom with a share of ownership in lucrative gas distribution networks in Germany through the joint company Wingas. Wintershall entered into negotiations with Gazprom on surrendering some of its stakes in extractive projects in the North Sea. Gazprom also seeks acquisition of Ruhrgas assets in other countries, including the UK and Hungary. At one point Ruhrgas offered to swap its holdings in Hungary to Gazprom for a 25 percent stake in Russia's Yuzhno-Russkoye gas and oil field in western Siberia. The Ruhrgas shares eventually ended up with Hungary's oil and gas company, MOL.

Gazprom has focused on acquiring stakes in electrical power firms in order to enter the British energy market. It plans to eventually extend Nord Stream into the North Sea and use Belgium as a regional hub for gas transmission to nearby countries, including the UK. It joined with the Belgian gas distribution company Fluxys to build a storage site at Poederlee and envisages laying a seabed pipeline from Belgium's Zeebrugge to the English coast. However, in August 2007 the Belgian government ruled against the storage agreement and the exclusive use of the site by Gazprom. Belgium's regulatory commission concluded that the project would contravene antimonopoly legislation.

In its planned division of labor for the major EU states, Moscow plans to construct a gas pipeline across the Baltic Sea with Germany, build another across the Black Sea with Italy, and develop the Shtokman gas field in the Barents Sea with France. In July 2007 a deal was signed between Gazprom and French oil company Total to develop Shtokman.[38] Total will receive 25 percent of a company that will develop the project's first phase but will not own any underground assets. Gazprom will maintain a 51 percent share of the management company, full control over the flow of gas, and 100 percent of the company that controls the project license. The agreement with Total stipulates the start of commercial production in 2013 if the required investments of $15 billion are secured. Total would have the role of a service company.

In July 2007 a report commissioned by the European Parliament was highly critical of Gazprom investments in EU distribution networks.[39] Neelie Kroes, EU competition commissioner, asserted that the new rules for energy liberalization would strictly separate energy-producing companies from the distribution business. As a result, Gazprom would have to sell its share in Nord Stream. However, Moscow has mobilized its WE energy lobby, including Germany's E.ON, French Gaz de France, and French Total, to oppose this legislation. Estonia, Finland, and Sweden have all objected to the Nord Stream pipeline on ecological grounds.[40] In September 2007 the Estonian government rejected a request by Nord Stream to conduct a seabed survey in Estonia's maritime economic zone with plans to construct the pipeline. Tallinn cited national sovereignty in its territorial waters and its wider economic zone as reasons for rejecting Nord Stream's request.[41] The proposed operations could reveal data about Estonia's natural resources and sensitive information about the configuration of its seabed.

In May 2008 a European Parliament panel concluded that Nord Stream must be approved by all countries whose coastline it will bypass. The panel responded to a petition by Lithuanian and Polish environmental associations. In June 2008 the Council of Baltic Sea States declared their opposition to Nord Stream owing primarily to its potential environmental effects. Polish premier Donald Tusk suggested that land pipelines such as the "Amber Stream" route along the Baltic Coast would be considerably cheaper, reliable, and practical. Danish prime minister Anders Fogh Rasmussen pushed for environmental reforms on energy projects in the region. The prime ministers of two other Baltic states, Angela Merkel and Vladimir Putin, did not attend the conference.[42]

Broader security concerns underpinned opposition to the pipeline among Baltic littoral states. Officials in Moscow indicated that the Russian navy may assist with surveying, construction, and security for the project, thus heightening fears of submarine surveillance. Moreover, the project was initiated without proper consultations in the Council of Baltic Sea States, a group mandated to focus on maritime and ecological issues. Nord Stream managing director Matthias Warnig also proposed that Estonia's port of Sillamäe be used as a staging area for pipeline construction and deploying a Russian work force. Tallinn strenuously opposed such plans, having already experienced a large influx of Russian colonists during the Soviet era.

The Baltic states and Poland assert that Moscow and Berlin forged a deal behind their backs in launching Nord Stream. They fear that the pipeline could set a precedent whereby Russia and Germany would combine to determine maritime and energy policies in the Baltic Sea basin. Far from being an EU initiative, Nord Stream remains an essentially bilateral project between the German and Russian governments; it has not qualified for EU financing, and it contradicts the EU's stated goal of energy diversification.

Energy Infrastructure: Southern Routes

Gazprom has lured several European countries to invest in the planned Russian-controlled South Stream project that would channel Kazakh and Turkmen gas under the Black Sea to the Balkans and on to southern and Central Europe.[43] Serbia, Italy, Greece, Bulgaria, and Austria all joined this Gazprom initiative, thus undercutting the EU's Nabucco project, intended to transmit Central Asian gas to Europe through Turkey.[44] Moscow courted all five countries with long-term guaranteed gas supplies, transit fees, and storage revenues. Gazprom has offered contracts to other smaller states, including Slovenia, Croatia, and Bosnia-Herzegovina, to solidify its energy dominance in the region.[45]

One branch of South Stream was projected to transit via Serbia either through Croatia and Slovenia to northern Italy or through Romania and Hungary to Austria. In April 2008, following contract disagreements with Austria's energy company OMV, Gazprom projected a route for South Stream from Serbia to Slovenia and northern Italy.[46] Declaring alternative proposals are a standard Muscovite ploy to gain more advantageous terms. The second branch of South Stream would run from Bulgaria to Greece and southern Italy, with Gazprom reserving the right to make final decisions on precise transit routes. The company has astutely involved several capitals in competition for gas supplies and to provide transit and storage services for Gazprom, while Western capitals have been unable to obtain the investment funds necessary to finance Nabucco.

If built, South Stream will enable Gazprom to control flows of Central Asian gas to Europe, even though it may prove unable to provide the declared gas volumes for all existing and planned pipelines. Nevertheless, Gazprom intends to accelerate pipeline construction in order to control European markets through its dominance over vital transportation routes. Some analysts suspect that South Stream may be a double gambit: to deactivate the Nabucco project, by monopolizing Central Asian supplies and disenchanting potential investors; and to pressure excluded transit countries such as Ukraine to surrender their pipelines to Russian control in order to guarantee steady gas supplies. Although Gazprom estimates an annual capacity of 30 billion cubic meters for South Stream, more than half of this volume will be needed to fulfill existing contracts with little remaining for additional customers.

According to Vladimir Socor of the *Eurasia Daily Monitor*, South Stream will have nine negative consequences for European security.[47] First, it will allow Russia to monopolize markets in CEE and significantly expand Gazprom's market share in WE states. Second, it will lock in Russia's state monopoly while shutting out competitors in parts of EU territory. Third, it will enable Gazprom to acquire critical infrastructure in Europe as part of its supply deals. Fourth, it will distort the market through price dictation on various forms of energy while forcing consumers to bear the high costs of Russian-delivered supplies. Fifth, it will perpetuate Russia's monopsony on Central Asian gas. Sixth, it may facilitate plans to create a cartel of gas exporters under Russian leadership. Seventh, it would enable Russia to control the southern gateway for Central Asian gas to Europe. Eighth, it will set the stage for Gazprom's continuing dominance in Europe through control of transport, even after Russia's own gas export potential declines. Ninth, it will pose risks to the integrity of political and financial systems in Europe, with nontransparent links to Gazprom and the Kremlin.

Moscow is also active in gaining control of oil and gas distribution facilities in Central Europe at the projected terminal of the South Stream pipeline. Austria's OMV became heavily dependent on Russia following agreements signed during Putin's May 2007 visit to Vienna.[48] The purpose of the agreements was to integrate Austria's gas transit and storage networks with Gazprom. OMV and Gazprom agreed in January 2008 to jointly develop a Central European gas hub (CEGH) and gas transit management center at Baumgarten near Vienna.[49] Baumgarten junction, the second-largest gas transmission center in Europe, is the designated terminus point for Nabucco. Once operational, the OMV-Gazprom deal will ensure preemptive Russian use of a key installation to the detriment of any competitors. Moscow promises to transform the facility into the largest hub in the EU if Gazprom can control its operations.

Gazprom plays Austria and Hungary against each other as regional hubs and entices Slovakia, Bulgaria, and Serbia with sections of the hub. OMV would also forfeit much of its decision-making independence, while assets it might acquire elsewhere would be vulnerable to Russian takeovers. Such attempts have already been made vis-à-vis Hungary's MOL.[50] Gazprom has also negotiated with Holland and Belgium by offering to transform them into gas distribution centers. Although Gazprom does not possess the sources or capacity to deliver on all these promises, it exploits the temptation of high revenues and steady energy supplies to convince WE corporations and governments to sign contracts and sell off key infrastructure.

The French government was also lured into the South Stream web as evident in the comments of French foreign minister Bernard Kouchner on October 28, 2008, following talks in St. Petersburg with Foreign Minister Lavrov. He stated that France was willing to join South Stream and that Russia could be included in the Nabucco project, thus contradicting the EU's declared policy of supporting Nabucco vis-à-vis its Russian rival South Stream.[51] The French government seeks access to Russian-delivered gas for the state-owned company Gaz de France. Gaz de France had earlier proposed joining the Nabucco consortium but was ruled out by Turkey in 2006, following a French parliamentary vote that recognized the Armenian genocide.

During 2007 the Hungarian government realized that OMV was attempting a hostile takeover of Hungary's strategic assets, whereby an OMV purchase of MOL could precipitate a full-scale Russian buyout of distribution networks and refineries. The result could be the creation of a regional monopoly that would control almost all oil refining and distribution in Central Europe. The EU itself has been in disarray over Gazprom's maneuvers. Some EU spokesmen accepted OMV's argument that Budapest's resistance violated EU regulations regarding the free movement of capital but failed to understand that Gazprom was maneuvering for an antimarket monopoly that could scuttle Nabucco.[52] OMV's attempt to take over MOL was eventually shelved because of Hungarian resistance.

MOL has also defended itself against Russian acquisitions by purchasing refining and retailing assets elsewhere in Central Europe.[53] It holds a 25 percent stake in INA, Croatia's largest energy entity; owns the Slovnaft refinery in Slovakia; and controls almost a quarter of the Czech Republic's market for oil products. Such assets increase MOL's capitalization and the value of its shares against nontransparent purchases by Russian proxies. Bratislava is concerned that an OMV takeover of Slovnaft would result in the refinery falling into Russian hands. Zagreb viewed MOL's actions as a defense against a Russian takeover. OMV and MOL already owned major oil refineries and fuel-distribution networks in Romania, Slovakia, and Croatia, in addition to Austria and Hungary. With OMV required to sell off some assets after a takeover of MOL, according to EU stipulations, Gazprom and the Gazprom Neft–Lukoil joint venture could be the main buyers.

Budapest is not opposed to MOL's foreign purchase but resists ownership by a foreign state-owned entity.[54] It challenges the spurious logic of some EU representatives who argue that any EU country has an obligation to hand over a highly efficient company to a state-controlled and less efficient firm because EU law requires the free movement of capital. Such a position ignores OMV's opaque relationship with Gazprom. To defend themselves against hostile state energy takeovers, some CEE countries may actually reverse the privatization process and even renationalize several energy companies.

In September 2007 Hungarian premier Ferenc Gyurcsány confirmed his backing for Nabucco while continuing to voice support for South Stream on the grounds that it was a more realistic option.[55] Critics charged that his government was embedded with Russian business interests and was undermining EU solidarity. In February 2008 Gyurcsány joined Putin and Dmitry Medvedev in Moscow to seal an intergovernmental energy agreement.[56] The new accord envisaged building an extension of South Stream through Hungary. Budapest would create a company with 100 percent state ownership to partner with Gazprom by establishing a 50-50 joint venture to build and operate a pipeline and an underground storage site on Hungarian territory. The signing of the agreement in the absence of any feasibility study indicates that it was rushed through for political reasons to strengthen Russia's strategic energy position.

Austria's OMV appeared to be the main culprit in undercutting Nabucco by seeking to turn the pipeline into a joint venture with Gazprom.[57] Austrian economics minister Martin Bartenstein and OMV executive Reinhard Mitschek, Nabucco's general director, suggested in early 2008 that Nabucco also carry Gazprom gas and become integrated with Gazprom's South Stream project. Such an arrangement would defeat the strategic rationale for the entire Nabucco initiative.

South Stream is intended to tie together three regions for Russia's energy dominance: the Caspian Basin, the Black Sea, and the Balkans. At a Balkan energy summit in Zagreb in June 2007, Putin announced that Gazprom and the Italian company Ente Nazionale Idrocarburi (ENI) had signed a memorandum on the construction of a gas pipeline under the Black Sea as the core component of South Stream.[58] He also declared that Moscow intended to build underground storage facilities in several Balkan states. Earlier that month, at a meeting of the Black Sea Economic Cooperation (BSEC) forum in Istanbul, Putin asserted, "The Balkans and the Black Sea has always been a sphere of our special interests."

In April 2008 Greece formally signed an agreement to join South Stream during Prime Minister Costas Karamanlis's visit to the Kremlin.[59] The accord involved the construction of the Greek section of the pipeline. Bulgaria had been included in South Stream in January 2008.[60] The project company for the pipeline's Bulgarian stretch would be registered in Sofia with Gazprom and Bulgargaz each owning a 50 percent stake. However, Gazprom and ENI retained the overall ownership and operating rights for the entire project. Pipeline construction was planned to start in 2009 with gas deliveries by 2013. However, following Russia's growing financial problems in the fall of 2008, construction plans were pushed back from 2013 to 2015.

The bilateral agreements were to be followed by multilateral deals with future consumers in countries along the South Stream route. Bulgaria was slated to become a linchpin country for the entire project, and the government was lured by the promise of a transit bonanza.[61] The pipeline was to bypass Turkey and divert gas volumes away from Ukraine's transit system. Bulgaria agreed to the deal even though the state pipeline company, Bulgargaz, was a partner in the Nabucco consortium, together with Turkey's Botas, Romania's Romgaz, Hungary's MOL, and Austria's OMV.

In January 2008 Serbian and Russian officials signed several agreements for the sale of Serbia's state oil monopoly, the Petroleum Industry of Serbia (NIS), to Gazprom subsidiary Gazprom Neft and for the construction of a pipeline through Serbia.[62] Putin also declared that Russia had designated Serbia as a key transit junction for energy supplies to Europe. Serbian finance minister Mlađan Dinkić commented that the government "humiliated" Serbia by selling NIS at a fraction of its market value of approximately $2 billion.[63] Prime Minister Vojislav Koštunica supported the transaction to reinforce Serbia's ties with Russia as a counterweight to Euro-Atlantic integration.

In October 2008 Gazprom officials proposed including Romania in South Stream and expressed willingness to build a section of the pipeline through Romania.[64] Gazprom also proposed constructing a gas storage site at Margineni in northeastern Romania. The South Stream offer was designed to increase

Russia's leverage vis-à-vis countries that had signed up for the pipeline and were negotiating commercial and financial terms with Gazprom. If Bucharest were to accept the proposal, more capitals in CEE would be competing for Russian gas supplies, pipelines, and storage sites, thus enhancing Moscow's bargaining position. Despite Gazprom's enticements, both President Băsescu and Prime Minister Călin Popescu-Tăriceanu publicly turned down Russia's offer.[65] Moscow was also frustrated with Belgrade's effort to eliminate the Gazprom-created intermediary YugoRosGaz, which was embroiled in a major corruption scandal in Serbia.

Within South Stream, Gazprom and Serbian Gas formed a 51 percent–49 percent joint company to build an arm of that pipeline through Serbia. The deal guaranteed a Russian supply and transit monopoly for thirty years. Gazprom would take over the Serbian Gas transmission network, including that in the Serb republic of Bosnia-Herzegovina. Moscow was also negotiating the inclusion of Croatia and the Bosnian Federation in the South Stream route. Additionally, Gazprom and Serbian Gas planned to create a joint company to develop the underground storage site at Banatski Dvor.

Throughout the Balkan region, Gazprom has adopted a novel acquisitions policy by acquiring oil assets and electricity-generating plants in addition to gas transport and storage infrastructure in return for guaranteed gas supplies.[66] To achieve these goals Gazprom operated through Gazprom Neft, which in 2007 formed a joint company with Lukoil under Gazprom Neft's control to pursue various projects in the oil sector.

A key element in Russia's energy expansion is the planned Burgas-Alexandropolis oil pipeline, and in March 2008 the Bulgarian and Greek prime ministers signed an agreement with Moscow to initiate construction. A Russian consortium, including Gazprom, will hold a 51 percent stake in the pipeline, with Bulgaria and Greece sharing the remaining 49 percent. The pipeline will be a prolongation of the Caspian Consortium's route that runs from Kazakhstan to Russia's Black Sea port of Novorossiysk.[67] Under the plan, Kazakh oil will be shipped from Novorossiysk by tankers to Burgas in Bulgaria and from there by pipeline to Greece. The project's strategic objectives are to increase Russia's control over the transit of Kazakh oil, to heighten political leverage over the major U.S. and European oil companies that have no other outlet from Kazakhstan, and to enhance Moscow's political influence in the Balkans.

Europe's Energy Security
The EU has failed to develop a coherent energy strategy despite its growing dependence on an authoritarian state with imperial ambitions. As a result, European consumers pay substantially more for energy than necessary, particularly for

natural gas, in an uncertain supply climate.[68] EU energy companies are nationally based and often protected by the state and are invariably competing for gas and oil resources that Russia can manipulate to its advantage. There is no pan-European energy grid, and there are no European storage facilities. The EU system consists of a number of national energy markets connected by pipelines owned by national companies, with little incentive for cross-border competition that would undermine the national monopolies. This leaves the EU highly vulnerable to Russian pressures, especially in gas supplies. Although the EU has developed a formula to reduce energy consumption by 20 percent and to utilize alternative sources by the year 2020, there is no agreement as to who will bear the costs.

Diversification in energy supplies and investment in alternative energy sources is more affordable among the WE states than among the CEE states. There is limited renewable energy potential in most CEE countries amid demands to scale back coal power plants for environmental reasons and broad resistance to developing nuclear power. The WE countries are also generally more efficient in energy usage than the CEE states. Moreover, alternative forms of energy are not commercially viable, while conservation measures are insufficient to ensure any significant reduction in dependence on hydrocarbon imports over the coming decade. These factors will actually increase CEE reliance on Russian gas supplies. Some analysts project that consumption of natural gas in CEE will increase threefold over the next fifteen to twenty years.

In October 2007 top officials from the three Baltic states, Poland, Ukraine, Romania, Georgia, and Azerbaijan, together with EU and U.S. representatives, attended an energy security conference in Vilnius.[69] Concerns were expressed about Russia's use of energy supplies as a political weapon. Czech deputy prime minister Alexandr Vondra underscored that "unjust manipulation or interruption of energy supplies is as much a security threat as is military action. Post-Soviet countries have been experiencing that on a daily basis, as Russia's appetite for using energy as a political weapon is growing."[70] Vondra warned about divisions in the EU between capitals arranging separate deals with Moscow and those seeking alternative energy sources.

Conference participants called for diverse energy flows by promoting cooperation among Europe, the United States, and the countries of the Caspian and Black Sea regions to bring energy from Central Asia and the South Caucasus to Europe. A set of policy recommendations called on the EU high representative for common foreign and security policy, the EU energy commissioner, and the EU's external affairs and neighborhood policy commissioner to work out a comprehensive road map for developing a European policy on energy security. The Vilnius document proposed that "member countries inform each other and the Commission before concluding any bilateral agreements with third parties that could affect EU interests." It asked the EU to intensify energy dialogue with countries in the Caspian Basin "in the common interest of creating a Central Asia–South Caucasus–Black Sea energy corridor directly to Europe and diminishing dependence on Russian transit."[71]

Romania and Ukraine have been especially concerned about the impact of the South Stream project. The pipeline is specifically designed to bypass Ukraine and thereby make Kyiv more vulnerable to Russia's pressure without disrupting supplies to WE. Romania turned down Gazprom's offer to join South Stream because it calculated that the political risks would outweigh the economic benefits. Both Kyiv and Bucharest may seek to block South Stream on legal and environmental grounds, as the underwater pipeline would have to traverse both countries' exclusive economic zones.[72]

An effective EU energy strategy needs several essential components, including the diversification of supply sources, routes, and downstream marketing; liberalization of Europe's energy industries; unbundling of national utilities; expansion and improvement of gas storage facilities; construction of more interconnecting pipelines and power lines; and greater investment in liquefied natural gas terminals. Such steps would lessen the dangers of transportation disruptions and political blackmail. A common EU energy policy will also need to determine long-term energy supplies based on economic and environmental criteria.

The European Commission has supported the creation of a unified gas transmission network named New Europe Transmission Systems (NETS), initiated by Hungary.[73] The gas market in Europe is characterized by national fragmentation, an absence of interconnections, and underfinancing of infrastructure development. NETS could improve capital efficiency, and its interconnectivity would improve the security of supplies by fostering risk-sharing. A unified regional network could also significantly strengthen each country's bargaining position vis-à-vis Gazprom, which is intent on gaining transmission and storage infrastructure in most European states.

The NETS project is intended to give southeastern Europe access to Azeri gas through existing infrastructure before the EU-backed Nabucco gas pipeline is completed. By the close of 2008 Austria, Bosnia-Herzegovina, Bulgaria, Croatia, Romania, Serbia, and Slovenia had signed on to the project. In developing the NETS plan, several CEE capitals backed the creation of a regional energy consortium to counteract the partnerships established by Russian companies with West European majors. The objective: to establish alternative energy routes not dependent on the East-West system. Hungary's MOL, having defeated the attempted takeover by Austria's OMV in August 2008, focused its attention on expanding operations in neighboring countries and interconnecting gas pipeline networks throughout CEE.[74] Interconnectivity can enhance the security of gas supplies through risk-sharing as NETS could unify national markets into a broader regional market to link up with non-Russian supply routes.

It is important for the EU to coordinate its energy policy with the United States, as the energy security of all allies is a strategic priority. Russian control over energy routes from the trans-Caspian region will undermine American interests throughout the Middle East and Central Asia by strengthening Moscow's political leverage over those states. A transatlantic energy security pact can oblige members of NATO and the EU to pool their resources during a crisis to prevent the political manipulation of energy. In March 2006 Warsaw submitted such a proposal to all NATO and EU states. EU-U.S. coordination can include a permanent consultative mechanism with NATO engaged in enhancing energy security.

While Russia seeks to monopolize the export of Central Asian gas, the EU needs to intensify negotiations with Central Asian governments and energy transit states for the construction of westbound pipelines from the trans-Caspian region. These include the Kazakhstan-Azerbaijan subsea oil pipeline and the Turkmenistan-Azerbaijan subsea gas pipeline that would link Central Asian energy resources with Europe through Turkey. The former can link up with the Baku-Tbilisi-Ceyhan oil pipeline, completed in 2005; the latter, with the Baku-Tbilisi-Erzurum gas pipeline that is currently under construction. Work must also be intensified on the Nabucco pipeline to pump Central Asian gas to southeastern Europe and beyond.

The success of all these routes remains dependent on sufficient foreign investment, political determination to stabilize Georgia after Russia's military intervention, as well as the resolution of legal disputes over the Caspian Sea's territorial delineations. The trans-Caspian route would enable the EU to fully bypass Russia and bring substantial gas reserves from Turkmenistan and Kazakhstan into Europe. In November 2008 the European Commission proposed the formation of a new company, the Caspian Development Corporation (CDC), to focus on developing the trans-Caspian connection.[75]

In the oil sector, investment in constructing the Constanta-Trieste oil pipeline could link this system with the Trans-Alpine Pipeline, which supplies crude to Austria and Germany. Up to 90 million tons of oil could be transported per year through this system, thus helping to ensure Europe's basic strategic energy needs and reducing tanker traffic through the Bosphorus. Investments could also be made in extending the Odesa-Brody oil pipeline across Poland to the Baltic Sea at Gdansk in order to supply European markets with Central Asian crude via the Black Sea rather than Russian oil through Ukraine.

The presidents of Ukraine, Azerbaijan, Georgia, Poland, and Lithuania agreed in May 2008 to create a Euro-Asian oil transportation corridor.[76] Its components would include an LNG terminal on Poland's Baltic coast to limit dependence on Russia and to increase supplies to CEE from North Africa and other sources. In a broader strategic document, the May summit approved a "Concept of the Caspian–Black Sea–Baltic Energy Transit Space," which focused on connecting Caspian producer countries with the EU via the South Caucasus and Ukraine.[77] The objective was to reduce Russia's transit monopoly by creating new transportation routes.

Assistance must be provided to the most vulnerable countries, including Ukraine and Moldova, to develop an effective energy strategy that would lessen their dependence on Russia. This should enable energy transit countries to maintain control over their energy infrastructure and limit takeovers by state-controlled Russian companies. Within Europe, EU member states need to ensure European control and supervision over energy transportation systems, strategic storage sites, refineries, and other critical infrastructures, with enhanced monitoring of supply and consumption across the region.

Additionally, international cooperation needs to be intensified in upgrading energy infrastructure, increasing the efficiency of energy usage, resolving cross-regional ecological problems, improving communication between government and business, devising a system of early warnings concerning potential cuts in supplies, and improving public education in energy conservation.

The EU has been unable to persuade Moscow to ratify the EU's Energy Charter Treaty, which Russia signed in 1994 and whose Transit Protocol requires that the government allow competitive access to its pipelines. The EU also failed to enforce the Rome Treaty's competition and antitrust rules in cross-border energy arrangements. Under the Putin regime, Russia classified much of its energy sector as strategic and therefore off limits to foreign investment. It renegotiated or terminated contracts in which foreign firms held substantial stakes. Despite these setbacks, the EU must take steps to promote transparency and fair competition in Moscow's energy investments. The EU and the United States possess some leverage in that Russia needs Western technology to increase energy extraction and modernize its energy-exporting infrastructure. This leverage should be used strategically to push for a transparent regulatory regime and the liberalization of upstream and downstream markets.

Russia's energy expansion could also be curbed by plans (styled as the "Gazprom clauses") the European Commission formulated to restrict foreign takeovers of the EU's energy sector, in particular the gas and electricity-transmission networks.[78] One option considered was a reciprocity clause that would keep out countries, such as Russia, where European companies face severe restrictions on investment. The proposals have been linked to the commission's plans to increase competition in the European energy market while easing fears about the consequences of liberalization and foreign takeovers.

In October 2007 Hungary's parliament approved legislation, known as "Lex MOL," designed to prevent hostile takeovers of private energy companies by state-controlled entities from outside the EU.[79] The law is designed to toughen conditions for purchases by foreign state-owned corporations that may be guided by nontransparent political influence. In September 2007 European Commission president José Manuel Barroso announced legislation aimed at liberalizing the EU's internal energy market by breaking up or "unbundling" utilities that control both the production and distribution of energy.[80] The legislation would bar foreign companies such as Gazprom from controlling energy networks unless their governments agree to open their domestic markets.

One unresolved policy problem that weakens Nabucco and serves Russia's neo-imperial designs is Washington's staunch opposition to the export of Iranian gas. Although the United States wants to promote Europe's energy security through supply diversification, its sanctions are also blocking gas development in Iran, which holds the world's second-largest reserves. The White House has threatened to impose sanctions against any state that engages in gas field development in Iran. Potential U.S. sanctions have persuaded major European companies, including Shell, Total, StatoilHydro, and OMV, to shelve their agreements of intent with Iran for gas development and turn their attention toward Gazprom.[81] The inclusion of Iranian gas in the Nabucco project would greatly enhance its capabilities and undermine Russia's monopolistic position. It could also serve to tie Tehran closer to the West and weaken its foreign policy radicalism. Not surprisingly, Moscow continues to court Tehran and does not welcome an Iranian-Western rapprochement.

The West has also moved too slowly in engaging Turkmenistan both politically and economically. Moscow, meanwhile, has pushed forward relentlessly to control Turkmeni gas exports and gas field development in sealing its position as the monopsonist purchaser of Central Asian energy. In addition, Western countries have failed to invest sufficiently in developing LNG terminals to diminish their dependence on Russian gas pipelines. A mechanism for transatlantic cooperation in the energy sphere also needs to be developed in which NATO could be entrusted with protecting pipelines, delivery systems, storage facilities, and other energy infrastructures. The lengthy list of failures in Western energy strategy seriously undermines the prospect of developing non-Russian energy supply and transportation routes and assists Moscow in its strategic expansion.

An unexpected blow hit the Russian regime in the fall of 2008 as global oil prices plummeted in reaction to the deepening economic recession and falling demand for energy. The price of oil fell from a high of over $140 a barrel in July to under $40 in December, while the price of gas was projected to drop by about 40 percent. The impact reverberated throughout the Russian economy, which had already been rocked by the global financial crunch, a steady devaluation of the ruble, and a major slowdown in economic growth. A prolonged spell of low gas prices and the rising cost of pipeline construction could prevent Gazprom from developing desperately needed new gas fields and could indefinitely delay the construction of the Nord Stream and South Stream pipelines.[82] Gazprom is heavily in debt, to the tune of $50 billion, and some observers believe it could be bankrupted by Nord Stream and South Stream. The worldwide recession is likely to starkly expose Russia's overreliance on energy exports as the basis for economic growth and test the stability and durability of the Putinist system. It may also strengthen EU commitments to the diversification of energy supplies as the momentum for a common EU energy network has been building.

7

Business as Policy

As a consequence of soaring energy prices during the past decade, Russia emerged as the third-largest holder of foreign reserves in the Asia Pacific region.[1] Under the Putin administration, the most productive large-scale sectors of the Russian economy were transformed into tools of government policy as Moscow nationalized the major energy concerns and other strategic industries. Between August 2004 and September 2006 the state regained control over twenty-two major businesses, particularly in the energy, banking, and engineering sectors.[2] By the end of 2007 state companies controlled 80 percent of Russia's gas industry, and government ownership of its oil industry increased from 19 percent in 2004 to 52 percent in 2007. These holdings enabled the Kremlin to pursue an increasingly vigorous foreign policy with economic instruments.

The precise scale of Russia's foreign direct investment (FDI) is difficult to measure, although a study released in early 2008 indicated that outward FDI stock outside the financial sector, which includes the ownership of foreign fixed assets, exceeded $70 billion.[3] The largest foreign investors are business groups with subsidiaries mainly in oil and gas, ferrous and nonferrous metals, telecommunications, and machinery. The main destinations for Russia's investment expansion are the European Union (40 percent) and the Commonwealth of Independent States (30 percent), with CIS investments concentrated in Ukraine, Belarus, and Kazakhstan.

Russia's Expanding Inventory

The core sectors of Russian business are closely tied to the Kremlin, through direct ownership, political appointment, or mutual interest. They aim to influence policymaking in targeted countries and have steadily expanded acquisitions of strategic assets in the European economies. Moscow displays a cynical view of economic transactions: the Kremlin considers business a pragmatic endeavor that can bypass any awkward legal regulations and believes corruption can enhance business development and the interests of the state. While it expands its business tools in Europe, the Kremlin has constrained Western investment in Russia's own strategic industries such as energy, mining, banking, telecommunications, machine building, arms manufacturing, and aviation. The Kremlin directly or indirectly controls all these sectors in order to block Western economic penetration that could allegedly undermine state interests.[4]

Russia's economic presence in Western Europe is largely a novelty. Never before have so many companies been so active with such large investments and engaged in "a form of political and economic imperialism."[5] The purchase by Russian companies of major stakes in strategic European industries has several negative consequences. First, asset buyouts in small economies such as in CEE can be readily translated into political influence. Second, quasi-legal and nontransparent business practices, commonplace among Russia's companies, retard economic development and hinder progress toward meeting the standards necessary for EU integration. Third, the main investor behind these buyouts is the Russian state, which is willing to incur losses for political advantage or prevent sectors of the targeted economy from developing by foreclosing Western investment prospects. Fourth, Russia's intense involvement in Europe's economies increases their exposure to technological, scientific, and military espionage.

The EU is Russia's most important trading partner, accounting for more than 50 percent of its foreign trade and nearly 70 percent of the accumulated foreign capital, while Russia is the fifth-largest exporter to the EU.[6] Nonetheless, Russia accounts for only approximately 5 percent of the EU's total foreign trade. The EU has become a primary destination of Russian capital: from an FDI total of approximately $55 billion by 2005, almost $10 billion was invested in Germany, Britain, Ukraine, and Cyprus.[7] According to the Central Bank of Russia (CBR), Russia's FDI abroad exceeded $100 billion by 2005. The statistical discrepancies can be accounted for by differing market value evaluations, by direct investment registered as portfolio investment, and by some investment avoiding registration altogether. A great deal of Russian investment is directed through holding companies registered in third countries, including Cyprus, the Bahamas, Panama, Luxembourg, Holland, Austria, and Ireland, thus masking the origin of the investor.[8]

A looming danger to Western economic and political interests comes from Russia's expanding sovereign wealth fund (SWF), which is believed to have exceeded $32 billion by early 2008.[9] This fund was separated from the stabilization fund created to protect the Russian economy against any downturn in oil prices. It consists of approximately 7 percent of Russia's total hard currency reserves, mostly accumulated from high oil revenues.[10] The SWF was expected to generate substantial investments abroad as President Medvedev pledged to make Russia one of the biggest financial centers in the world.

Analysts feared that Russia's SWF, as an essentially governmental entity, could be used for political purposes on the capital market through the acquisition of public and private equities and strategic assets, including defense industries, or for a large-scale speculative attack on another currency. Moscow could use its expanding market access to exert financial leverage in order to achieve various political objectives. Without transparency, oversight, and binding codes of conduct, concern over the impact of Russia's SWF could also encourage financial protectionism that would curtail the process of globalization.

In his speech at the St. Petersburg International Economic Forum in June 2008, Medvedev asserted that the world was in the throes of the worst economic crisis since the Great Depression and that a newly revived Russia could offer solutions because the United States had overreached its economic capabilities and could not fulfill the role of a global government.[11] In a parallel assault, Putin criticized the World Trade Organization, the International Monetary Fund, and the World Bank as archaic and undemocratic organizations controlled by the United States and the EU as their private clubs. The escalating financial crisis at the close of 2008 reinforced Moscow's contentions that the global economy had to be multipolar and not revolve around Western financial and business interests.

At the World Policy Forum in France in October 2008, Medvedev charged that the global economic crisis sparked by the contraction of financial markets was precipitated by America's "economic egoism."[12] This was evidently a consequence of the "unipolar vision of the world" and of the "desire to be its megaregulator." He called for extensive changes in the "global financial architecture" and the creation of new international institutions in which Russia would become a primary player. Given the steady meltdown in Russia's financial reserves and its abandonment by foreign investors, Medvedev's words rang increasingly hollow as the global recession deepened. Nonetheless, the major Russian companies continue to penetrate the Western economies.

On the eve of the March 2008 presidential elections, Putin's closest allies secured their positions on major corporate boards.[13] The twenty-two companies involved control some 40 percent of the Russian economy. The list includes presidential administration deputy chair Igor Sechin as head of Rosneft; then–prime minister Viktor Zubkov as chairman of Gazprom; presidential aide Viktor Ivanov as head of Aeroflot; presidential aide Igor Shuvalov as head of Sovkomflot; former presidential administration head Aleksandr Voloshin as chair of Unified Energy System; Deputy Prime Minister Sergei Ivanov as head of the United Aircraft Corporation (OAK); Deputy Prime Minister Sergei Naryshkin as head of Channel

One; and presidential aide Sergei Prikhodko, nominated to retain positions on the boards of two companies in the military-industrial complex, Technical Military Armaments and the military aircraft manufacturer Sukhoi.

The largest Russian corporate investors in Europe are Lukoil and Gazprom (Russia's two most powerful energy giants) and several other natural resource–based companies. Under Putin's presidency, Gazprom and its subsidiaries, acting in league with various European partners, "systematically created an elaborate web of opaque companies throughout Europe and Russia."[14] Gazprom focuses on investing in downstream energy infrastructure rather than raising upstream production. It has spent more capital on purchasing companies outside the gas sector than on developing new gas fields inside Russia. It is largely able to claim staggering profitability by gaining productive new acquisitions while its own operations show evidence of mismanagement, underinvestment, and large-scale corruption.

Under Putin, Russia's energy companies adopted an "asset-for-debt" or "asset-for-supplies" policy toward neighboring states. In this scheme, state-controlled companies acquire infrastructure and other strategic assets while guaranteeing long-term energy supplies and increasing economic dependence on Moscow. Russian companies purchase foreign assets and infrastructure for both profit and politics. Owning distribution infrastructure and refining assets in countries dependent on Russian energy supplies can reduce transportation and other logistical costs. However, ownership of an entire chain of distribution also provides state-linked companies with enormous leverage over a country's economy and political leadership.

Several EU governments express concern about losing strategic industries to Russian interests as well as the corrosive effect of Russian acquisitions where there is little transparency and an absence of Western business standards in company strategy, accounting, taxation, financial reporting, and auditing.[15] Authorities in a number of states have launched investigations into the origins of incoming capital, as Russian firms often camouflage their presence behind offshore firms, complex joint ventures, or subsidiaries registered in third countries, and thereby avoid governmental and legal oversight. Such schemes and the presence in most companies of a small cluster of individuals linked with the Russian government indicate money laundering, kickbacks to officials, and ties with intelligence services.

Moscow also engages in grossly unfair business competition, whereby Gazprom has profited from the EU's market liberalization while Russia practices protectionism. The gas giant has established joint venture marketing companies in nearly all EU states; has acquired nonenergy equity in manufacturing, media, and financial services; and plans to build large natural gas storage depots in Hungary, Germany, Belgium, Serbia, and Romania.[16] In February 2008 Luxembourg finance minister Jean-Claude Juncker, chairman of the Eurogroup of finance ministers, asserted, "It is unacceptable that while Russia's government-affiliated fund is sweeping into Europe, European companies are unable to conduct similar activities in Russia." As a result, it will be necessary to take "strong political action to strengthen surveillance and ensure transparency in financial markets."[17]

Gazprom's ambitions would be reduced if proposed EU legislation is enacted banning non-EU companies from controlling Europe's gas networks while unbundling ownership in production, transport, storage, and distribution. These proposals would prevent Gazprom from purchasing parts of the EU's transmission network and force the company to sell its assets in EU transport, distribution, and storage infrastructures. Rather than surrendering its assets, Gazprom is likely to forge contracts with nominally independent companies and seek to disguise its controlling influence. Moreover, EU legislation is unlikely to be accepted by the European Parliament and the Council of the European Union because of resistance by German and French officials who protect their own national monopolistic energy companies and privileged business relations with Moscow.

Several EU governments are concerned that Russian business contracts in the West have helped to enrich the Kremlin elites, significantly raised the level of corruption and other illegal practices within their economies, and enticed various European leaders with lucrative business deals. These contracts have also spawned interest groups that favor Russia over other countries in a range of transactions. Moreover, the clandestine connections between Russian foreign intelligence officers and business networks enable Moscow not only to penetrate industrial lobbies throughout Europe, but to bribe and blackmail politicians, legislators, businesspeople, and journalists and thereby expand its political influences.[18]

Gazprom and other Russian corporations have established dummy companies, especially in CEE, that channel money into election campaigns and political parties favoring Russian interests. Gazprom has put enormous effort into covering its tracks by using subsidiaries or shell companies to evade resistance to its investments, avoid taxation, and strip assets.[19] For example, Gazprom used an Ireland-based sham company for a hostile takeover of Hungary's chemical manufacturer BorsodChem in 2000. Despite opposition by the Hungarian government, the company was able to acquire a 25 percent stake in the firm. Dummy companies and a maze of intermediaries also prevent the detection of corrupt practices involving local officials. The slowdown or even stagnation in structural reform visible in some CEE countries following EU accession has the potential to develop into a more lasting recession that could be nurtured by Russia's corrupt business practices.

To appraise the scale of Russia's purchasing power, it is informative to survey the growth of Russian investment throughout Europe both within and outside the energy sector during the past decade.[20] This is not an exhaustive listing but a selective compendium that primarily pinpoints the penetration or outright buyouts of strategic industries by state-connected Russian enterprises or individual investors with close ties to the Kremlin.

Western Europe: Political Investments

Russian authorities have adopted a "stalking horse" strategy toward much of Western Europe. The Kremlin strategizes with Russia's large state-controlled corporations to form links with Western companies so the latter can lobby for Moscow's interests inside the EU. Gazprom and other Russian energy giants entice key Western corporations into their foreign operations to obtain political support from Western governments. They also offer the prospect of investment inside Russia to Western firms if they sell distribution and other networks in the EU to Russian companies.

For instance, Germany's Ruhrgas owns about 7 percent of Gazprom and has a seat on Gazprom's board.[21] In December 2007 President Putin and German foreign minister Steinmeier inaugurated the Yuzhno-Russkoye oil and gas field in northwestern Siberia.[22] Steinmeier believed that the project would ensure Germany's gas supplies for many years. Gazprom CEO Aleksei Miller noted that Gazprom and Germany's E.ON Ruhrgas were planning to exchange assets. E.ON is Europe's largest private electric power and gas concern. E.ON Ruhrgas is a subsidiary of E.ON and is responsible for the group's gas business in Europe, including production, sales, transport, and storage of natural gas. E.ON Ruhrgas is the largest foreign shareholder in Gazprom, currently owning about 6.5 percent of its shares.

On October 2, 2008, Gazprom and E.ON, with the presence of Merkel and Medvedev in St. Petersburg, signed an agreement to develop Yuzhno-Russkoye.[23] The agreement foresees an exchange of assets giving E.ON 25 percent minus one ordinary registered share in the share capital of Gazprom subsidiary Severneftegazprom and the right to participate in the development of Yuzhno-Russkoye. Severneftegazprom has a license to engage in infrastructure construction, field development, and oil and gas extraction. Gazprom was to receive 49 percent in Gerosgaz, a joint venture formed in 1999 with the participation of Gazprom Export. Meanwhile, the Russian subsidiary of British Petroleum (BP), TNK, obtained a license to develop the Kovytka gas field in eastern Siberia. Although the deal was later blocked and BP was forced to sell its stake, BP was given promises that it could retain some share in the development of the field.

Italy's ENI bought the expropriated gas assets of Russia's Yukos company in April 2007 in a controversial auction and then agreed to cede control to Gazprom. In return, two Italian energy enterprises were given a foothold in Russia's gas fields and the prospect of a seat on the board of Gazprom's oil subsidiary.

Gazprom also maintains long-term gas contracts with ENI and has forged similar arrangements in France, Germany, and Holland. As a result of these cartel contracts between wholesale sellers and buyers, EU consumers pay gas bills several times higher than the wholesale prices that Gazprom charges the national companies.

GERMANY

Russia is a rapidly growing trading and investment partner for Germany. German exports reached over €23 billion in 2006, and more than four thousand German companies are represented in the Russian economy. The influential Eastern Committee of German Industry, chaired by Klaus Mangold, lobbies the government in Berlin to maintain good relations with Russia and protect its investments. German energy companies lubricate close relations between Moscow and Berlin and generally support Russian energy policy, as evident in the planned construction of Nord Stream. Former German chancellor Gerhard Schroeder is chairman of the Nord Stream management committee. Nord Stream is owned by Gazprom (51 percent), Wintershall (20 percent), E.ON Ruhrgas (20 percent), and Gasunie (9 percent). Ruhrgas is a leading German company and a top European public utility company. Wintershall is the largest oil and gas producer in Germany and a subsidiary of the German giant BASF. Gasunie is a Dutch natural gas infrastructure and transportation company, and it owns Holland's gas transmission network.

Gazprom owns 50 percent of Wingas, a German gas distribution and storage company and a subsidiary of Wintershall, itself a subsidiary of BASF and Gazprom. Since October 2007 Wintershall has owned 50 percent plus one share of Wingas, while Gazprom's stock is 50 percent less one share. Analysts believe that through such purchases Gazprom is positioning itself for future energy liberalization in the EU to increase its assets and revenues. Gazprom-Wingas established a joint venture to market Russia's gas throughout the EU, and Gazprom plans to acquire shares in Wintershall's North Sea operations. To create the impression of interdependence, Wintershall was permitted a 25 percent stake in Russia's Yuzhno-Russkoye gas field. Similarly, in return for Germany's Ruhrgas gaining a 7 percent stake in Gazprom, Gazprom wanted a substantial share in Ruhrgas's gas and electricity distribution networks in Germany.

Gazprom's German subsidiary Germania announced in November 2007 that it had purchased mining rights north of Berlin that could enable it to construct the largest natural gas storage site in Europe.[24] Gazprom will have rights to rock layers at Hinrichshagen and Schweinrich to store gas delivered through Nord Stream, which is expected to begin functioning in 2010. Kremlin-connected oligarch Oleg Deripaska bought a 10 percent stake in Hochtief, Germany's largest construction company, while his holding company, Basic Element, bought 30 percent of

Strabag, Europe's largest tunnel and bridge builder. In the telecommunications sector, the Moscow firm Sistema tried to acquire a 25 percent stake in Deutsche Telekom (DT), Germany's dominant telco.[25] The German authorities, who own almost 32 percent of DT, prohibited the deal as a stake of that magnitude would give Sistema veto powers over major DT decisions.

Norwegian shipbuilder Aker Yards announced in March 2008 that it sold 70 percent of two German and one Ukrainian shipyard to the Russian investment group FLC West.[26] The Baltic yards are located at Wismar and in the Rostock suburb of Warnemuende, while the Black Sea facility is at Mykolayiv. The yards will build specialized ships for Russian oil and gas drilling and transport companies. FLC West is based in Luxembourg, with the Russian state holding a 50 percent share; the remaining 50 percent is held by a Cyprus-based group of private shareholders.

UNITED KINGDOM

Russia's regime, working through Gazprom, forced British Petroleum and Shell to sell their controlling stakes in the Sakhalin II and Kovytka gas fields for less than market value. It retained both companies as minority partners, however, with the prospect of further contracts to promote a Russian lobby in the UK. This was a valuable example of how Moscow failed to respect business contracts in pursuit of its political interests, was not held accountable for its actions, and used strategic firms to assist in advancing its foreign policy.

Britain is the second-largest source of FDI in Russia, and bilateral trade reached $16.3 billion in 2006. As a result, British business ties with Russia are expanding and enable greater scope for political lobbying. Gazprom executives announced in November 2004 their goal of gaining at least 10 percent of the UK natural gas market by 2010.[27] The British government is aware of the dangers posed by Russian companies and discouraged Gazprom from bidding for the country's major power company, Centrica, after the deputy director of Gazexport announced Gazprom's interest in acquiring the corporation. In April 2006 Gazprom executives threatened to divert gas supplies away from the UK when UK trade secretary Alan Johnson insisted that London would block Gazprom from acquiring Centrica. Gazprom also submitted bids for several British electricity-generating facilities.

FRANCE

By 2007 trade between Russia and France reached more than $13 billion. French companies account for about 4 percent of the Russian market and have been permitted to invest in several projects, including transportation, aircraft manufacturing, electricity, and construction. In turn, Russian companies have steadily increased their investments in the French economy. Atomenergomash formed a partnership with Alstom, a global leader in equipment and services for power generation and rail transport. Joint projects have been initiated between Russia's Inter RAO UES, the import-export operator of the electricity monopoly UES, and Électricité de France, the main electricity generation and distribution company in France.[28]

In mid-September 2008, only a few weeks after EU criticism of Russia's invasion of Georgia, the French-Russian intergovernment commission met in the Black Sea resort of Sochi, near the Georgian border, to discuss joint projects in the energy, high tech, and space sectors. Prime Minister Putin and French prime minister François Fillon attended the meeting. Putin underscored that the Georgian crisis did not affect bilateral relations as not a single joint project was suspended between the two countries.[29]

Moscow has stealthily tried to penetrate the European arms market. In September 2006 the EU expressed serious concern over the purchase by Russia's Vneshtorgbank of 5 percent of shares of the European Aeronautic Defence and Space Company (EADS), the multinational airplane manufacturer and defense contractor that owns the civilian plane manufacturer Airbus.[30] Even Paris and Berlin decried such a move as an aggressive act, thus precipitating Putin's denial that this was a hostile move to gain influence over EADS's policy.

In the car manufacturing industry, in December 2007 the Russian automobile manufacturer, AvtoVAZ (Volzhsky Automobilny Zavod), which has one of the largest facilities in the world, announced plans for a partnership with the French manufacturer Renault. The partnership would allow AvtoVAZ and Renault to accelerate the development of AvtoVAZ, renew and expand its vehicle range, and share technological expertise. In February 2008 Renault signed an agreement to pay $1 billion for a 25 percent stake in AvtoVAZ. Russian Technologies and Renault will become equal shareholders of AvtoVAZ, and their combined production would make them the world's number three automaker behind Toyota and General Motors.

In July 2007 the French oil company Total, one of the world's six oil majors, signed a framework agreement with Gazprom giving Total a 25 percent stake in an operating company to finance exploration and infrastructure in extracting and transporting gas from Russia's Shtokman reserves. In November 2007 Gazprom announced plans to establish a joint operating company with Total and Norway's StatoilHydro to develop the first phase of the Shtokman project. The company, in which Total and StatoilHydro will hold 25 and 24 percent, respectively, is projected to pump 23–24 billion cubic meters of gas annually by 2013. In February 2008 Gazprom, Total, and StatoilHydro signed an agreement establishing the Shtokman Development Company. Gazprom holds a 51 percent stake of the Switzerland-based company while Total holds 25 percent and StatoilHydro 24 percent.

ITALY

Under Prime Minister Silvio Berlusconi strong economic links were developed between Italy and Russia with Rome becoming Russia's second-largest trading partner, just behind Germany but ahead of the United States. In June 2007 Italy's multinational energy company ENI, the largest enterprise in the country, signed an agreement with Gazprom to construct the South Stream pipeline under the Black Sea.[31] The two companies were to own the venture equally. In May 2005 ENI signed a contract that would have permitted Gazpromexport to participate in selling Russian gas to Italian consumers. The agreement came under investigation by an Italian parliamentary commission and was subsequently blocked.[32] Investigators believed that various opaque deals with Italian officials and the sale of a portion of former Yukos assets to ENI enabled the Kremlin to recruit the Italian major as a leading supporter of Russia's energy interests.

In early December 2008 Lukoil and the Italian energy group ERG signed a final agreement on establishing a joint venture to operate the giant ISAB oil-refining complex in Sicily. Presidents Medvedev and Berlusconi witnessed the signing during Berlusconi's November 6 visit to Moscow. Lukoil will pay a mere €1.35 billion ($1.72 billion) for the 49 percent stake because it has guaranteed it will supply crude oil for refining.[33]

SPAIN AND PORTUGAL

In September 2006 Gazprom and Endesa SA, the largest utility company in Spain and involved in nuclear, hydroelectric, fossil fuel, and renewable energy resources, had agreed to explore opportunities in the gas and electricity sectors. In October 2006 Gazprom and Repsol YPF, an integrated Spanish oil and gas company with operations in twenty-nine countries, signed a draft agreement to jointly develop oil and gas projects. In October 2008 Gazprom announced that it was on track to acquire a 29 percent stake in Repsol, Spain's national champion oil and gas company. The purchase would turn Lukoil into the single largest shareholder in Repsol, a corporation supported by the Moscow-friendly Spanish Socialist government.[34]

In Portugal in February 2007 Galp Energia SGPS, the leading Portuguese energy corporation and responsible for the import, transportation, and distribution of natural gas, began negotiations with Gazprom for gas supplies and the acquisition of Gazprom shares in the company. In October 2007 Gazprom acquired a stake equivalent to 6.6 percent of Galp by buying shares in companies that control Amorim Energy, which holds about 33 percent of Galp's capital.

BENELUX

In addition to offering Belgium an incentive as a regional hub for natural gas distribution to the North Sea states, Gazprom signed a twenty-five-year deal with Fluxys, one of Belgium's largest gas distribution companies, to build an underground storage site at Poederlee. Gazprom also owns 10 percent of the interconnector pipeline between Belgium and Britain and is seeking a similar share of a Dutch-British link. The Russian authorities pressured Royal Dutch Shell into relinquishing control of the Sakhalin II project, blocked British BP plans to develop a gas field in eastern Siberia, and prevented foreign companies from developing the Shtokman field in the Barents Sea. All these measures were part of the Kremlin's strategy to maintain Russian monopolies over upstream and downstream gas operations. Lukoil also plans to acquire from ConocoPhillips its network of 156 gasoline service stations in Belgium. Further, Luxembourg has become a haven for Russian capital and offshore investments, and by 2008 it had emerged as the fourth-largest foreign investor in Russia.

AUSTRIA AND SWITZERLAND

Austria has been a traditional destination of Russian business and espionage. In recent years Vienna burgeoned as the center for several Gazprom-connected companies that "provided the Russian gas monopoly closer entrée to government circles."[35] Moscow has manipulated the incentive of turning Austria into an energy hub in Central Europe to gain a growing share in the local economy. Russian companies have participated in the construction of a large underground gas storage installation near Salzburg, and Gazprom acquired a major ownership share in the facilities. Vienna has also allowed Gazprom to acquire shares in several gas distribution networks and to construct a joint gas transit management center with OMV. In return, OMV has been promised shares in upstream assets in Russia. The Austrian police are investigating the role of Raiffeisen Zentral Bank (RZB) in massive money laundering from Russia through offshore accounts held by high-level managers in the Russian energy industry.[36]

In Switzerland, Russia's VSMPO-Avisma, the world's leading titanium company, bought Tirus International, a major Swiss titanium producer.[37] Russian oligarch Victor Vekselberg became the largest shareholder in the Swiss engineering company Sulzer. He also owns 14 percent of OC Oberlikon, a Swiss tech-nology group. In October 2006 Russian Aluminum (RusAl), the world's largest aluminum producer, and Siberian-Urals Aluminum Company (SUAL), Russia's second-largest aluminum producer, signed a cooperation agreement with Glencore International AG, the world's major commodity corporation. Glencore is a privately owned company headquartered in Baar, Switzerland, with fifty offices in over forty countries, and is one of the world's largest suppliers of raw materials to industrial consumers. Its customers include automotive, power generation, steel production, and food-processing companies.

SCANDINAVIA

In February 2008 Gazprom, Total, and Norway's StatoilHydro signed a share-holders agreement for the creation of Shtokman Development for phase one of the Shtokman field located in Russia's sector of the Barents Sea. The new field is projected to supply gas for Nord Stream. Gazprom will maintain a 51 percent share of the company, which was registered in Switzerland.[38] In June 2008 Norway's Tschudi Shipping extended an invitation to Russian mining company Norilsk Nickel to use its facilities in Kirkenes on the Barents Sea. The two firms expressed interest in cooperating on infrastructure and training projects.[39]

Finnish state-owned oil, chemicals, and gas group Neste formed a new gas company called GasumOy in the 1990s in which Gazprom gained a 25 percent stake. GasumOy is responsible for the supply and distribution of gas in Finland. The Russian company Rosenergoatom owns the Helsinki-based energy company United Power. United Power plans to build power cables connecting Vyborg in Russia and Lappeenranta in Finland, although Helsinki has opposed the project because of the proposed route of the cables.[40]

In the forestry and paper industry, the main assets of Investlesprom, the second largest European paper sack producer, are located in Sweden, with subsidiaries in Italy, Holland, and other European countries. Russia's Tractor Plants conglomerate also owns a forestry machinery factory in Denmark.

GREECE AND CYPRUS

Greece has become increasingly important for Russia in the energy sphere and is participating in the construction of the first Russian-controlled oil pipeline in the EU, the Burgas-Alexandroupolis line. Athens is also an important partner in the Gazprom-controlled South Stream gas pipeline. The Russian firm Sitronics, part of the Sistema group, has major holdings in Greece, Ukraine, and the Czech Republic.

Cyprus remains the most important shelter for Russian capital within the EU. By 2004 Russian investment on the island had reportedly reached $6 billion with more than three thousand Russian companies registered.[41] In 2006 the country was formally the biggest investor in Russia, supplying almost one-fifth of all foreign FDI, which reached $9.8 billion. The main reason for this volume is that Russian companies have used Cyprus for offshore investments and tax shelters.

Central Europe: Boosting Dependence

LATVIA

The Baltic states have been a prime destination of Russian capital during the past decade. This is especially true in Latvia and Lithuania, where by 2004 Russia's share in FDI reached 7.3 and 8.4 percent respectively. Gazprom maintains stakes in all three national gas monopolies in the Baltic republics (Latvijas Gaze, Lietuvos Dujos, and Eesti Gaas). It holds 37 percent of Eesti Gaas, and a further 10 percent is owned by Russia's Itera company. Lukoil maintains a substantial presence through its subsidiary Lukoil Baltija Group, managed by Lithuanian Lukoil Baltija and consisting of seven companies. Lukoil Baltija operates in the wholesale and retail market in Latvia and by 2006 was the third-largest fuel trader with a 9 percent market share.[42]

Russia's Gazprom and Itera Latvija are the main players in the Latvian gas industry. They are co-owners in Latvijas Gaze, with stakes of 34 and 16 percent respectively. This is the only Latvian enterprise engaged in gas transportation, storage, distribution, and sales. About 80 percent of Latvia's gas imports are from Gazprom and the rest are from Itera Latvija. In April 2008 Gazprom announced that it would seek at least a 25 percent plus one stake in a proposed gas-fired power plant in Latvia. The project would involve the construction of two new power plants, one gas-fired and one coal-fired, as the country sought to increase its overall power-generating capacity. Gazprom directors asserted that they would be interested in the project only if the company received at least a blocking share in the plant, which would run on Russian supplies provided by Gazprom.[43]

Lukoil Baltija owns two oil depots (in Tukums and Olaine) and thirty-four fuel filling stations, of which twenty-five stations are equipped with modules for selling liquefied petroleum gas (LPG).[44] The next step for Lukoil is to purchase ninety filling stations from Estonian Alexela, which owns a gas station chain in the Baltics. The goal is to increase the number of gas stations owned in the Baltic region to match the leading Scandinavian companies Statoil and Neste.

LatRosTrans manages the Polotsk-Ventspils and Polotsk-Mazeikiai crude oil and oil product pipelines that cross the country from Belarus to western Latvia and Lithuania. It is owned by Latvia's oil transit concern Ventspils Nafta and Russia's oil product pipeline operator Transnefteprodukt, with the latter holding 34 percent of shares.

In pressuring Latvia to sell major energy assets, in January 2003 Russia's oil pipeline monopoly Transneft removed Latvia's Ventspils Nafta oil terminal from the Russian oil export schedule. Oil shipments through the LatRosTrans pipeline operated by Ventspils Nafta were halted after Transneft decided to transport petroleum products mainly by rail, resulting in substantial losses for Ventspils Nafta. In May 2003 Sergei Grigoryiev, vice president of Transneft, claimed that the pipeline operator was willing to resume oil shipments to Ventspils Nafta in exchange for a stake in the oil terminal—in an oil for equity deal.

After Riga refused to sell the terminal, in July 2005 Transneft declared that it had no interest in acquiring a stake in Ventspils Nafta as it was developing alternative routes to the Baltic Sea. The Latvian government, with a 38.6 percent stake in Ventspils, decided to divest its stake in an effort to restart oil supplies to the terminal. Transneft redirected crude oil supplies to the port of Primorsk, Russia's first oil outlet on the Baltic, following the commissioning of the Baltic Pipeline System (BPS).

In July 2006 Russia's Transmashholding bought Latvia's Riga Electric Machine Building Works. The company produces components for electric loco-motives. Russia is also heavily involved in Latvia's banking sector, where Mos-cow's Municipal Bank and the Bank of Moscow hold almost 100 percent of the Latvian Business Bank (LBB). Both banks are closely tied to Moscow's municipal government. LBB was reported to be one of the most dynamically developing banks in the country, specializing in servicing trade with Russia, Belarus, and Ukraine.

ESTONIA

Lukoil Eesti, Lukoil's subsidiary, owns 39 filling stations in Estonia, 31 in Latvia, and 116 in Lithuania, providing it with a sizeable market share in the retail sector. The chairman of the supervisory council and purported owner of the chemical corporation Nitrofert, based in northeastern Estonia, is Dmitry Firtash, who owns 45 percent of the Russian-Ukrainian gas transit company RosUkrEnergo. Nitrofert processes Russian natural gas into ammonia and prilled urea and is one of the major employers in northeastern Estonia. Analysts believe that Nitrofert may be a cover for suspects wanted by the FBI, including alleged criminal boss Semyon Mogilevich and his subordinate Igor Fisherman, who is the financial head of Mogilevich's business empire. Fisherman has managed Highrock Holdings, and Firtash is president of Highrock Holdings' subsidiary Highrock Properties, headquartered in Cyprus.

In the chemical sector, in October 2006 the Russian company Akron purchased 50.01 percent of the shares of the Estonian enterprise Baltic Chemical Terminal and planned to build other terminals in the country. In the construction sector, in November 2006 LSR Group, one of the largest construction companies in Russia's Northwest Federal District and composed of thirty subsidiaries, acquired Aeroc AS (Estonia) and Aeroc Poribet SIA (Latvia). Their total annual production capacity makes LSR Group the largest concrete manufacturer in Russia and northern Europe.

Russian companies active in Estonia also possess majority shares in a rail-way rolling stock assembly plant in Ahtme and several transportation projects through Severstaltrans. This included Spacecom, which runs a fleet of locomo-tives and tanker cars for shipment of oil and gas and is a major competitor for the largest rail freight carrier, Estonian Railways. Severstaltrans also bought 70 percent of Estonian Oil Service (EOS) and became the leading player in Estonia's oil and transit-trade market. In August 2006 Severstaltrans merged its Estonian subsidiaries EOS, Turmoil, and Trendgate, creating the largest oil transit company in the country.

The steady penetration of Russian capital and the opaque profile of many Russian investors and managers led the local government of Viimsi municipality, adjoining Tallinn, in May 2006 to request that the security police investigate whether the accumulation of Russian capital in the Muuga port area could pose a threat to Estonia's security.[45]

LITHUANIA

Russia's share in the Lithuanian economy is believed to be significantly higher than the official 8.4 percent, as its investors often act through third parties. Russian firms have acquired several Lithuanian oil and gas companies, chemical and power plants, and banks and are heavily involved in purchasing real estate in Vilnius and other cities and resort areas. The Yukos company, which was appropriated and divided by the Russian state, owned a majority stake in Mazeiku Nafta, including the only oil refinery in the Baltic states, the Birzai pipeline system, and the Butinge terminal on the Baltic coast. Yukos became the fourth-biggest investor in the country. Russia's state-owned Rosneft appropriated most of Yukos's assets in Lithuania in 2005.

Gazprom obtained a third of the shares of the gas import, transmission, and distribution monopoly Lietuvos Dujos in December 2003, and by 2005 its stake had grown to 37.1 percent. Gazprom also holds a 30 percent stake in Stella-Vitae, a major gas importer, which was replaced by Dujotekana in 2001. Gazprom, in a consortium with a Lithuanian power engineering company and a U.S. company, purchased a heat and power plant in 2003 that supplies Kaunas, Lithuania's second-largest city, with heating and hot water. AB Lifosa, the largest phosphate fertilizer plant in the Baltic region, became part of EvroKhim, which was owned by Moscow's mineral and chemical corporation, the MDM Group. In the metals sector, the Russian company Mechel acquired a 75 percent stake in the metallurgical plant UAB Mechel Nemunas and bought the remaining shares shortly after.

In the banking sector, Lithuania's Snoras Bank was acquired in 2003 by Conversbank Financial Group, which included Conversbank-Moscow. Snoras was the third-largest bank in the country in capital size and turnover and fourth in the volume of assets. Conversbank wanted to use Snoras as a bridgehead to expand European business deals, with plans to buy banks in Latvia, Austria, and Cyprus. In 2005 Snoras bought an 83 percent stake in Latvia's oldest commercial bank, Latvijas Krajbanka.

POLAND

Most of Russia's FDI in Poland is connected with Gazprom, which by 2004 was the seventh-largest investor in the country. It has since dropped in importance and divested some of its assets, as the climate in Poland was not conducive to Russian investment. In 2006 Gazprom failed to gain a significant stake in PGNIG, Poland's gas distribution monopoly. Nevertheless, Gazprom maintained a 48 percent stake in EuRoPol Gaz, a 16 percent share in Gaz Trading, and a 32 percent stake in the telecom network operator Polgaz Telekom. EuRoPol Gaz owns the Polish section of the Yamal-Europe gas pipeline. In January 2002 Russia's Vneshtorgbank signed agreements with Poland's Bank Gospodarki Zywnosciowej and Kredyt Bank, with a view to joint participation in the financing of Polish-Russian business projects.[46]

In October 2007 Poland's Intelligence Services coordinator Zbigniew Wassermann announced, "Russia is taking steps to rebuild its imperial position using energy resources to achieve this goal."[47] The Polish government is applying preventive measures, including protecting Polish refineries from possible hostile Russian takeovers. One such case involved Lukoil's attempted purchase of the Gdansk refinery in which a Russian agent was alleged to have used his connections with former officials, including ex-premier Józef Oleksy, who had purportedly been recruited by the KGB in 1982. Polish prime minister Leszek Miller successfully blocked the Lukoil bid.[48]

HUNGARY

Russian FDI in Hungary has steadily increased, with Gazprom as the largest investor. Together with Hungary's oil and gas company MOL, Gazprom, through its subsidiary Gazexport, established Panrusgaz Hungarian-Russian Gas in 1994. Panrusgaz, selling natural gas purchased through Gazprom, became Hungary's eighth-largest company by 2003. In 2005 Gazprom subsidiary Gazprombank also acquired the General Banking and Trust Company (AEB), and the Russian Megdet Rakhimkulov became AEB's chairman. Rakhimkulov was reputed to be the richest person in Hungary and had interests in media broadcasting and chemicals, often operated through offshore companies. AEB maintained an 18 percent stake in DKG-East, a major supplier of equipment to Hungary's oil and gas industry.

Through various subsidiaries and middlemen, Gazprom expanded its stake in Hungary's chemical industry, including two of the largest companies, Borsod-Chem and Tiszai Vegyi Kombinát (TVK). In November 2005 Rakhimkulov gained representation on the board of directors of BorsodChem, through Firthlion, Rakhimkulov's family enterprise, which owns 10 percent of the chemical giant. Representing Firthlion on the BorsodChem board was his son Timur, managing director of another Rakhimkulov family enterprise, Kafijat Kft, the 100 percent owner of Firthlion that held a 10 percent stake in OTP Bank, the biggest commercial bank of Hungary with branches in several CEE countries. In 2003 Lukoil established Lukoil Downstream Magyarorszag Kereskedelmi (DMK) and acquired several dozen filling stations in the country. Lukoil also controls the chemical trading company Stavrochem.

Gazprom pursues major stakes in MOL's various subsidiaries, including gas transmission and storage. In October 2007, in response to Gazprom and Austria's OMV working in tandem, Hungary's parliament passed a law aimed at protecting national interest in the energy and water-related sectors. The law was dubbed "Lex Mol," as it was essentially drafted to prevent MOL from falling into OMV's and Gazprom's hands.[49] By September 2007 OMV declared it owned 20.2 percent of MOL and would seek approval of its $19.75 billion takeover bid directly from shareholders. OMV and Gazprom agreed to long-term Russian gas supplies to Austria in return for the joint development of a European gas distribution center such as the one owned by MOL. Budapest is particularly concerned that the Kremlin is working through Gazprom and the Russian oligarch Oleg Deripaska to pressure MOL into selling the company.

In addition to Gazprom, several Russian banks have offices in Budapest, including Rossiyskiy Kredit Bank, Baltiyskiy Bank, and Vnesheconombank. Rakhimkulov, the billionaire former Gazprom executive, also became the CEO and owner of the Hungarian bank AEB and acquired a 5.29 percent stake in OTP Bank.

CZECH REPUBLIC

Since 2004 FDI flows from Russia into the Czech Republic have largely increased. At the close of 2003, hotels and restaurants accounted for 35 percent of Russian investments, transport equipment for 17.9 percent, and health services for 19.9 percent. Significant capital has also been invested in the hotel industry in the Czech spa resort of Karlovy Vary. Investments soared in 2004 as a result of the sale of three Skoda Holding subsidiaries, including plants producing equipment for nuclear power facilities, to OMZ. OMZ is the largest heavy engineering company in Russia and has established a strong international presence. The company controls a 25 percent share of the world market for equipment for atomic power stations. OMZ has affiliates and subsidiaries in several CIS and WE countries. The Czech acquisition provided the company with improved access to Central European markets.

During 2005 Gazprom's German subsidiary ZMB purchased a 37.5 percent stake in Czech gas wholesaler Gas-Invest. In April 2008 Vemex, a Czech subsidiary of Gazprom, initiated talks to buy almost the entire annual domestic gas production of Czech natural gas producer MND.[50] Russia's Tatneft has sought to purchase Czech Unipetrol and several other petrochemical companies. In the metals sector, in August 2006 Russia's Evraz Groups, one of the largest mining businesses in Russia and a major producer of steel products, whose assets include three of the leading steel plants in Russia, completed the acquisition of Vitkovice Steel, the biggest platemaker in the Czech Republic. In addition, Ilim Pulp Enterprises, the largest pulp and paper producer in Russia, and Europe's fourth largest, owns the Czech company Plzenska Papirna.

SLOVAKIA

Until the early 2000s, the largest Russian investment in Slovakia, by Yukos's Trans-petrol, was made through a Dutch-based subsidiary that acquired a 49 percent stake of the Slovak state-owned pipeline company. Gazprom currently owns 50 percent of Slovrusgas, which is involved in gas transportation and marketing.[51] In July 2002 the European Commission approved the purchase of a 49 percent stake in Slovakia's SPP pipeline system by Gazprom, Ruhrgas, and Gaz de France. The deal was worth $2.7 billion and was financed by Ruhrgas and Gaz de France. The SPP pipeline network transmits about 70 percent of all gas supplied from Russia via Ukraine to Europe.

Russia's Rosenergoatom, a nuclear generator company, intends to acquire a controlling stake in Slovakia's state power utility Slovenske Elektrarne, including its nuclear assets. At the founding meeting of the Russian-Slovak Business Council in Moscow in August 2007, Georgi Petrov, vice president of Russia's Chamber of Commerce and Industry, announced that Russian companies were interested in renovating or building nuclear power facilities in Slovakia.[52]

In July 2008 the European Commission granted conditional approval for two new reactors at the Mochovce nuclear power plant, designed to offset the loss of power production in Slovakia after the shutdown of two units at the Jaslovske Bohunice plant. The Mochovce and Bohunice plants, both Russian designed, will be supplied with nuclear fuel by Russian TVEL. The Russian company won the tender over U.S.-based Westinghouse.

SLOVENIA

Slovenia is a relatively small market for Russian FDI. Nevertheless, Russia remains active in the energy sector, and Gazprom has obtained a 7.6 percent share in Slovenia's gas trading company Tagdem. Also, Russia's Koks Group owns a steel plant in Slovenia.

Southeast Europe: Valued Enticements

BULGARIA

Russia has deeply penetrated the Bulgarian economy and maintains close relations with Socialist government officials. Russian business seeks greater access to the energy sector, including the electric and nuclear industries, and aims to use Bulgaria as a major transit country for gas supplies. Gazprom is present in Bulgaria through Topenergo and Overgas. Topenergo, a gas trading and transportation enterprise, is a wholly owned subsidiary of Gazprom, and Gazprom owns a 50 percent stake of Overgas, the largest private gas retailer and transporter in Bulgaria.[53] In July 2007 Bulgaria's power regulator added seven new southern Black Sea municipalities to the license of local gas distributor Overgas, and its subsidiary Burgasgaz will build the gas distribution network. In 2005 Russia's Unified Energy System bought the Varna and Ruse thermal power plants, although both purchases were delayed by antitrust investigations.

By May 2005 Lukoil held 93.82 percent of the shares of Neftochim Burgas, the largest refinery in the Balkans. Neftochim Burgas accounts for 9 percent of Bulgaria's GDP, and its sizeable petrochemical complex produces fuels, polymers, and petrochemicals. Lukoil Bulgaria, the company's commercial outlet, specializes in the export and trade of its products. In March 2008 Lukoil signed a major deal with a Greek construction group to build two desulphurization units at the plant.[54] In March 2006 Lukoil Bulgaria inaugurated the first of seven regional wholesale depots near Sofia to facilitate the supply of fuel, oils, and natural gas. By early 2007 Lukoil controlled more than 10 percent of Bulgaria's oil retail market. Russian investments will also increase with the planned construction of the Burgas-Alexandropoulis oil pipeline and the South Stream gas pipeline.

Lukoil has announced plans to spend $300 million through 2011 to expand its retail presence in Bulgaria by purchasing a greater volume of petrol stations. In April 2008 the company declared that it was acquiring a number of petrol stations and oil and gas storage facilities from local fuel retailer Petrol. By operating a network of 180 petrol stations, Lukoil possessed a 17 percent market share in Bulgaria. Petrol operated over 440 petrol stations and held 25 percent of the retail fuel market. Observers predicted that Lukoil might purchase seventy retail units from Petrol as well as the company's Iliantza oil storage facility.[55]

In 2005 a decision was made to resume construction of the Belene Nuclear Power Plant, and in May 2007 a contract was signed with Russia's Atomstroiexport to build two power-producing units at Belene, with a capacity of a thousand megawatts each.[56] Atomstroiexport, established in 1998, is one of the largest companies in the world involved in building nuclear plants and the leading Russian company involved in constructing nuclear facilities abroad.[57] The deal was signed in January 2008 during Putin's visit to Sofia for an agreed sum of €4 billion. The German company Siemens and the French Areva are subcontractors for the project. The power plant will host two thousand-megawatt nuclear reactors to be commissioned in late 2013 and in 2014 respectively.

A statement released by the Bulgarian government in February 2008 revealed plans to merge eight power companies into one of the largest energy entities in the region. Bulgarian Energy Holding will include the gas company Bulgargaz, National Electric Company, Kozloduy NPP, Maritza East II TPP, and Mini Maritza Iztok.[58] The consolidation was completed in September 2008, with assets totaling $8.5 billion and an estimated annual profit of $2.63 billion. The Economy and Energy Ministry will hold up to 75 percent of shares in each of the five energy companies while minority shares will be transferred to the newly established company.

The successor of Multigroup (MG), a company founded by the Russian tycoon Iliya Pavlov (murdered in March 2003) in 1988, is still active in Bulgaria with suspected criminal connections. In 2000 it was renamed MG Corporation. The MG holding company comprises eight large enterprises in the energy sector, sugar factories, the crystal sea-salt production enterprise Chernomosrki Solnici, and three wineries. The crown jewel of the company is its tourist business, which includes St. Ilia's resort on the Black Sea, Grand Hotel Varna, and Grand Hotel Bulgaria in Sofia. At the end of 2002, the Polish magazine *Wprost* estimated Pavlov's personal wealth at $1.5 billion, ranking him the eighth-richest businessman in CEE.

ROMANIA

Russian companies, often through subsidiaries, are focused on Romania's oil, gas, steel, and aluminum sectors. Gazprom, through its German-based subsidiary ZGG, holds a 26 percent stake in Wirom Gas, which imports and distributes gas in Romania. Gazprom wants to purchase Romania's two main gas distributors, Distrigaz Nord and Distrigaz Sud, as well as Rompetrol, which possesses two oil refineries and a large network of filling stations and terminals.

In February 2008 Russia's trade representative in Bucharest announced that Moscow was considering increasing the price of natural gas imports by 7 percent. Romania currently purchases gas from Russia through an agreement with the Russian-German company Wintershall that is due to expire in 2012. Moscow contends that Bulgaria paid lower prices than Romania for gas because it provided incentives to Russian companies, and it hinted that Gazprom would lower gas costs only if foreign competition with Russian firms was curtailed.[59]

By 2004 Lukoil had invested more than $500 million in Romania. In 1998 it purchased a 51 percent stake in the Petrotel refinery in Ploesti, which subsequently increased to over 94 percent. Petrotel became one of the three major refineries that Lukoil controlled outside Russia; the other two were Neftokhim Burgas in Bulgaria and the Lukoil-Odessa refinery in Ukraine. Lukoil-Petrotel ran almost three hundred filling stations in the country, controlled almost 20 percent of Romania's market for petroleum products, and planned to expand into oil processing. Talks are under way for Gazprom to acquire a majority stake in Romgaz, Romania's state-owned company. However, the privatization of Romgaz was postponed until late 2009, when domestic gas prices will be aligned with EU levels. Gazprom has also expressed interest in building a gas storehouse at Margineni in northeastern Romania.[60]

In the metals sector, RusAl, which accounts for 75 percent of Russia's aluminum output and 10 percent of global supplies, purchased Cemtrade, a Romanian alumina refinery. The company controls an extensive network of production outlets in neighboring countries, including two giant alumina refineries in Ukraine.[61] Romania's intelligence service viewed Russia's efforts to acquire the aluminum industry with growing concern. It reported in 2006 that oligarch Oleg Deripaska had attempted to take over the entire industry when three state-owned aluminum enterprises were slated for privatization.[62] Although Deripaska failed to win the tenders, the Russian-Israeli magnate Vitaliy Machitski, who has close ties to Gazprom, subsequently acquired two aluminum companies, Alum Tulcea and Alro Slatina. Machitski planned to gain a range of industries, including a power plant and a factory producing primary products.

Bucharest was also concerned that Machitski controlled a substantial percentage of Romania's gas imports from Russia. In April 2007 Gazprom signed gas supply contracts with three Romanian gas companies, Romgaz, Transgaz, and Conef, which provided Gazprom with long-term access to gas shipping facilities. Gazprom also agreed to increase gas deliveries to the Alro Slatina aluminum plant owned by Machitski's Marco Group at an undisclosed price. By June 2008 Machitski's seemed poised to take advantage of the Gazprom deal and produce aluminum below the costs of other European manufacturers.

In the fall of 2008 Russian companies intensified their acquisition of gold mining assets in CEE. For instance, in November 2008 Russia's largest gold mining corporation, Polyus Gold, made a bid to purchase Kazakhstan's Kazakh-Gold, which owns the rights to mine Romania's Baia Mare gold mine.[63] Polyus Gold is owned by oligarch Mikhail Prokhorov, who is reportedly tied to Kremlin officials. The company is under investigation in the EU for alleged asset stripping.

Russia's TMK Pipe Metallurgical Company, one of the world's three largest pipe producers, acquired a controlling stake in the ArtRom pipe plant in 2001 and in 2004 a 90 percent stake in the Combinatul Siderurgic Resita steelworks, the third-largest manufacturer of rolled steel in Romania. Mechel, which produces 40 percent of Russia's steel output, holds an 81 percent stake in Industria Sarmei, which manufactures steel products, and in COST SA, a Romanian manufacturer of specialty steel products. In 2002 Russia's OMZ acquired a 66 percent interest in SC UPET, which specializes in the production of metal valves and components for offshore rigs. Russian companies are also looking to invest in further Romanian privatizations, including Electrica Mutenia Sud, Romania's largest electricity distributor.

SERBIA

In June 2007 in Brussels, European Enlargement Commissioner Olli Rehn told Serbia's deputy prime minister, Božidar Đjelić, that "one has to be careful that even when hugging a friendly big bear, one wouldn't [want to] be suffocated."[64] According to unofficial figures, the combined amount of Russian investment in Serbia reached $400 million by 2005.[65] In May 2007 Belgrade invited Russian investment in the energy, metallurgical, and financial industries. During a meeting with Putin in St. Petersburg in June 2007, Serbian prime minister Vojislav Koštunica urged Russian businesses to invest in Serbia.[66] Deputy Prime Minister Đjelić promised that Russian investors would receive "special attention," specifically linking this to Russia's stance on Kosovo. Russia also sought to settle its Soviet-era debt to the former Yugoslavia by committing itself to modernizing a Serbian power plant and writing off part of Serbia's gas bill.

The most important deal in the energy sector, signed in January 2008, involved the sale of Serbia's state oil monopoly, NIS, to a Gazprom-led group and the planned construction by Gazprom of a gas pipeline through Serbia. The sale of NIS took place at a fraction of its market value. However, before the parliamentary elections in May 2008, ministers loyal to President Boris Tadić blocked moves by the caretaker cabinet to begin ratification procedures for the NIS deal.[67] A final decision was to be made after the formation of a new Serbian government. In November 2008 Economy Minister Mlađan Dinkić asserted that Serbia would not sell its energy monopoly unless it received firm guarantees from Moscow that it would build the South Stream pipeline through Serbia after Gazprom refused to sign a contract.

Among other Russian energy acquisitions in Serbia, Gazprom owns 50 percent of the gas company Progresgaz and 75 percent of the gas company YugoRosGas, and in 2007 the Moscow-based Harvinter bought the Belgrade-based Termoelektro. The largest investment was the purchase of Beopetrol by Lukoil in 1993 for €117 million. Further penetration by Lukoil could include the Novi Sad and Pancevo oil refineries and a large network of filling stations across Serbia. In February 2008 President-elect Medvedev, as chairman of the Gazprom board and accompanied by Foreign Minister Lavrov, witnessed the signing of an agreement with Serbia Gas to create a joint company for a feasibility study to construct Serbia's section of the South Stream gas pipeline.

In April 2008 the Serbian government cancelled an agreement to sell RTB

Bor, Serbia's largest copper mining and metallurgical company, to the Austrian consortium A-Tec Industries and agreed to restart talks with the Russian company SMR, owned by oligarch Oleg Deripaska.[68] A previous agreement to sell Bor, which owns the largest copper mine in the Balkans, to Romania's Cuprom for $400 million fell through in April 2007.

The Russian carrier Aeroflot negotiated to buy the Serbian national carrier JAT, while the owners of Moscow's Heremetyevo Airport expressed an interest in buying Belgrade airport. In the telecommunications sector, Moscow-based BK Trade held a 51 percent stake in the mobile telephone operator Mobtel. In the tourism sector, Russia's Metropol purchased significant shares in the Putnik tourism agency and Russian purchases have fueled a real-estate boom in central Belgrade.

Montenegro

Russia's regime views Montenegro as a useful target along the Adriatic, where it can profit from the country's eagerness for foreign investment. Russian companies have gained a major position in the Montenegrin economy. Kremlin-linked oligarch Oleg Deripaska and his En Plus group, working through Russia's aluminum giant RusAl, purchased the Kombinat Aluminijuma Podgorica aluminum factory, which produces a fifth of Montenegro's GDP and generates 80 percent of its exports. During 2007 Montenegro's parliament blocked the sale to Deripaska of the Thermal Power Plant in Pljevlja, which produces a third of Montenegro's electricity, as well as the Rudnik coal mine.[69] If En Plus gains these facilities, it will in effect control 25 percent of Montenegro's GDP and major parts of the economy. Russian investment in Montenegro reached €780 million in 2006, and the two countries signed a free trade agreement in September 2008 that may complicate Montenegro's aspirations to EU membership.[70] Actual Russian capital investment is believed to be significantly higher than the official figure as much of it is conducted by companies registered in other countries.

Montenegro reportedly receives more foreign investment per capita than any other country in Europe, and the bulk comes from Russia and a handful of European states.[71] Russians have bought up hotels, real estate, and extensive stretches of the Montenegrin coastline. Among the major purchasers is Moscow mayor Yuriy Luzhkov and the Mirax Group, a company owned by Russia's billionaire developer Sergei Polonsky. The European Commission repeatedly warned that Russian-linked money laundering is a critical problem that has to be tackled if Montenegro is to qualify for EU entry. In a report issued in 2007, the commission complained that there is "no proper monitoring of financial transactions," especially in real estate, and "considerable room for corruption in land-use planning, construction, and privatization."[72] Montenegrin authorities also planned to permit Russian companies to invest in infrastructure and hydroelectric power plants.

CROATIA

Rosneft, Lukoil, and Sibneft have expressed strong interest in acquiring stakes in Croatia's major oil company, Industrija Nafte (INA). INA operates two fuel refineries and two lube refineries together with a network of four hundred petrol stations across Croatia. Lukoil, aiming to create a network of 150 filling stations through acquisitions and building new stations, plans to expand its market share in Croatia from 3 to 20 percent by the end of 2011. It also has proposed building an oil import terminal and storage tanks on the Adriatic coast.[73] Additionally, in 2008 Zagreb planned to conduct a second stage of privatizing INA.

MACEDONIA

Russia has been exploring energy projects with Macedonia, but its political leverage remains limited. Bilateral trade in 2006 amounted to only $500 million, and Russia's direct investment reached only $15 million in 2006. Putin observed that Russian companies are prepared to invest more than $180 million in Macedonia.[74] Lukoil is to build several dozen filling stations and three oil storage bases. Itera and the Macedonian government also signed agreements on investment projects in energy infrastructure. The Russian company Itera and Macedonia's Toplifikacija established a joint venture in 2004 to construct a gas thermal power plant that would generate a fifth of the country's annual electricity output.

BOSNIA-HERZEGOVINA

In 2007 the Serb Republic's government in Bosnia-Herzegovina sold a package of majority stakes in Bosanski Brod oil refinery and the Modrica and Petrol fuel retailers to Russia's state-owned oil company Zarubezhneft for $1.4 billion through its subsidiary Neftegazinkor. Zarubezhneft now owns 80 percent of Brod, 75.65 percent of Modrica, and 80 percent of Petrol. Milorad Dodik, the Serb Republic's prime minister, expanded the entity's links with Russia by signing a series of economic and cultural agreements in St. Petersburg in September 2007.[75] The agenda for the high-level delegation in Russia, which included the finance and economy ministers, involved meetings with leaders of Russia's electricity companies. Other Bosnian energy assets slated for privatization include the fuel retailer Energopetrol. In February 2008 Dodik met with Medvedev and canvassed for including the Serb Republic in Gazprom's various projects in Serbia.

Eastern Europe: Consolidating Control

UKRAINE

In November 2007 the Swiss-registered RosUkrEnergo was created as an intermediary owned 50 percent by Gazprom. The accord established a joint venture between RosUkrEnergo and the Ukrainian gas firm Naftogaz that granted the former access to half of Ukraine's domestic market. Ukraine's intelligence services calculated that the owners of RosUkrEnergo were using their control over energy supplies to secure ownership of energy-intensive industries such as fertilizer and titanium plants. Analysts were also concerned about the possible involvement of organized crime groups in RosUkrEnergo, as well as corrupt links with Russian and Ukrainian officials. Ukrainian prime minister Yulia Tymoshenko called for the elimination of RosUkrEnergo as a middleman.[76] In February 2008 Ukraine's chief audit agency declared as illegal the agreements giving RosUkrEnergo exclusive rights to import natural gas in Ukraine and asked the Justice Ministry to annul them.[77]

In other contracts, Russian Aluminum owns 25 percent of the Nikolayev Alumina Refinery, while Lukoil acquired a controlling share in the Odessa oil refinery. Russia's Tractor Plants conglomerate owns agricultural machinery plants in Ukraine, Belarus, and Moldova.

BELARUS

Russian capital has heavily penetrated Belarus's banking sector. Belrosbank is almost wholly owned by Russia's Rosbank. Rosbank was founded in 1993 and is the parent company for a banking group that includes Rosbank (Switzerland), Belrosbank, BaikalRosbank, and Rosbank-Volga.[78] Moscow-Minsk Bank, the seventh-largest bank in Belarus and the fourth most profitable, was registered in April 2000 to promote trade with Russia. By 2007 it was fully owned by the Bank of Moscow. In November 2007 VTB, the large Russian state-owned bank, increased its share in Belarus's Slavneftbank to 64.9 percent.[79] In 2007 Russia's Vnesheconombank acquired a controlling stake of Belnevsheconombank, a joint stock commercial bank.[80] Shareholders of the bank included National Space Bank (Russia), National Bank of the Republic of Belarus, Belarusian Steel Works, and the Belarusian Ministry of Economy.

Russia's VTB Bank announced in March 2007 that it would invest in the authorized fund of VTB Bank (Belarus) and provide investment support to Belarus's petrochemical and energy industries, including the Mozyr and Naftan refineries.[81] The Russian Group PECO announced plans to set up a mortgage bank in Belarus in December 2007 and purchased a 100 percent stake of the Belarusian Insurance Company AIVeNa.[82]

Gazprom has endeavored to purchase a controlling stake in Belarus's energy infrastructure, and in April 2008 Gazprom and the Belarusian government signed a protocol on the purchase of a 50 percent stake in Beltransgaz by Gazprom, which already held a 25 percent share in the state company.[83] In December 2006 Gazprom and Beltransgaz signed an updated agreement on the supply and transit of gas in the period between 2007 and 2011.

Moldova

Energy debts among neighbors provide Russia with valuable economic and political leverage.[84] Facing demands to repay debts in a short period of time, the indebted government has few options and may offer Russian companies shares in energy enterprises or other domestic infrastructure. During 2002 Moscow pressured the Moldovan government to sell substantial shares in gas delivery companies and electricity-generating power stations in exchange for cheaper Russian electricity supplies.

Gazprom acquired a controlling stake in MoldovaGaz, which controls the country's entire gas infrastructure. In January 2006 Gazprom severed gas supplies to Moldova after Chisinau rejected demands to double the price. Supplies were restored after a few weeks with a price increase from $60 to $110 per thousand cubic meters. Moldova also agreed to give Gazprom, already the majority shareholder, Transnistria's 13 percent stake in MoldovaGaz. Gazprom took over majority shares in the major Transnistrian gas company, as the separatist region had incurred massive debts. Gazprom currently holds 63.4 percent of MoldovaGaz's shares and effectively controls Moldova's domestic gas infrastructure.

Gazprom increased the price of gas to $170 per thousand cubic meters in 2007 and plans to make further increases until 2011, when the price will reach the level paid by EU members. However, as the price is set yearly, Moscow could increase costs more rapidly for political reasons.[85] Russia's trade embargo on wine imports in April 2006 cajoled the Voronin government to grant various privileged investment concessions to Moscow, tying the country even more closely to the Russian market.[86]

Georgia

Lukoil-Georgia is the largest petroleum product seller in Georgia. In the telecommunications sector, by September 2007 Russia's mobile telephone operator VimpelCom had invested $30 million in the Georgian cellular operator Mobitel. In July 2006 VimpelCom acquired 51 percent of Mobitel and an option for the remaining 49 percent. Georgia became the fifth CIS country outside of Russia in which VimpelCom ran operations. In March 2008 VimpelCom announced plans to invest $800 million in the CIS countries other than Russia: $300 million in Kazakhstan, $180 million in Uzbekistan, $160 million in Ukraine, and $160 million in Tajikistan, Armenia, and Georgia.[87]

ARMENIA

In February 2008 Atomredmetzoloto, a uranium mining subsidiary of Russia's nuclear monopoly Rosatom, established a joint venture in Armenia to develop uranium reserves estimated at thirty to sixty thousand tons.[88] Russia has also pledged to build a new nuclear power plant in Armenia and to invest over $800 million between 2008 and 2010.[89]

Conclusions:
Revitalizing the West

Developments during the Putinist imperial restoration have demonstrated that the West has limited means to influence politics and policy inside Russia, particularly since Moscow became emboldened by its growing energy revenues. The Putin era indicates that Western aspirations to democratize Russia were unrealistic and misguided. Instead of transitioning to a free-market democracy, Russia has transitioned to a state-capitalist authoritarianism; and instead of emerging as a benign and cooperative regional power, Russia has reasserted its neo-imperial ambitions. Both developments have important implications for the policies of various regional and global players, particularly the major Western countries and multinational organizations, including the United States, NATO, and the European Union.

Although Putin was replaced as Russia's president by Dmitry Medvedev and assumed the position of prime minister in May 2008, the Putinist strategy has persisted and expanded as Russia seeks a more prominent global role. The impact of the global financial crisis and economic recession could turn Russia into an even more aggressive actor, especially in its immediate neighborhood. This will present Western institutions with continuing challenges in promoting their interests and deflating any negative pressures emanating from Moscow. In framing some helpful recommendations for a more effective EU, NATO, and U.S. strategy toward Russia, it is worthwhile to briefly evaluate the shortcomings of current Western policy approaches.

Western Strategic Imperatives

In sum, there is no common EU or NATO strategy toward Russia, and wide divergences are visible across the Continent and within the alliance. A loose coalition of larger Western European countries, including France, Germany, and Italy, are apprehensive about provoking disruptive disputes with Moscow and are willing to overlook negative trends in Russia's domestic and foreign policies and even to sacrifice some basic European values and interests. The more assertive policies of several Central-Eastern European capitals are resisted in Paris, Berlin, and Rome, where commercial pragmatism generally prevails over geostrategic calculation. Such an approach toward Russia has at least four negative consequences:

• It allows Moscow to continue fracturing the European Union and NATO by bilateralizing or nationalizing its relations with individual states and increasing its leverage by offering diplomatic and economic incentives to some capitals and exerting pressure on others.
• It generates disputes between individual Western states in their approaches toward Russia and undermines the development and implementation of a common EU and NATO foreign and security policy on a broader range of issues.
• The overly accommodationist policies of countries such as Germany, France, and Italy can restrict any further EU or NATO enlargement eastward for fear of antagonizing Russia. Such an approach can unsettle the reformist prospects of aspirant states in Eastern Europe and the Black Sea region.
• EU division, inconsistency, and acquiescence toward Moscow can harm relations with the United States and disable the pursuit of a common Western strategy toward Russia and toward the wider transatlantic and pan-European zones.

Two general approaches to EU-Russia relations emerged at the onset of the Medvedev presidency with significant implications for policymaking: the grand bargain and national bilateralization.[1] The *grand bargain* position envisages the EU and Moscow seeking a comprehensive agreement to stabilize their relations that could culminate in the emergence of a vaguely formulated strategic partnership. The objective would be to centralize EU policy toward Russia but base such cohesion on lowest-common-denominator agreements through which sufficient consensus could be reached. The French and German governments in particular have pursued such a policy, while Washington has been opposed and seeks a broader strategic framework with Russia before any Europe-Russia grand bargain can be negotiated.

Several CEE capitals are adamantly opposed to any strategic bargaining or an institutional partnership that implicitly legitimizes antidemocratic tendencies in Russian politics and tolerates Moscow's neo-imperialist policies toward its neighbors. They assert that such a strategy would dilute both the EU and NATO and weaken their security capabilities. They also calculate that Russia's negative influences in the region must be curtailed by pursuing a realistic prospect of international institutional integration for all European states aspiring to join Western political and security structures.

These differing European policies could precipitate new transatlantic tensions. Indeed, some Western European capitals are reviving the notion of a European "balance of power" between the EU and Russia. This would suit Moscow's interests by assigning much of the "post-Soviet space" to predominant Russian influence while curtailing Western influence in the eastern part of the Continent and steadily reducing the U.S. role throughout Europe.

The *national approach* to EU-Russia relations focuses on developing strong bilateral ties between Moscow and selected EU capitals alongside a weak and restricted common EU policy. Indeed, Putinist Russia has focused on "bilateralizing" the EU-Russia relationship to extract economic and diplomatic benefits and on minimizing the emergence of a more concerted and assertive EU approach or a broader long-term Western strategy.

Both policy options, institutional bargains or national bilateralism, will preclude the emergence of a coherent Western strategy that can simultaneously expand the democratic European space, pursue cooperative relations with Russia when it serves EU and NATO interests, develop competitive and law-bound economic interchanges with the Russian economy, and help forge a more unified and effective EU and NATO foreign and security policy.

The new alliance and Union members monitor and highlight Moscow's ambitions in countries that are most prone to destabilizing Russian influences. They continue to urge both the EU and NATO to respond in unison to a concerted Kremlin-directed strategy aimed at redividing Europe and forestalling further NATO and EU expansion. Several CEE governments struggle to prevent the emergence of new divisions with their Eastern European neighborhood, claiming that this will damage interstate relations, undermine economic development, obstruct structural reform, encourage Russian revanchism, and unsettle a wider region.

CEE capitals also remain wary of EU compromises with the Kremlin that could weaken the U.S. role in European affairs and endanger their own security interests. In the absence of a unified Europe with a realistic and effective strategy toward Putinist Russia, the United States remains the most credible protector against growing Muscovite aspirations toward any part of Europe, regardless of U.S.-Russian collaboration in arenas of mutual interest in counterterrorism and against nuclear proliferation.

The Obama administration will need to restore America's prestige and rebuild the country's most important alliances if it is to play a more effective role in countering various security threats. Revitalizing the transatlantic relationship will also necessitate a thorough review of American and European policies toward Russia and all the states that are vulnerable to pressures from Moscow. While Russia has reemerged as an authoritarian and neo-imperialist power under the Putinist doctrine, Western policies have lacked a clear objective and an effective strategy to curtail Russia's expansionism and deter, diminish, or defeat its escalating national security threats to neighboring countries.

Since Russia's military campaign and attempted partition of Georgia in August 2008, two broad strategic approaches regarding relations between the West and Russia have been germinating among policymakers and analysts on both sides of the Atlantic: the passive and the active.

The *passive* spheres of influence position that may envisage a grand bargain with Russia endeavors to accommodate Moscow's ambitions to delineate Western and Russian zones of predominant influence within Europe. As underscored by the new Russian president, Moscow is intent on dominating its former Soviet supplicants in a broad region from the Baltic to the Caspian seas. Although acceptance of such a geopolitical division across the continent may not be explicit in any European capital, it could become increasingly evident through the forestalling of any further enlargement of NATO and the EU and the acceptance of Russian claims that its national interests are more important than those of its neighbors.

Such neo-appeasement couched as a realpolitik balance of power by some Western capitals will have far-reaching implications for the security orientations and foreign policies of states that are included in one or the other sphere. It would signal a Yalta-like acceptance of Russia's aggrandizement by assigning the post-Soviet states to Moscow's indefinite suzerainty.

In marked contrast, the *active* wider Europe position dismisses Russia's zero-sum geopolitical calculations with respect to Europe's security and focuses on the sovereign decisions of all European states to accede to multinational institutions, including NATO and the EU. Such moves do not objectively threaten the security of any nearby power but help to stabilize member states. Although the "wider Europeanists" and Atlanticists do not seek to provoke outright confrontation with Moscow, they are more willing to challenge Russia's great power ambitions and empire-building objectives throughout Europe. Indeed, the activist strategic position recognizes that Moscow will not feel restricted by any "privileged sphere of influence" but will seek to undermine and suborn other European regions.

Georgia, Ukraine, Moldova, Belarus, Armenia, and Azerbaijan are positioned in the middle of this conflictive debate, which will have major ramifications for their international relations and security priorities. In addition, Central-Eastern Europe's current frontline states, such as Poland, Romania, and the three Baltic countries, have felt especially vulnerable to Moscow's growing assertiveness and are concerned over a potential spillover of instability from neighboring states where Russia has claimed that its own national interests must prevail.

To devise effective forms of protection against Russia's advances, discussions in several CEE capitals are likely to intensify on how to forge closer regional collaboration while eliciting more direct U.S. security guarantees. This has become especially urgent as questions have been raised over the practical validity of NATO's article five security guarantee, given the accommodationist approach toward Russia exhibited by several older alliance members such as Germany and France and growing questions over their commitment to joint allied defense.

In early October 2008 NATO's highest military commander, General James Craddock, requested the authority to draw up full defense plans for Estonia, Latvia, and Lithuania in the event of attack.[2] Other NATO newcomers may also request full defense plans from the alliance. Although the United States and Britain reportedly supported the measures, Germany and France evidently opposed Craddock's request. The primary concern of several older NATO members, whose own security was assured by the United States throughout the Cold War, was to pacify Russia rather than provide credible security to new alliance members.

Deliberations have also intensified in CEE over the potential hosting of U.S. and NATO military infrastructure on their territories, following the Polish and Czech acceptance of components of the U.S. missile defense system. This could include a NATO antimissile shield to complement the U.S. system, the stationing of a NATO rapid reaction force in the Baltic region, as well as army, air force, and naval bases to counteract and deter Russia's threatening posture in the Baltic and Black Sea zones.

For instance, Romania seeks military equilibrium between NATO and Russia in the Black Sea, which is currently perceived throughout CEE as a Russian-dominated lake or a Russian-Turkish condominium. The reorientation of national security and force structures toward territorial or homeland defense in order to deter or confront the perceived Russian menace will also grow in significance. Additionally, CEE members will seek a more prominent policy role vis-à-vis Russia within both the EU and NATO.

The apprehensions and aspirations of America's newest European allies as well as those states that seek NATO and EU membership will require a creative U.S. and allied approach. Europe's new democracies will need to have their security ensured at the same time that the West manages its multifaceted relationship with Russia and endeavors to maintain cooperative links with Moscow in areas of mutual interest.

Policy Recommendations

An effective, realistic, and concerted long-range strategy toward Putinist Russia would consist of a combination of practical engagement and strategic assertiveness. Practical engagement involves the pursuit of cooperative relations where Western and Russian interests evidently coincide: in countering international jihadist and other forms of terrorism, reducing stocks of nuclear weapons, curtailing WMD proliferation, confronting the deleterious effects of climate change, and resolving regional conflicts where Moscow can play a positive role.

It would also need to include specific incentives for the Kremlin to adopt constructive approaches where Western interests are directly at stake, whether in energy security, arms control, or missile defense. Dialogue and compromise may be possible in some areas in order to achieve the more important targets. For instance, arrangements could be made to involve Russia in the planned missile defense system in Europe, to resolve standoffs in various arms control regimes, and to enmesh Russia's energy companies in a competitive economic environment in Europe that will enhance the security of each country. If Russia is unwilling to make adjustments and compromises in those arenas, the Western powers will need to assert their interests regardless of Moscow's opposition.

An essential complementary approach toward Russia must focus on important strategic questions where Western institutions and member states face unconstructive trends in Kremlin policy that challenge or undermine Western interests. The EU and NATO must not compromise fundamental principles by arranging any agreements with Russia that sacrifice one important security interest to gain Kremlin acquiescence on another security issue. Additionally, Russia needs to be held accountable to international legal commitments and regulations in a range of areas from human rights and energy contracts to arms control, peacekeeping missions, and military deployment agreements. Having decided on their overarching objectives under such a two-pronged strategy, Europe and the transatlantic alliance can pursue a number of specific initiatives.

Transatlantic Initiatives

1. The Barack Obama administration needs to underscore that progress toward stability and democracy in a widening Europe and an expanding transatlantic alliance is in America's national interests and serves NATO's long-range strategic goals. The creation of a wider institutional Europe and a broader multinational alliance would help expand and consolidate democratic systems, open up new markets, and increase the range of U.S. allies in dealing with numerous global challenges.

2. Washington needs to develop a mechanism for EU and NATO consultations on Russia policy and specify some realistic policy objectives toward Moscow. The urgent need for such a mechanism became starkly apparent after Russia's invasion of Georgia in August 2008, for which Western institutions were

glaringly unprepared. Washington should also consider appointing a special envoy for Russia and the Black Sea and Caspian regions.

3. The security of all NATO newcomers must be substantially strengthened to deter Russia's assertiveness toward potentially vulnerable neighbors. The U.S. missile defense shield in Poland and the Czech Republic, if proved to be effective, accompanied by the modernization of their militaries, the enhancement of their defense capabilities, and the reaffirmation of NATO and U.S. security guarantees to all frontline states from Estonia to Romania, can become the initial steps in this process.[3] Further initiatives could include positioning NATO and U.S. infrastructure from Western to Central Europe, whether army, navy, or air force facilities; basing a NATO rapid reaction force in CEE; and rebuilding the territorial defense forces and naval capabilities of NATO's newest members and alliance aspirants.[4]

4. Each NATO state must obtain a comprehensive defense plan from the alliance to confirm the latter's intent to honor the article 5 defense guarantees.[5] CEE countries must also construct a more robust homeland defense by increasing defense spending, ensuring large manpower reserves for territorial defense, and amassing defensive weapons, including portable missile systems, such as the Stinger and Javelin, "capable of inflicting great damage on Russia's lumbering air and armor forces" in case of an attack.[6] The United States should offer to sell CEE capitals these relatively inexpensive defensive systems.

5. NATO should devise a more coherent and long-range approach toward the aspirant states in Eastern Europe in terms of steps toward future membership, beginning with the issuing of MAPs or some alternative membership track, and affording them heightened status, such as the formula of a major non-NATO ally (MNNA).[7] As NATO takes on a global role in such areas as peace enforcement, humanitarian support, and state stabilization, countries that fulfill the general criteria for inclusion, including democratic development and security sector reform, need to obtain specific tracks for accession.[8] Countries that request military assistance should be afforded the opportunity to construct more effective capabilities in deterring or confronting conventional and unconventional military threats. Russia's pressures on its neighbors to become neutral states, as evident in Georgia, Ukraine, and Moldova, must not be allowed to determine NATO policy, otherwise Moscow will feel emboldened to expand its interference in alliance decision making.

6. The United States and the EU must improve consultation and coordination in energy policy as a common strategic security concern. Russia's control over energy routes will undermine U.S. interests from the Caspian to the Mediterranean while enhancing Moscow's regional leverage. The appointment of Ambassador Richard L. Morningstar as special envoy for Eurasian energy

in April 2009 is an important move in improving U.S.-EU coordination. The new envoy will provide the secretary of state with strategic advice on policy issues relating to development, transit, and distribution of energy resources in Eurasia. Plans should also be made to dispatch an energy protection force under NATO auspices that can enforce security and respond quickly to any threats against pipeline and shipment operations between the Caspian Basin and Europe.

7. A transatlantic energy security strategy can direct more substantial investment toward alternative energy routes and oblige members of NATO and the EU to pool their resources during a crisis. This will lessen dependence, instability, and potential future conflicts with Russia. The EU and the United States possess some leverage in that Moscow will presumably need Western technology to increase energy extraction and to modernize its infrastructure. This leverage should be used strategically to ensure fair competition and transparency in energy policy and avoid the monopolization of supplies and infrastructure. Such a strategy must also include a clear set of regulations that Russia needs to abide by in any economic, commercial, or energy transactions with EU and NATO countries. Russia cannot be held to lower standards than any other state.

8. The EU and the United States need to increase assistance to CEE to develop alternative pipelines and non-Russian sources of energy supplies.[9] Development of the South Stream and Nord Stream pipelines can also be slowed down or indefinitely postponed by countries along the Black Sea and Baltic Sea coasts claiming exclusive economic zones and demanding environmental impact investigations. This will give the EU more time to devise an effective long-term energy policy. According to some analysts, the West has a window of opportunity until 2010, when Russian gas supplies will begin to seriously decline and Moscow will seek to place Central Asian suppliers under firmer control.[10]

9. Support for Russia's accession to the World Trade Organization must be dependent on Moscow's ratification of the EU's Energy Charter.[11] The European Parliament's foreign affairs committee and the European Commission have proposed linking the two issues. Brussels must press Russia to agree to basic ground rules on energy policy, including the Transit Protocol requiring Moscow to open up access to its pipelines.

10. Both the United States and the EU must pay more attention to human rights conditions in Russia and place democratization, the rule of law, as well as human, civil, and minority rights more firmly on the international agenda in exposing Russia's inadequate record in these domains.

11. NATO must directly address the anti-alliance propaganda generated by

Moscow, especially among Russia's neighbors, and better inform local societies about NATO's actual missions and the benefits of cooperation and
membership in the alliance. NATO has evolved into an organization that
projects stability and is actively engaged in resolving conflicts and crises.
It is not simply a military alliance but a political organization and a security
advocate for members, aspirants, and neighbors.[12] NATO leaders must
also speak out when Russia is conducting military deployments without
any international institutional mandate and condemn Moscow's military
pressure against its neighbors. This will help contrast NATO's and the West's
multilateralism with Russia's unilateralism.

12. Russia's unilateral recognition of South Ossetia and Abkhazia as independent
    states will rebound against Moscow. Although it claims to be following
    the Kosova model, in reality Russia established its own precedent for
    separatism within the newly independent states by sponsoring rebel groups
    in Transnistria, South Ossetia, and Abkhazia in the early 1990s, long before
    NATO intervened in Kosova in 1999. This precedent can be turned against
    Russia, which consists of dozens of federal units and aspirant nations who
    deserve to decide on their own statehood. Until now, the West has tread softly
    with regard to Russia's suppression of independence movements in the North
    Caucasus, especially in Chechnya and Ingushetia. Diplomatic and political
    support should be provided to all nations within the Russian Federation that
    were forcibly incorporated in the Russian or Soviet empires and that seek to
    achieve genuine national sovereignty.

EUROPEAN INITIATIVES

1. If the Treaty of Lisbon or its foreign policy components are agreed on and
   implemented, EU policy toward Russia can become more coherent to undercut
   Russia's pursuit of divisive bilateralism. Under the treaty's provisions a new
   high representative of the EU for foreign affairs and security policy will be
   created together with a new European External Action Service. These innovations would enable a more unified long-range EU approach in a number
   of external arenas.

2. To make European Union policy more consistent and coherent, a Russia
   office should be established at the European Commission or a separate EU
   commissioner for Russia policy should be appointed. This would help coordinate strategy within the commission, between various commission
   departments, and with other EU bodies, including the Council of the EU. The
   office or the commissioner would then be directly responsible to the new EU
   foreign minister once he or she is appointed.

3. The EU needs to leverage its numerous incentives and disincentives, particularly its large share in Russia's foreign trade, to encourage Moscow to

pursue more constructive policies.[13] This will be essential if a free trade area is negotiated through the new EU-Russia agreement. There needs to be greater scrutiny of Russian assets in the EU and the United States, both individual and corporate, and thorough investigations of illicit deals, especially those involving EU companies. Moscow should be pressured to close down the operations of opaque intermediary companies active in Europe, such as Gazpromexport. The EU must also defend the contractual obligations of EU companies vis-à-vis Russia and not allow Moscow to alter contracts or arbitrarily seize assets.

4. The EU should adopt an internal code of conduct with specific guidelines on contracts and mergers with Russian energy companies. This would help avoid further monopolization of the EU energy market and encourage open competition and the rule of law.[14] The EU must equally campaign for the demonopolization of Russia's energy industry. It can also promote the energy interconnection of neighboring CEE states such as Ukraine and Moldova, especially in their electricity grids; involve them in Nabucco and other EU energy transmission plans; promote energy efficiency; and limit their dependence on Russia.

5. Europe's energy market must be liberalized and national utilities unbundled in order to cut profit margins in gas distribution and reduce acquisition of EU energy assets. This would encourage national operators to invest in multinational energy networks and weaken Russia's ability to play off one customer against another. The European Commission has already urged EU members to break up vertically integrated energy companies.

6. In the aftermath of Russia's occupation of Georgian territory in August 2008, the EU must ensure freedom of transmission through the Azerbaijan-Georgia oil and gas pipelines and rail corridor and resist any Russian interference in their operations. A multinational EU peacekeeping contingent should be dispatched to the Russian-carved buffer zones outside of South Ossetia and Abkhazia. The EU can confer a mandate for the force within the framework of the European security and defense policy (ESDP) after an invitation from the Georgian government. Seeking a mandate from the UN or the OSCE would allow Russia to use its veto to delay the contingent's arrival or reduce its size and mission.[15]

7. The EU needs to develop its European Partnership Program (EPP) with Ukraine, Moldova, Georgia, Belarus, Armenia, and Azerbaijan. Belarus's inclusion in the program can encourage the Minsk government to pursue basic democratic reforms. An effective EPP, through which the benefits of cooperation become evident to elites and the public alike, could entice Belarus to establish closer relations with the EU. Moreover, EPP may be viewed as

a first step toward potential EU accession. Enlargement has been the EU's most important foreign policy success, while in the long term the costs of nonenlargement may prove higher than the price of admission. The prospect of membership coupled with specific criteria for entry will encourage reforms that effectively stabilize the political and economic systems among candidate countries.

8. The final status of the separatist entities in Georgia and Moldova must become a priority for the EU.[16] Following Russia's recognition of South Ossetia and Abkhazia as separate states, the EU needs to develop a coherent policy to block their international recognition and commit itself to Georgia's territorial integrity and economic development. The EU can also strengthen the conflict resolution instruments of its policies in Moldova and provide more powers and resources to the EU special representatives in the South Caucasus and Moldova. The EU needs to adopt a more prominent role in promoting democratization, civil society development, and the rule of law without legitimizing the status of any separatist entity. The Union must also act more resolutely on the diplomatic front in mobilizing a multinational peacekeeping mission for deployment to Moldova's Transnistria region to prevent any repetition of the Georgian separatist scenario.

9. More resources need to be earmarked for conducting an effective public awareness campaign throughout Eastern Europe about the European Union, including its structure, institutions, principles, values, programs, capabilities, and membership benefits. CEE countries can be extremely helpful in this process as they have recent firsthand experience regarding the impact of accession.

Additionally, the Western allies need to draw up contingencies for a potentially unstable period in Russia's development. One cannot assume that Putinism has ensured a stable and durable authoritarian system. Russia confronts several looming crises: demographic (with a declining population of productive age and serious health problems, including high death rates and declining birthrates), ethnic and potentially religious (especially in the North Caucasus), economic (with overreliance on the price of primary energy resources), social (as the stifling of democracy restricts flexibility, adaptability, and modernization), and political (as power struggles may become manifest between Kremlin oligarchs and security chiefs who gained control over large sectors of the economy).

Russia is clearly not immune from global financial disruptions. This was vividly demonstrated during the escalating financial credit crunch in the fall of 2008. Investor confidence in the Russian economy evidently falls dramatically during global financial turmoil and especially when this is followed by a drop in demand for energy with a severe downturn in crude oil and natural gas prices.

Russia's military intervention in Georgia also contributed to investor concerns that West-East confrontations were mounting and this could affect the stability of the Russian economy. It remains uncertain whether potential economic stagnation will constrain Moscow's agenda to undermine Western cohesion and ensure its political dominance among neighbors. Russian officials calculate that the West will continue to view the country as an important international player as well as a substantial market and key energy provider regardless of its internal turmoil.

The long-term political impact of the global financial crisis on the Russian economy may take time to materialize. However, the lack of Western investor confidence has been evident in the meltdown of the Russian stock exchange, whose value fell by more than 70 percent between May and October 2008, making it one of the world's worst performers. This was coupled with falling oil prices, shrinking energy revenues, a plummeting of the exchange rate, with the ruble losing over 12 percent of its value by November 2008, and a steep decline in Russia's hard currency reserves. Russia's economy was projected to shrink by 6 percent in 2009. Financial restraints will further curtail investments in energy extraction and lead to supply problems in the years ahead.

Demands on government financial reserves, accumulated during the period of high oil prices, were rising fast in the latter part of 2008 and early 2009 as the central bank was spending billions of dollars each week to support the national currency. Moscow's social spending is also set to rise sharply in 2009. By the end of October 2008 Russia's reserves fell below the $500 billion mark for the first time in eight months. The Kremlin also spent $8 billion from its foreign exchange reserves to help several favored oligarchs to refinance their foreign debts. A number of leading billionaires have transferred stakes in some of their most prized firms from Western banks to the Russian state as collateral, handing the Kremlin the means to keep them under closer control by appropriating their assets if they fail to repay loans or fall out of favor with the regime.[17] A greater share of the banking sector also fell under state control as several smaller banks went out of business.

Financial factors could precipitate growing competition between Kremlin-connected oligarchs for scarcer cash flows and may lead to even tighter state control of the economy. It could mushroom into struggles for power between interest groups that were pacified or balanced throughout the Putin presidency and even result in pressures to streamline the military budget. The legitimacy of the system itself and the popularity of President Medvedev could seriously erode if living standards decline precipitously as economic growth stagnates. Some Russian experts have even warned about the serious possibility of an abrupt collapse of living standards and economic disintegration leading to social unrest and political upheaval.[18] Rumors have abounded in Moscow that following a constitutional amendment in December 2008 that extended the presidential term from four to six years, a new election would be called in 2009 or 2010 to return Putin as head of state, strengthen central control, and contain any potential unrest.

In an indication of growing concern about the country's stability, on December 20, 2008, Prime Minister Putin, in celebrating the creation of the Cheka on the annual Day of Security Officers, warned Russia's foes against trying to destabilize the country. In his words, "any attempts to weaken or destabilize Russia or harm the interests of the country will be toughly suppressed." The authorities were in the process of passing legislation to impose high treason charges on people accused of "harming the constitutional order." Critics believe this could lead to a major political crackdown as the role of the security services is likely to grow if Russia experiences prolonged economic decline.[19]

Some Western officials and security analysts contend that Russia's neo-imperialism and strategic expansionism remain illusory as Moscow does not possess the capabilities to effectively challenge the West, either in military or economic terms, and is increasingly interconnected with the West through energy, trade, finance, and business. Such arguments highlight the lack of understanding about the damage that Western interests can sustain from an aggressive and opportunistic Russia.

Irrespective of Russia's evident structural weaknesses, including over-dependence on hydrocarbon revenues and potentially serious domestic economic and demographic problems, in the immediate future Russia remains a serious threat to its weaker neighbors whether through political subversion, energy entrapment, or purposeful destabilization. Such persistent threats, even toward new NATO and EU members, are compounded by a disunited and unfocused West that remains preoccupied with numerous other global and regional crises.

Moscow continues to exploit and deepen Western disunity to undermine the effectiveness of multinational institutions and neutralize allied reactions to its destabilizing policies. Furthermore, a serious crisis inside the Russian Federation may have even more damaging consequences along the country's long borders. Moscow is likely to manipulate perceptions of besiegement and outside threat to deflect attention from its mounting domestic challenges by applying additional pressures on, if not engaging in outright aggression against, its near neighbors.

President Barack Obama will face two stiff challenges in his transatlantic agenda: revitalizing the NATO alliance and dealing with a neo-imperialist Russia. Above all, Washington must reject any moves toward redividing Europe into Cold War zones or sacrificing the security of any European state. This can be accomplished by intensifying links with all of Europe's new democracies and offering NATO aspirants a road map toward inclusion.

If handled adroitly by a united and determined West, the ultimate failure of Russia's Orwellian "sovereign democracy" and Moscow's inability to construct durable spheres of influence and Eurasian dominance will provide an important boost for the reanimation of democratic and pro-Western development along Russia's overextended borders. Although Washington and Brussels have few direct tools available to influence or accelerate Russia's internal developments, they can deploy their substantial economic, diplomatic, and security resources to prevent and contain any instabilities emanating from Russian territory that challenge the security and sovereignty of various European countries, whether they are already EU and NATO members or are currently only aspirants. Ultimately, the most effective tool in disarming Russia's attempts to expand and dominate Eurasia is a united allied strategy to consolidate and enlarge the zone of democratic security.

Postscript

While it is understandable in the current global turmoil that policymakers and analysts in Europe and the United States wish to see Russia transformed from a strategic adversary to a strategic partner, it is important to base such a transformation on a realistic appraisal of Moscow's actual geopolitical objectives.

On May 9, 2009, Russia's self-identification and international assertiveness was on display in the annual celebrations of Soviet victory in World War II. Under Putinism this solemn ceremony has been converted into a display of Russia's machismo and self-glorification reminiscent of Soviet days. This year's Red Square parade included a mass military exhibition with armored vehicles, long-range missiles, and combat aircraft. However, the entire exercise is based on a monumental national delusion fostered by the Kremlin, all branches of state propaganda, and the educational system.

Although Russia was one of the victorious powers at the end of World War II, its current rulers studiously disguise and avoid the historic record, which demonstrates that the Soviet Union itself contributed to launching World War II in alliance with Nazi Germany. Moscow implemented plans to carve up Eastern Europe through the Ribbentrop-Molotov Pact with Berlin. Russia's authorities also disguise the fact that Stalin murdered more Russians and other Soviet citizens than Hitler did. Hence, instead of admitting that it was a perpetrator and an opportunist in the destruction of Europe, Russia, as the successor state to the Soviet Union, depicts itself as a victim and a victor.

Interpretations of the past are important for legitimizing the current government as one committed to Russia's greatness. This was underscored with the formation in May 2009 of a presidential interdepartmental commission to tackle alleged anti-Russian propaganda, which damages the country's international image, and to promote the Soviet version of history. The committee is bereft of independent historians but is made up of high-ranking bureaucrats from various government ministries, representatives from the military and intelligence agencies, several pro-Kremlin spin doctors, and nationalistic lawmakers.

The chairman of the "historic truth" commission, Sergei Naryshkin, is also the chief of President Medvedev's administration and a loyal supporter of Prime Minister Putin. The commission's mandate is to formulate policy initiatives for the president and to "neutralize the negative consequences" of historical falsifications aimed against Russia. Russian liberals have compared the commission to Soviet institutions that established a monopoly over scientific and scholarly truth.

Legislators from the ruling United Russia Party have also proposed amendments to the penal code that will make the "falsification of history" a criminal offense. If passed by the Duma they could result in mandatory jail terms for anyone in the former Soviet Union convicted of "rehabilitating Nazism." In the proposed legislation individuals could be prosecuted for questioning the alleged Soviet liberation of Eastern Europe at the close of World War II or the purportedly voluntary annexation of countries such as Georgia by the tsarist empire. The prospect of legal campaigns against political leaders in neighboring countries, including Ukraine, Georgia, and the Baltic states, who challenge the distorted official Russian version of history will become another source of information warfare and political pressure.

Moscow is likely to intensify its disinformation campaign during preparations and celebrations of the 1989 democratic revolutions by claiming that Moscow voluntarily gave up communism and the Soviet bloc and that the Cold War ended in a draw. It will also claim that the USSR did not occupy Central-Eastern Europe after World War II and play down the Kremlin's imposition of a repressive totalitarian system over the entire region. In reality, the 1989 revolutions not only overthrew communism but also liberated each state from Moscow's overlordship.

Systematized historical distortions have profound contemporary repercussions. Not only is Moscow's May parade symbolically reminiscent of Soviet days, Russia is also substantively imitating its predecessor and sending unmistakable imperial signals to its former satellites. Although Moscow does not possess the military wherewithal to challenge U.S. or NATO preponderance, it can still threaten its immediate neighbors. During the May display Medvedev issued a warning to those adversaries who were contemplating "military adventures" against Russia. Presumably, he had in mind the further enlargement of NATO. The tsarist-style uniforms visible on Red Square together with the hammer-and-sickle red flag were intended to send a message to all formerly occupied territories that Russia was once again the strongest continental power and would continue its tsarist and Soviet traditions.

After the May parade Moscow released its new national security doctrine, which in effect claimed that the expansion of NATO and the modernization of the U.S. military were the chief threats to Russia's security. It also claimed that competition over energy could provoke military conflicts in several key regions, including Central Asia and the Arctic. Moscow has signaled its intent to annex a vast swathe of the continental shelf between northern Siberia and the North Pole that is estimated to contain over ten billion tons of oil and natural gas deposits. Moscow is also believed to be readying a claim to an eighteen-thousand-square-mile section of the Bering Sea, which separates Alaska from Russia's Chukotka province.

In addition to the combative oratory, symbolic displays of empire building, and official statements of intent, tensions between Russia and NATO and the EU have persisted in a series of disputed areas. They include Moscow's condemnation of NATO's Partnership for Peace exercises in Georgia in May; the expulsion of two Russian spies from Brussels and the subsequent eviction of two Canadian diplomats from Moscow; renewed threats to cut off gas supplies to Ukraine, which would negatively affect EU consumers; and President Medvedev's vehement criticism of the EU's Eastern Partnership Program at the EU-Russia Summit in May.

The EPP with six former Soviet republics (Armenia, Azerbaijan, Belarus, Georgia, Moldova, and Ukraine) is designed to facilitate closer relations with the EU by developing association agreements and registering progress on visa liberalization. The authorities in Moscow are determined to view it as an anti-Russian initiative that will avowedly create new dividing lines in Europe. For Kremlin leaders, both NATO and the EU present threats to Russia's security as they pull former satellites away from Moscow's orbit and diminish its room for exerting predominant influence.

In these conditions, the much-touted American "reset button" with Russia may not be sufficient to establish a genuine partnership, despite President Barack Obama's objective to forge new avenues of cooperation. Strategic partners not only share particular policies but are also bound by common interests and joint goals. While Russia can be a partner with the transatlantic alliance in dealing with specific threats, such as nuclear proliferation or counterterrorism, or in negotiating arms control accords, the government in Moscow does not share the long-term strategic goals of either NATO or the EU.

Despite periodic transatlantic disagreements over such issues as U.S. policy toward Iraq, NATO partners are committed to respecting the will of sovereign states to enter multinational institutions of their choice. They also favor and support the development of democratic systems and legitimate governments that combine stability with respect for human and civil rights. The same foreign policy principles do not apply for the Russian authorities.

Contrary to Western interests, Kremlin goals and strategies revolve around a form of "pragmatic reimperialization" in which zero-sum calculations prevail. Russia's administration seeks to be a global player, but to achieve this goal it remains intent on rolling back American influence; neutralizing the EU as an effective institution by focusing on bilateral ties with selected states; engaging in a postcommunist version of "salami tactics," in which adversaries are sidelined or silenced; reestablishing zones of "privileged influence" around its long borders; and curtailing the further expansion of Western multinational institutions.

Russia's neoimperial project no longer relies on Soviet-era instruments such as ideological allegiance, military force, internal security sector control, or the implanting of proxy parties and governments. Instead, the primary goal is to exert predominant influence over the foreign and security policies of disparate states that the Kremlin wants to remain neutral or that directly support Russia's ongoing reimperialization. Moscow has not embarked on a new cold war with the West but pursues opportunistic alliances with an assortment of states whatever their political coloration in order to undercut U.S. and NATO interests.

While its goals are imperial, Kremlin strategies are pragmatic. It employs elastic and eclectic methods involving a mixture of enticements, threats, incentives, and pressures where Russia's national interests are seen as predominating over those of its neighbors and individual European capitals. The Russian administration aims to discredit Western institutional enlargement, postures as the defender of the international legal order, seeks to emasculate or alter the mandate of democracy-promoting institutions such as the Organization for Security and Cooperation in Europe, pursues economic dependency relations with neighboring governments, manufactures security disputes with NATO to gain concessions and advantages in other arenas, and promotes its diplomatic indispensability in resolving conflicts that it has contributed to creating.

Russia's brewing domestic problems precipitated by the global financial crisis will not ensure that its expansionist ambitions are curtailed. On the contrary, to deflect attention from mounting social and regional disquiet inside the Russian Federation, the Kremlin may further cultivate the sense of besiegement to threaten and destabilize various neighbors in Central-Eastern Europe and the Caucasus and to test Western reactions to its assertive policies.

While official statistics released in May 2009 indicated that the Russian economy had contracted by 9.5 percent year-on-year and unemployment exceeded 10 percent, Moscow's ambitious foreign policy agenda showed little sign of abating. Indeed, the Kremlin may be calculating that its economic woes are only temporary as the market price of oil steadily rose during the spring of 2009 and the Russian stock exchange began to rebound as foreign investment began to return to the country. Nonetheless, Russia has a highly volatile and vulnerable economy that is overdependent on oil revenues and commodity price cycles. This boom-and-bust system could actually stimulate a more expansive appetite during the boom cycle to compensate for potentially more restricted foreign policy capabilities during economically leaner periods.

Russia's ambitions, depicted as its justifiable national interests, threaten the primary national interests of its neighbors to remain as sovereign states. To forestall coercion, absorption, conflict, or the creation of broader Russian-led alliances that could undermine Western security interests, it is important for the Allies to work more closely with a range of countries along Russia's borders. In particular, the emphasis should be on ensuring their independence and stability during a time of political uncertainty and economic crisis. For instance, an independent Ukraine is vital to prevent political and ethnic conflicts from unsettling a wider region, while the independence of Kazakhstan remains key for the alliance in its mission to ensure security in Central and South Asia and prevent the spread of terrorism, WMDs, and narcotics trafficking.

While Russia applies pressures on its neighbors to stay within its orbit and remain outside of NATO, many of the incumbent governments are increasingly wary of Moscow's long-range aspirations and are looking to the West for strategic balance and support in preserving their sovereignty and statehood from Russia's encroachments.

Most of Russia's CEE neighbors fear that instead of simply pursuing avenues of cooperation where there are genuine common interests with NATO, Washington may ignore or accommodate Russia's imperial drive in order to gain support from Moscow in a multitude of global challenges, from arms control and nonproliferation to counterterrorism and climate change. The Kremlin views President Obama's outstretched hand as an opportunity to expand Russia's influences and will drive hard bargains to gain far-reaching advantages from Washington, especially in regions where it claims to have privileged interests. It will also continue to drive wedges between EU and NATO states to forestall the emergence of a common and effective Western strategy toward Russia.

Despite this inauspicious setting, President Obama, especially through the broad support he has generated in Europe, has a unique opportunity to rebuild transatlantic relations by basing them on three core principles: first, common security provided by the NATO alliance; second, openness to new members that meet the standards necessary for accession; and third, a cooperative approach toward all other powers, including Russia, but one that does not sacrifice the first two principles.

WASHINGTON, D.C., MAY 25, 2009

Acknowledgments

I would like to express my utmost gratitude to all the assistants and interns at the Center for Strategic and International Studies (CSIS) in Washington, D.C., who tirelessly conducted volumes of research, in both the written and spoken word. I would especially like to thank Milena Staneva, my program manager and research associate, and Besian Bocka, program coordinator and research assistant, during the duration of this project. Invaluable help was also provided by all the research interns in our New European Democracies (NED) program, including Brigitta Stumpf, Jasenka Jocic, Fadil Aliriza, Loren Puette, Kathleen Miskovsky, Thomas Shonosky, Michelle Warren, and Daniel Palazov. I am also grateful to my stalwart deputy at CSIS, Ilona Teleki, for always keeping all of our flags flying high.

An earlier and more condensed version of this manuscript, titled "Expanding Eurasia: Russia's European Ambitions," was published in November 2008 by the CSIS Press Significant Issues Series. Permission was obtained from CSIS to expand and develop the original monograph into a full-length book for Potomac Books, Inc.

Notes

Chapter 1. Russia's Revival

1. Gyorgy Schopflin, "Russia and the West Are a World Apart," *Moscow Times*, September 1, 2008.
2. For a valuable discussion of Russia's state imperialism see Vera Tolz, *Russia: Inventing the Nation* (London: Arnold, 2001).
3. Andrzej Nowak, "Was the Polish-Lithuanian Commonwealth an Empire?" in *History and Geopolitics: A Contest for Eastern Europe* (Warsaw: Polish Institute of International Affairs, 2008), 40.
4. For a valuable recent analysis of the ideology of Eurasianism see Marlene Laruelle, *Russian Eurasianism: An Ideology of Empire* (Washington, DC: Woodrow Wilson Center Press, 2008).
5. Dmitry Medvedev, "Speech at Meeting with German Political, Parliamentary, and Civic Leaders" (Berlin, June 5, 2008), http://www.kremlin.ru/eng/speeches/ 2008/06/05/2203_type82912type82914type84779_202153.shtml.
6. A valuable analysis can be found in Marcin Kaczmarski, "The Russian Proposal for a New European Security System," *CES Commentary*, no. 11 (October 16, 2008).
7. For instance, see Thomas Graham, *U.S.-Russia Relations: Facing Reality Pragmatically* (Washington, DC: Center for Strategic and International Studies, July 17, 2008), 1. One wonders whether the same principle should apply to Germany's loss of the Third Reich or the dissolution of the British Empire.
8. Russia's self-justification for expansion has included the concept of the "third Rome," the savior of Europe against barbarism, pan-Orthodoxy, pan-Slavism, and international communism. Putinism added two further pretexts for intervention against neighboring states: the defense of Russian speakers, compatriots, and passport holders; and the protection of Russia's infrastructure abroad.
9. In addition, the Kremlin relishes highlighting the shortcomings in America's democracy promotion and focuses on scandals such as the Abu Ghraib prison abuses by U.S. troops in Iraq. It thereby claims that Washington does not hold the moral high ground in campaigning for human rights.

10. For example, see Sergei Karaganov, "The New Epoch of Confrontation," *Russia in Global Affairs* 5, no. 4 (October–December 2007).

11. See the article by Russian foreign minister Sergei Lavrov, "The Present and the Future of Global Politics," *Russia in Global Affairs* 5, no. 2 (April–June 2007). Lavrov claimed that Washington measures the level of democracy according to how willing a country is to follow in the United States' footsteps. Also check Kremlin ideologist Vladislav Surkov, "Our Russian Model of Democracy Is Called 'Sovereign Democracy,'" June 28, 2006, http://www.edinros.ru/news.html?id=114108.

12. It is estimated that the Russian state has appropriated an estimated $100 billion in assets from private hands since Putin assumed power in 2000. See Bill Powell and Li You, "How the KGB (and Friends) Took Over Russia's Economy," *Fortune* 158, no. 5 (September 10, 2008): 84–94.

13. Lilia Shevtsova, "Anti-Westernism Is the New National Idea," *Moscow Times*, August 7, 2007.

14. Putin's landmark Munich speech on February 10, 2007, can be found at http://www.securityconference.de/konferenzen/rede.php?sprache=en&id=179.

15. Russia is a neo-imperial state regardless of its aspirations toward its neighbors and former satellites. The Russian Federation consists of eighty-three federal subjects and dozens of nationalities that were conquered and colonized by Moscow during the periods of czarist and Soviet imperialism. Unlike all the European empires, from which dozens of new states emerged, Russia has never dismantled its internal empire and maintains its political dominance over other nations while continuing its Russification process. According to the federal constitution, the non-Russian nationalities are not entitled to vote for secession or for the creation of independent states.

16. Among useful recent book-length studies of Russia's political development see Andrew Wilson, *Virtual Politics: Faking Democracy in the Post-Soviet World* (New Haven, CT: Yale University Press, 2005); Vadim Volkov, *Violent Entrepreneurs: The Use of Force in the Making of Russian Capitalism* (Ithaca, NY: Cornell University Press, 2002); Stephen K. Wegren, ed., *Russia's Policy Challenges: Security, Stability, and Development* (Armonk, NY: M. E. Sharpe, 2003); Stephen White, *Russia's New Politics: The Management of a Postcommunist Society* (New York: Cambridge University Press, 2000); and Richard Rose and Neil Munro, *Elections without Order: Russia's Challenge to Vladimir Putin* (Cambridge: Cambridge University Press, 2002).

17. The VeCheka (All-Russian Extraordinary Commission for Combating Counter-Revolution, Speculation, Sabotage, and Misconduct in Office) was the political police established in December 1917 by Lenin's Bolsheviks after their seizure of power. It was founded by Felix Dzerzhinsky and evolved during Communist rule through several name changes, including the KGB. For a valuable analysis see George Leggett, *The Cheka: Lenin's Political Police* (Oxford: Clarendon Press, 1981). Putin and his colleagues in the FSB, the institutional descendent of the Cheka and the KGB, take pride in its heritage and purportedly patriotic credentials.

18. Julie Anderson, "The Chekist Takeover of the Russian State," *International Journal of Intelligence and Counterintelligence* 19, no. 2 (May 2006): 227–88.

See also Daniel Treisman, "Putin's Silovarchs," *Orbis* 51, no. 1 (Winter 2007): 141–53. The KGB and its counterparts in the Soviet bloc states were instrumental in organized crime, including drugs and weapons smuggling, years before the collapse of communism. See Misha Glenny, *McMafia: A Journey through the Global Criminal Underworld* (New York: Knopf Books, 2008), 3–20.

19. Zbigniew Brzezinski, "Putin's Choice," *Washington Quarterly* 31, no. 2 (Spring 2008): 95–116. Brzezinski asserts that the economic system shaped by Putin was designed to strengthen the state rather than to modernize Russian society.

20. Stephen Blank, "Power Struggles in the Kremlin—How Stable Is the New Regime?" in *Russia after Putin: Implications for Russia's Politics and Neighbors*, Policy Paper (Stockholm-Nacka: Institute for Security and Development Policy, March 2008), 12–18.

21. According to Andrew Wilson, Medvedev "remains the willing servant of a system where power rests on shadowy deals and methods unacceptable in any true democracy." See Andrew Wilson, *Meeting Medvedev: The Politics of the Putin Succession*, Policy Brief (London: European Council on Foreign Relations, February 2008), 9–10.

22. For a standard Medvedev apologetic, check Nadia Alexandrova-Arbatova, "Russia after the Presidential Elections: Foreign Policy Orientations," *EU-Russia Centre Review*, no. 8 (October 2008): 10–19.

23. See George Bovt, "Russian Foreign Policy under Dmitry Medvedev," *EU-Russia Centre Review*, no. 8 (October 2008): 21.

24. Some experts dismiss depictions of Putinist Russia as "neo-imperial" and claim such a description contains an "ideological bias" that hinders understanding of Moscow's policy. For instance, see Dmitri Trenin and Bobo Lo, *The Landscape of Russian Foreign Policy Decision-Making* (Washington, DC: Carnegie Endowment for International Peace, 2005). Trenin and Lo contend that analysts should not extrapolate grand strategy from "individual developments" such as "Moscow's interest in developments in Georgia."

25. For seminal pro-Putin apologetics that depict Russia as a "pragmatic" power consult Andrei P. Tsygankov, "Vladimir Putin's Vision of Russia as a Normal Great Power," *Post-Soviet Affairs* 21, no. 2 (2005): 132–58; "New Challenges for Putin's Foreign Policy," *Orbis* 50, no. 1 (January 2006): 153–65; and "Projecting Confidence, Not Fear: Russia's Post-Imperial Assertiveness," *Orbis* 50, no. 4 (Fall 2006): 677–90. Tsygankov argues that the primary driver of Russia's foreign policy is domestic (despite the fact that political dissent is largely irrelevant); that Russia is taking "precautions against encroachment on its sovereignty" (although no neighbor or multinational organization has challenged Russia's independence and integrity, unless Russia's "sovereignty" extends throughout the post-Soviet space); that Russia feels "encircled" by Western powers (even though Russia encircles its own neighbors through economic, diplomatic, political, and military tools); and that Russia's "engagement" with the West precludes neo-imperialism (the author is unfamiliar with "pragmatic empire building" as practiced by imperial powers throughout history).

26. For an incisive synopsis of the Putinization of Stalinism see Leon Aron, "The Politics of Memory," *Russian Outlook*, AEI Online, September 8, 2008, http://www.aei.org/publications/pubID.28503/pub_detail.asp. According to Aron, for

the Kremlin "the overarching agenda that is to shape this and future historical narratives is the 'normalization' of the monstrosity of Soviet totalitarianism—the procurement of justifications and excuses for its crimes."

27. Edward Lucas, *The New Cold War: The Future of Russia and the Threat to the West* (New York: Palgrave Macmillan, 2008), 10.

28. According to Konstantin Kosachyov, chairman of the Duma Committee on International Relations, in a speech delivered on March 1, 2006, Russia has always been treated unequally by the West and Moscow was unable to receive any real economic or financial assistance after the termination of communism. See Konstantin Kosachyov, "Russia's Presidency at the G8, Energy Security and Other Foreign Policy Priorities for 2006" (speech given at Geneva Center for Security Policy, March 1, 2006), http://www.gcsp.ch/e/meetings/Issues_Institutions/Russia-CIS/Public_Disc/2006/Kosachev/Kosachev-speech.htm.

29. Lilia Shevtsova, "The End of Putin's Era: Domestic Drivers of Foreign Policy," in *U.S.-Russian Relations: Is Conflict Inevitable?* (Washington, DC: Hudson Institute, June 26, 2007), 50.

30. See Dmitri Trenin, "Russia Redefines Itself and Its Relations with the West," *Washington Quarterly* 30, no. 2 (Spring 2007): 95–105. In a variant of the economistic argument, one analyst suggests that Moscow seeks to restore a regionally dominant Greater Russia but is modeling this dominance on the EU integration process. The author does not contrast Russia's approach with that of EU enlargement: the latter is accomplished voluntarily, without outside pressure and internal subversion, where each capital surrenders elements of sovereignty and where no single power dominates. See Bertil Nygren, *The Rebuilding of Greater Russia: Putin's Foreign Policy towards the CIS Countries* (New York: Routledge, 2007). Nygren does conclude that one of Putin's major goals was to "regain actual political and economic control of much of the former Soviet space" (p. 238).

31. See "A Survey of Russian Federation Foreign Policy," Ministry of Foreign Affairs of the Russian Federation, Information and Press Department, 2006, http://www.ln.mid.ru/brp_4.nsf/e78a48070f128a7b43256999005bcbb3/89a30b3a6b65b4f2c32572d700292f74?OpenDocument.

32. Consult the accusations by Putin against former U.S. national security adviser Zbigniew Brzezinski in an interview with newspaper journalists from G-8 member countries on June 4, 2007, in http://www.kremlin.ru/eng/speeches/2007/06/04/2149_type82916_132716.shtml.

33. A useful Russian-focused analysis of U.S. approaches to EU-Russia relations can be found in Vitaly Merkushev, "Relations between Russia and the EU: The View from Across the Atlantic," *Perspectives on European Politics and Society* 6, no. 2 (2005): 353–71.

34. Harvey Sicherman, "A Clarifying Act of Violence: Russia, Georgia, and the West," *E-Notes* (Foreign Policy Research Institute), August 20, 2008.

35. Check the rambling piece by Richard Sakwa, "'New Cold War' or Twenty Years' Crisis? Russia and International Politics," *International Affairs* 84, no. 2 (2008): 241–67. Among his numerous questionable conclusions, Sakwa believes that Moscow seeks "accelerated integration with the EU"; that Putin's "realism," "pragmatic Eurasianism," and "accommodationism" do not envisage a neo-imperial

revival; that Moscow is not setting itself up as an "alternative to the West"; and that Putin's policy resembles that of Charles de Gaulle. The historical record demonstrates that France under de Gaulle did not threaten any of its neighbors with nuclear strikes, ethnic turmoil, administrative fragmentation, military invasion, territorial annexation, energy blackmail, or political interference. Sakwa also displays a simplistic understanding of Soviet foreign policy, which included "realism" where necessary together with "balancing" and confrontation where it was advantageous for an expansive global role.

36. For a poignant analysis of anti-Westernism among contemporary Russian intellectuals see Nowak, "History as an Apology for Totalitarianism," in *History and Geopolitics*, 235–64.

37. This point was highlighted in an official document titled "Medium-Term Strategy for the Development of Relations between the Russian Federation and the EU (2000–2010)." It was issued in 1999 and presented by Prime Minister Putin before his selection as Russia's president. The document is usefully described in Dov Lynch, "Russia's Strategic Partnership with Europe," *Washington Quarterly* 27, no. 2 (Spring 2004): 99–118.

38. According to Professor Stephen Blank from the U.S. Army War College during his presentation at a conference on U.S.-CEE relations at the Center for Strategic and International Studies on October 2, 2008.

39. Even in terms of historical precedents there is general misunderstanding of Russian intentions. For instance, Czar Peter the Great is often depicted as a great Westernizer even though an essential component of his strategy was to neutralize the Polish-Lithuanian Commonwealth and make Central Europe dependent on Russia. For a valuable analysis see Nowak, *History and Geopolitics*, especially the chapter titled "Russia and Europe, or Geopolitical Orientations in Russian Thought," 14–35.

40. Marshall Goldman points out that Moscow's use of energy resources is part of "a carefully thought out grand strategy" to place the strategic economic sectors in the service of the state. Check Marshall I. Goldman, *Petrostate: Putin, Power, and the New Russia* (New York: Oxford University Press, 2008), 15.

41. Katinka Barysch, *The EU and Russia: Strategic Partners or Squabbling Neighbours?* (London: Centre for European Reform, May 2004), 9.

42. For details on the institutional aspects of EU-Russia relations consult European Commission, *The European Union and Russia: Close Neighbours, Global Players, and Strategic Partners* (Luxembourg: Office for Official Publications of the European Communities, May 2007), http://ec.europa.eu/external_relations/russia/docs/russia_brochure07_en.pdf.

43. "EU-Russia Relations in 'Crisis': Polish Foreign Minister," Agence France Presse, May 17, 2007. For an analysis of the EU-Russia agreement and proposals for future arrangements see Michael Emerson, Fabrizio Tassinari, and Marius Vahl, "A New Agreement between the EU and Russia: Why, What, and When?" Policy Brief no.103 (Brussels: Centre for European Policy Studies, May 2006). The authors conclude that any strategic treaty between Moscow and Brussels would require Russia to become a real democracy and to redefine its security doctrine so as not to threaten its neighbors.

44. Cynthia A. Roberts, *Russia and the European Union: The Sources and Limits of "Special Relationships,"* (Carlisle Barracks, PA: Strategic Studies Institute, U.S. Army War College, February 2007), 21. While critical of the EU's approach toward Russia, the author offers little of substance for restructuring the relationship other than working groups to develop "deeper cooperation" and a "new bargain" with "positive incentives." By offering dialogue and bargains as the solution, the author contradicts her own observation that Russia's leaders believe that "Russia's convergence to EU norms would diminish its power and unique 'Euro-Asian' role" (p. 79).

45. Ibid., viii. For a sober Russian assessment of EU-Russia relations see E. Kuznetsova, "Will the Roadmaps Lead Russia to Europe?" *International Affairs* 51, no. 4 (2005): 67–71.

46. Mark Leonard and Nicu Popescu, *A Power Audit of EU-Russia Relations*, Policy Paper (London: European Council on Foreign Relations, November 2, 2007), 2.

47. The EU's economy is approximately fifteen times larger than that of Russia, while Russia's GDP is the size of Holland's and Belgium's combined. See World Bank, Key Development Data and Statistics, http://www.worldbank.org/data/countrydata/countrydata.html.

48. See Yuri Borko, head of the Center of European Integration Studies at the Institute of Europe of the Russian Academy of Sciences, in "Rethinking Russia-EU Relations," *Russia in Global Affairs* 2, no. 3 (July–September 2004): 168–78.

49. A helpful analysis of EU-Russia relations can be found in Paul Flenley, "Russia and the EU: A Pragmatic and Contradictory Relationship," *Perspectives on European Politics and Society* 6, no. 3 (2005): 435–58. One feasible solution is a free trade agreement between the EU and Russia once Moscow has been admitted into the World Trade Organization.

50. For details on how Russia has complicated the visa facilitation process for EU citizens see Barysch, "The EU and Russia," 45–50.

51. Leonard and Popescu, *A Power Audit of EU-Russia Relations*, 16.

52. Jonathan Eyal, "European Appeasement Will Worsen Russian Aggression," *Financial Times*, May 17, 2007. Eyal is the director of international security at the Royal United Services Institute for Defense Studies in London.

53. Timofei Bordachev and Arkady Moshes, "Is the Europeanization of Russia Over?" *Russia in Global Affairs* 2, no. 2 (April–June 2004): 90–102.

54. Tanguy de Wilde and Gaelle Pellon, "The Implications of the European Neighbourhood Policy (ENP) on the EU-Russian 'Strategic Partnership,'" *Helsinki Monitor* 17, no. 2 (2006): 119–31.

55. Differences in Russia policy have also been evident between the Council of the EU's high representative for foreign policy and the European Commission's commissioner for foreign affairs. Moreover, the various departments in the European Commission conduct their own uncoordinated policies, and each EU presidency in the six-month rotating system exhibits a differing approach toward Russia.

56. For a useful analysis of attempts to make EU foreign policy more effective consult Brian Crowe, "The European Action Service: Roadmap for Success," Chatham House Report, May 2008, http://www.chathamhouse.org.uk/publications/papers/view/-/id/621/.

57. According to Mikhail Margelov, head of the Russian Federation Council's International Affairs Committee, Interfax, October 19, 2007.

Chapter 2. Confronting the United States

1. Despite Moscow's contentions, democracy promotion and the inclusion of new democracies in NATO and the EU are not Cold War concepts. Much of the Cold War was based on distinct spheres of influence and a clear division between West and East. As sovereign states, all European countries can now qualify for membership of the Atlantic alliance and the European Union.

2. According to Russian foreign minister Sergei Lavrov, quoted in Oleg Shchedrov, "Georgia Crisis Defines New Russian Defense Policy," Reuters, September 1, 2008.

3. Pavel Felgenhauer, "Russia Is Stronger and More Aggressive," *Eurasia Daily Monitor*, July 17, 2008.

4. See Sergei Lavrov, "Containing Russia: Back to the Future?" an article that Russian spokesmen claim was censored by *Foreign Affairs*, August 8, 2007. The full article can be found at http://www.voltairenet.org/article15303.html. Also check Fyodor Lukyanov, "The Tymoshenko Doctrine: The Orange Princess Proclaims a Concept for Containing Russia," *Vremya Novostey*, April 11, 2007.

5. See Justin Burke, "Mismatch of the Century," *Transitions Online*, May 11, 2006, http://www.tol.cz/look/TOL/article.tpl?IdLanguage=1&IdPublication=4& NrIssue=166&NrSection=2&NrArticle=17096.

6. Quoted in "The Shadowy Hand of Uncle Sam," *Rossiyskaya Gazeta*, September 16, 2008, and reported by BBC Monitoring, September 29, 2008.

7. Carol R. Saivetz, "Making the Best of a Bad Hand: An Assessment of Current Trends in Russian Foreign Policy," *Post-Soviet Affairs* 22, no. 2 (2006): 170.

8. Boris Piadyshev, Aleksandr Bessmertnykh, and Boris Shmeler, "Realpolitik from Munich," *International Affairs* 53, no. 3 (2007): 50–80.

9. "Russia Will Withdraw from Farcical Arms Agreement," RIA Novosti, July 16, 2007.

10. Michael Radu, "Make Love Not War? Anti-Americanism and the Presidential Election," *E-Notes* (Foreign Policy Research Institute), October 10, 2008, http://www.fpri.org/enotes/200810.radu.lovewarantiamericanism.html.

11. "New Draft Resolution on Kosovo Unacceptable—Kosachyov," *ITAR-TASS Daily*, July 13, 2007.

12. M. Cekerevac and M. Albunovic, "Kosovo Kazachok," *Politika*, December 20, 2007.

13. Alexander Konovalov, "Russia Will Never Negotiate with Terrorists—Ivanov," *ITAR-TASS Weekly News*, April 5, 2004.

14. *Balkan Watch* (Public International Law and Policy Group) 10, no. 9 (May 26, 2008).

15. Patrick Moore, "Are UN, EU Part of the Problem in Kosovo?" *Radio Free Europe/Radio Liberty Analysis*, May 28, 2008.

16. AFP, Reuters, AP, June 13, 2008.

17. "NATO Expands KFOR's Mission," *Southeast European Times*, June 13, 2008.

18. John R. Bolton, "After Russia's Invasion of Georgia, What Now for the West?" *Telegraph* (London), August 15, 2008.

19. Reuters, October 29, 2008.
20. Arkady Moshes, "Russia and Europe in the Aftermath of the Georgian Conflict: New Challenges, Old Paradigms," REP BN 08/04 (London: Chatham House, September 2008), 3.
21. Sergey Markedonov, "Caucasus Conflict Breaks Old Rules of the Game," *Russian Analytical Digest*, no. 45 (September 4, 2008): 3.
22. Emil Danielyan, "Iran to Supply Armenia with Gas and Armenia to Export Electricity to Iran," *Eurasia Daily Monitor*, September 29, 2008.
23. An assessment can be found in Valery Dzutsev, "Lessons from Kosovo," *Transitions Online*, January 21, 2008, http://www.tol.cz/look/TOL/article.tpl?Id Language=1&IdPublication=4&NrIssue=252&NrSection=2&NrArticle=19291.
24. Wojciech Górecki, "Russia Concludes Interstate Treaties with Abkhazia and South Ossetia," *EastWeek*, no. 30 (139) (September 24, 2008): 1–3.
25. For an analysis of Russia's provocations and buildup to invasion see Vladimir Socor, "The Goals behind Moscow's Proxy Offensive in South Ossetia," *Eurasia Daily Monitor*, August 8, 2008; and Pavel Felgenhauer, "The Russian-Georgian Was Preplanned in Moscow," *Eurasia Daily Monitor*, August 14, 2008; and Felix K. Chang, "Russia Resurgent: An Initial Look at Russian Military Performance in Georgia," *E-Notes* (Foreign Policy Research Institute), August 13, 2008, http://www.fpri.org/enotes/200808.chang.russiaresurgentgeorgia.html.
26. "Ukraine Offers West Radar Warning," BBC News, August 16, 2008, http://news.bbc.co.uk/go/pr/fr/-/2/hi/europe/7566070.stm.
27. A. Wess Mitchell, "America's New Eastern Problem," *Central Europe Digest,* August 15, 2008.
28. For example, see Paul J. Saunders, "Georgia's Recklessness," *Washington Post*, August 15, 2008.
29. For a useful analysis, see John Roberts, "Georgia Falls Victim to Pipeline Politics," BBC News, August 12, 2008.
30. Vladimir Socor, "Moscow Summit on Karabakh Falls Short of Kremlin's Goals," *Eurasia Daily Monitor*, November 4, 2008; and "Nagorno-Karabakh Agreement Signed," BBC News, November 2, 2008, http://news.bbc.co.uk/2/hi/europe/7705067.stm.
31. Thomas Grove, "Turkey in Tight Spot between Russia and NATO," Reuters, August 28, 2008; and Gareth Jenkins, "Ongoing Trade Crisis Demonstrates Turkey's Lack of Leverage against Russia," *Eurasia Daily Monitor*, September 9, 2008.
32. Ercan Ersoy and Orhan Coskun, "Turkey-Russia Energy Links Thaw," Reuters, July 22, 2008.
33. Gareth Jenkins, "More Speed, Less Haste Results in Turkish Nuclear Tender Fiasco," *Eurasia Daily Monitor*, September 25, 2008.
34. *Alman Mir Ismail*, "Responding to Georgia Crisis, Turkey Seeks New Security Initiative in the Caucasus," *Eurasia Daily Monitor*, August 22, 2008.
35. Vladimir Socor, "Russia Neutering the Council of Europe after Invasion of Georgia," *Eurasia Daily Monitor*, September 25, 2008.
36. Reuters, August 17, 2008.
37. For details on instability in the North Caucasus check issues of *North Caucasus Weekly* published by the Jamestown Foundation.

38. Consult the *North Caucasus Weekly*, formerly the *Chechnya Weekly*, Jamestown Foundation.

39. President Putin centralized Russia's arms sales under the control of a single agency, Rosoboronoexport.

40. "Russia and Brazil Heads Push Ties," BBC News, November 26, 2008, http://news.bbc.co.uk/2/hi/americas/7750837.stm.

41. For a valuable critique of "pragmatology" see Robert Kagan, "The End of the End of History: Why the Twenty-First Century Will Look Like the Nineteenth," *New Republic*, April 23, 2008. According to Kagan, "The rulers of China and Russia may indeed be pragmatic, but they are pragmatic in pursuing policies that will keep themselves in power. Putin sees no distinction between his own interests and Russia's interests."

42. Robert Skidelsky, "Russia's Role as the 'Awkward Partner,'" *Japan Times*, December 9, 2007.

43. ITAR-TASS, September 12, 2008. Nonetheless, some Western analysts doubt whether the Russian navy will have combat ships available for deployment in the Mediterranean in the foreseeable future and are using their renewed ties with Syria and Libya largely as propaganda ploys.

44. Ariel Cohen, "The Real World: The Russian Navy Back in the Med," *Middle East Times*, October 17, 2008, http://www.metimes.com/International/2008/10/17/the_real_world_the_russian_navy_back_in_the_med/1111/. Among the vessels that could be deployed to Tartus are Russia's only aircraft carrier, the *Admiral Kuznetsov*, the missile cruiser *Moskva*, and several nuclear power attack submarines (SSNs) or nuclear guided missile submarines (SSGNs).

45. Isabel Gorst, "Russia Baulks at Selling Missiles to Syria," *Financial Times*, August 22, 2008.

46. Hannes Adomeit, "Russia's Iran Policy: Global and Regional Objectives, Political and Economic Interests," *SWP Comments* (German Institute for International and Security Affairs) 9 (March 2006).

47. Ray Takeyh and Nikolas Gvosdev, "U.S. Must Engage in Direct Negotiations with Iran," *International Herald Tribune*, September 9, 2008.

48. Kamal Nazer Yasin, "Iran: U.S.-Russian Tension Creates New Diplomatic Options for Tehran," *Eurasia Insight*, August 22, 2008, http://www.eurasianet.org/departments/insight/articles/eav082208.shtml.

49. "Libya Seeks Russian Arms Worth $2 Billion," Reuters, October 20, 2008.

50. "Gaddafi Seeks Russia Energy Pact," BBC News, October 31, 2008, http://news.bbc.co.uk/2/hi/europe/7702488.stm.

51. See, for example, Siraj Wahab and Samir Al-Saadi, "Russia Embraces Muslim World," *Arab News*, October 29, 2008; and Siraj Wahab and Samir Al-Saadi, "Russian-Muslim Alliance Picks up Momentum," *Arab News*, October 30, 2008.

52. "Russia and Venezuela Boost Ties," BBC News, September 26, 2008, http://news.bbc.co.uk/go/pr/fr/-/2/hi/europe/7636989.stm.

53. Jeff Franks, "Talk of Russia-Cuba Ties Seen as Warning to U.S.," Reuters, August 22, 2008; and Tony Halpin, "Nuclear Bomber Base Raises Fears of a New Cuban Crisis," *Times* (London), July 25, 2008.

54. "Putin Offers Nuclear Energy Help to Chavez," Reuters, September 25, 2008.

55. "Russia-Venezuela Nuclear Accord," BBC News, November 27, 2008, http://news.bbc.co.uk/2/hi/americas/7751562.stm.

56. Arthur Herman, "Russia and the New Axis of Evil," *Wall Street Journal Europe*, August 29, 2008.

57. "Moscow Intensifies Contacts with Latin America," *EastWeek*, no. 30 (139) (September 24, 2008): 5.

58. John C. K. Daly, "Naval Implications of the South Ossetian Crisis," *Eurasia Daily Monitor*, September 10, 2008.

59. Tony Halpin, "Russia Engages in 'Gangland' Diplomacy as It Sends Warship to Caribbean," *Times Online*, September 22, 2008, http://www.timesonline.co.uk/tol/news/world/europe/article4804157.ece.

60. "Russia's Zimbabwe Sanctions Veto Angers West, Raises Questions about Medvedev," Associated Press, July 15, 2008.

61. "Zimbabwe President and the Leaders of the Opposition Agreed on Power-Sharing," *Nezavisimaya Gazeta*, September 18, 2008. President Mugabe has publicly thanked Moscow for opposing sanctions against Zimbabwe in the UNSC.

62. For an assessment of the Kremlin model of economic development see Michael McFaul and Kathryn Stoner-Weiss, "The Myth of the Authoritarian Model," *Foreign Affairs* 87, no. 1 (January–February 2008): 68–84. According to the authors, the emergence of Russian democracy in the 1990s coincided with economic decline and state breakdown but did not precipitate either. Likewise, the reemergence of autocracy under Putin coincided with economic growth but did not cause it. High energy revenues and postcommunist economic recovery account for most of the success. The authors conclude that economic growth would have been more impressive if democracy had survived in Russia. However, increased energy earnings for the state have allowed for the return of autocracy, the elimination of political opposition, and the curtailment of economic competition.

63. By 2007 the Russian economy measured only the same size as the Benelux countries combined and would probably not catch up with Portugal for another decade. See Stephen Sestanovich, "Russia by the Numbers," *Wall Street Journal*, December 17, 2007.

64. "Cheney Swipes at Russia, EU Vows to Help New Democracies," Agence France Presse, May 4, 2006. For a Lithuanian defense of Vice President Cheney's comments see Virginijus Savukynas, "Has 'Cold War' with Russia Started in Vilnius?" *Vilnius Lietuvos Rytas*, May 10, 2006.

65. For a pro-Kremlin reaction following the election of Barack Obama and warning about the dangers for Russia of an invigorated transatlantic alliance see John Laughland, "Russia Versus Europe—The Same Old Story," RIA Novosti, November 5, 2008.

Chapter 3. Weakening the Alliance

1. Alexander Golts, "Taking Aim at the New NATO," *Moscow Times*, July 19, 2005.

2. "Putin Accuses U.S. of Starting New Arms Race," RIA Novosti, May 31, 2007.

3. Flenley, "Russia and the EU," 435–61.

4. Interview with Aleksandr Sharavin, director of Russia's Institute for Political and Military Analysis, in *Vremya Novostey*, June 15, 2007.

5. In a speech commemorating the sixty-second anniversary of the defeat of Nazi Germany, Putin compared U.S. foreign policy to that of the Third Reich. See Andrew E. Kramer, "Putin Likens U.S. Foreign Policy to That of the Third Reich," *International Herald Tribune*, May 9, 2007.

6. See "The Foreign Policy Outcomes of 2005: Reflections and Conclusions," Ministry of Foreign Affairs of the Russian Federation, Information and Press Department, http://www.ln.mid.ru/brp_4.nsf/f68cd37b84711611c3256f6d005410 94/4e2913a74a69adf7c32570e6004d151a?OpenDocument.

7. Simon Saradzhyan, "Russia Sees Kosovo as the Answer," *Moscow Times*, March 29, 2006.

8. For instance, see the misleading formulation by Thomas Graham that parrots Kremlin assertions, in "U.S.-Russia Relations: Facing Reality Pragmatically," 4.

9. Details on the NATO-Russia Council can be found in "NATO-Russia Council," Russian Federation Ministry of Defence, http://www.mil.ru/eng/1864/12075/ 12096/12099/index.shtml. Russian troops have also participated in NATO-led peacekeeping missions in Bosnia-Herzegovina and Kosovo.

10. Tuomas Forsberg, "The EU-Russia Security Partnership: Why the Opportunity Was Missed," *European Foreign Affairs Review* 9, no. 2 (2004): 247–67.

11. Dmitry Danilov, "The Potential Ally of Moscow: Militarization of the EU Is Objectively Advantageous to Moscow," *Nezavisimoe Voennoye Obozreniye*, no. 47 (1999).

12. Forsberg, "The EU-Russia Security Partnership," 253. According to the Lisbon treaty, the ESDP will be renamed as the common security and defense policy (CSDP). The new EUHR will have a more prominent role in civil-military relations and in the CSDP.

13. See "Russia Seeks No Accession to NATO; Warns Its Expansion Is a Mistake," *ITAR-TASS Weekly News*, March 31, 2004.

14. "NATO Expansion Fraught with Risks," ITAR-TASS, February 9, 2007.

15. Radio Free Europe/Radio Liberty (RFE/RL), *Newsline*, January 10, 2008.

16. Ibid., November 21, 2007.

17. See the transcript of the press conference by Putin with Russian and foreign media in the Kremlin on February 1, 2007, in G. Feifer, *Foreign Dispatch*, National Public Radio, February 1, 2007. A study by the Finnish Institute of International Affairs (FIIA) warns that Helsinki could face military remonstrations near its borders by an assertive Russia if Finland were to join NATO. Although about 50 percent of Finns oppose NATO membership, there is a growing view that NATO membership would provide insurance in the face of Russian assertiveness. See RFE/RL, *Newsline*, December 12, 2007.

18. Julie Anderson, "The HUMINT Offensive from Putin's Chekist State," *International Journal of Intelligence and Counterintelligence* 20, no. 2 (June 2007): 169.

19. "NATO Spy Could Have Passed on Missile Defence, Cyber-War Secrets to Russia," *Russia News.Net*, November 17, 2008, http://www.russianews.net/ story/431133.

20. RFE/RL, *Newsline*, February 6, 2008; and Judy Dempsey, "New NATO Intelligence Chief Was Trained by KGB," *International Herald Tribune*, February 4,

2008. The main task of NATO's intelligence committee is to analyze and share intelligence from all the secret service chiefs of NATO countries.

21. Pavel K. Baev, "Moscow Lambastes West during Election Lull," *Eurasia Daily Monitor*, December 10, 2007.

22. Piadyshev, Bessmertnykh, and Shmeler, "Realpolitik from Munich," 77.

23. Check the interview with Konstantin Kosachyov, chairman of the State Duma International Affairs Committee, in Sofia Filippova, "Ukraine, Georgia Gain Nothing from Entry into NATO," *ITAR-TASS Weekly News*, September 20, 2006.

24. For an analysis of the report see Victor Yasmann, "Russia: Kremlin Sees Its Foreign-Policy Star on Rise," RFE/RL, March 21, 2007.

25. "Global Partnership," Russian Ministry of Defence, www.mil.ru/eng/1864/12075/index.shtml.

26. Vladimir Chizhov, "Russia-EU Cooperation: The Foreign Policy Dimension," *International Affairs* (Moscow) 51, no. 5 (2005): 134–38. See also Vladimir Socor, "Russia-Led Bloc Emerges in OSCE," *Eurasia Daily Monitor*, November 16, 2007. Moscow mobilized members of the CSTO to refocus the OSCE on its military-political dimension. According to Socor, "this move continues Moscow's long-standing attempts to endow the OSCE with functions that could duplicate or interfere with those of NATO and maintain a Russian-influenced grey area in Europe's East."

27. Vladimir Mukhin, "Defense Minister Ivanov's Proposal to Divide World Between NATO, ODKB Commented Report," *Nesavisimaya Gazeta*, December 4, 2004.

28. Nikolay Proskokov, "NATO Russian Style," *Vremya Novostey*, January 19, 2007.

29. "NATO Unwilling to Cooperate with CSTO for Political Reasons—Official," Interfax, March 1, 2007.

30. "NATO's Infrastructure in Europe, Asia Targeting CSTO Member States," Agentstvo Voyennykh Novostey, May 15, 2007.

31. "NATO Planes Collect Reconnaissance Data on Russia," *ITAR-TASS Weekly News*, February 19, 2004.

32. Roger McDermott, "New CSTO Military Force Planned," *Eurasia Daily Monitor*, September 22, 2008.

33. RFE/RL, *Newsline*, March 7, 2008.

34. See paragraph 23 of the "Bucharest Summit Declaration," issued by the North Atlantic Council in Bucharest on April 3, 2008, http://www.nato.int/docu/pr/2008/p08-049e.html.

35. Vladimir Socor, "Putin's 'Near Abroad' Is 'NATO's East' as Disagreement Continues," *Eurasia Daily Monitor*, April 10, 2008.

36. Vladimir Socor, "Chancellor Merkel's 'Alleingang' in Moscow Ahead of the NATO Summit," *Eurasia Daily Monitor*, March 20, 2008. Socor believes that blocking the Georgian and Ukrainian MAPs can become a precedent-setting case for a few NATO countries to block allied decisions in the perceived interest of upholding relations with Moscow, whether in business, energy, or security. See Vladimir Socor, "Is NATO Facing a Russian Veto through Franco-German Hands?" *Eurasia Daily Monitor*, March 20, 2008.

37. Viktor Volodon, "They Are Seeking Nuclear Superiority over Russia," *Vremya Novostei*, December 6, 2007.

38. Statement by Putin at a press conference in the Kremlin following talks with Greek president Karolos Papoulias, May 31, 2007, from the Russian embassy in Athens, Greece, website, www.greece.mid.ru/pol-12_e.html. See also "Deployment of U.S. ABM Sites in Europe Threat to Russia," *ITAR-TASS Daily*, March 20, 2007.

39. See "Russia, U.S. May Sign New START Treaty in Mid-2009," RIA Novosti, November 6, 2008. Since the START-1 Treaty was signed in July 1991, Russia and the United States have reduced the number of delivery vehicles to sixteen hundred each, with no more than six thousand nuclear warheads each.

40. Anca Simina, "Putin Turns His Back on Basescu," *Evenimentul Zilei*, June 28, 2007.

41. Denis Zhuikov, "The Americans Recollect the CFE Treaty," *RBC Daily*, May 28, 2007.

42. Vladimir Socor, "Russia Demands a Totally Changed Treaty on Conventional Forces in Europe," *Eurasia Daily Monitor*, June 13, 2007; and "NATO Holds Firmly at Extraordinary CFE Conference with Russia," *Eurasia Daily Monitor*, June 18, 2007.

43. In April 2007 Putin announced a moratorium on Russian observance of the CFE Treaty, and in July 2007 he signed a decree suspending Russia's participation to take effect after 150 days. Consult President Putin's "Annual Address to the Federal Assembly" (speech given at the Marble Hall in the Kremlin, April 26, 2007), http://www.kremlin.ru/eng/speeches/2007/04/26/1209_type70029type82912_125670.shtml.

44. See "Full Text of Putin's Decree to Suspend Operation of CFE Treaty," Interfax, July 14, 2007; and RFE/RL, *Newsline*, July 16, 2007. Russia's military leaders called for steps to beef up the military presence in northwestern Russia and the Caucasus, as CFE would no longer hamper Moscow.

45. RFE/RL, *Newsline*, November 8, 2007. Also consult "Reasons for Russia's Suspension of CFE Treaty Listed in Explanatory Note," RIA Novosti, July 14, 2007.

46. RFE/RL, *Newsline*, November 19, 2007.

47. Vladimir Socor, "OSCE's Year-End Conference Not Coping with Security Issues," *Eurasia Daily Monitor*, December 4, 2007.

48. Vladimir Socor, "NATO Summit Sends Ambiguous Message on Russian Troops in Moldova and Georgia," *Eurasia Daily Monitor*, April 11, 2008.

49. Bagila Bukharbayeva, "Russia Setting Up Think Tank in U.S., France to 'Expose' Flaws of Western Democracy," Associated Press, January 28, 2008. According to a founder of a Russian institute based in Paris and New York, Andranik Migranian, in Russia "civil society is not detached from state bodies," thus underscoring the Kremlin's understanding of democracy.

50. See the interview with Russia's minister of foreign affairs Sergei Lavrov in *Rossiiskaya Gazeta*, February 21 and 28, 2007.

51. Denis MacShane, "Putin's Tories: Welcome to the Vlad and Dave Show," *Spectator* (London), January 12, 2008. According to MacShane, "The Kremlin is reverting to the old Soviet line of insisting that the West's record on democracy and human rights can be criticized, but to apply the same standard to Russia amounts to external interference."

52. Sergei Ivanov, "Russia Must Be Strong," *Wall Street Journal*, January 11, 2006.
53. Conor Humphries, "Russia Test-Fires New-Generation Strategic Missile," Agence France Presse, September 18, 2008.
54. Pavel K. Baev, "Chimera of a 'New Cold War' in the Russia-U.S. Relations," NewsNet, October 2007.
55. RFE/RL, *Newsline*, August 20, 2007. On August 17, 2007, British RAF Eurofighter Typhoon aircraft intercepted a long-range Russian Tupolev Tu-95 "Bear" reconnaissance aircraft over the North Atlantic. The first indications that Russia was flexing its muscles were in May 2007, when Bears flew toward British airspace during an exercise off Scotland to spy on Royal Navy warships. RFE/RL, *Newsline*, July 18 and August 16, 20, and 27, 2007.
56. Ibid., October 2, 2007.
57. Ibid., February 1, 2008.
58. Ibid., December 6, 2007.
59. Ibid., January 23, 2008.
60. John Vinocur, "Europe's Unlikely Attempt to Renew a 'Partnership' with Russia," *International Herald Tribune*, April 21, 2008.
61. John C. K. Daly, "Russia and Its Allies Conduct Eurasian Air Defense Drill," *Eurasia Daily Monitor*, April 25, 2008.
62. RIA Novosti, July 25, 2008.
63. "Russia to Upgrade Nuclear Systems," BBC News, September 26, 2008, http://news.bbc.co.uk/go/pr/fr/-/2/hi/europe/7638356.stm.
64. For an analysis of Moscow's Arctic strategy see Pavel Baev, "Russia's Race for the Arctic and the New Geopolitics of the North Pole," *Occasional Paper* (Washington, DC: Jamestown Foundation, October 2007).
65. See the article by Russia's chief of General Staff Yuriy Baluyevskiy, "Russia Main Target of U.S. Missile Defence in Europe," *Rossiyskaya Gazeta*, May 4, 2007.
66. Major General Vladimir Belousov, "Russian Expert Details Three-Pronged Response to U.S. Missile Defence Plan," *www.utro.ru*, August 1, 2007, from BBC Monitoring International Reports, August 5, 2007.
67. Chris Baldwin, "Russia Long-Range Missile Test a Success," Reuters, August 28, 2008.
68. Oleg Shchedrov, "Russia Test-Fires Ballistic Missile to Mid-Pacific," Reuters, October 11, 2008.
69. Yevgeny Primakov, "Does Europe Need Protection?" *Moscow News Weekly*, July 19, 2007.
70. Russia reported successfully testing an RS-24 multiple-warhead ballistic missile in December 2007. This is intended to replace the RS-18 and RS-20 multiple-warhead missiles (known as the SS-19 and SS-20, respectively) and, together with the single warhead RS-12M2 Topol-M (SS-27) truck-mounted missile, will form the core of Russia's Strategic Missile Forces. See RFE/RL, *Newsline*, December 6, 2007; and Luke Harding, "Russia Threatening New Cold War over Missile Defence," *Guardian*, April 11, 2007.
71. "Yuriy Baluyevskiy, Chief of General Staff Says Russia 'Main Target' of U.S. Missile Defense in Europe," *BBC Monitoring*, May 4, 2007.

72. Viktor Litovkin, "Abroad: NATO Advances to Russian Borders," *Moscow News*, April 7, 2004.
73. "Europe's Space Wars," *Economist*, February 23, 2007. The *Economist* points out that "the only real damage to Russia from this episode will be self-inflicted: Mr. Putin and his generals have reminded the Czechs and the Poles, and others queuing outside the door, why they wanted to join NATO in the first place."
74. On July 6, 2007, Czech foreign minister Karel Schwarzenberg stated that Moscow's criticisms of missile defense are merely Russia's games with America and did not concern Prague. See "Moscow Plays Games with U.S.A. about Missile Shield—Czech Foreign Minister," Czech News Agency (CTK), July 6, 2007.
75. See Putin's interview with newspaper journalists from G-8 member countries on June 4, 2007, http://www.kremlin.ru/eng/speeches/2007/06/04/2149_type82916_132716.shtml.
76. Yevgeny Primakov, "Another Confrontation?" *Moscow News*, March 2, 2007.
77. Czech intelligence officers suspect that Russia's secret services are funding Europe's anti-missile defense campaign. The public relations offensive in Prague and elsewhere is supported by the advertising agency BigBoard, which is also active in Moscow and Minsk. See Petr Suchý, "Putin's Peaceniks in Prague?" *Central Europe Digest,* June 16, 2008.
78. Judy Dempsey, "Poland Seeks Equal Role in Europe: Foreign Minister Complains of EU Critics' Double Standards," *International Herald Tribune*, August 15, 2007.
79. "Lithuania Not Planning to Host MD Elements—Ministry," Interfax, May 30, 2007.
80. Viktor Yadukha, "Ukraine Is Being Readied for War with Russia," *RBC Daily*, March 14, 2007.
81. RFE/RL, *Newsline*, September 24, 2007.
82. Ibid., June 14 and July 26, 2007.
83. Dmitry Litovkin, "What Is So Dangerous about American Interceptor Missiles in Europe?" *Izvestia*, August 23, 2007.
84. RFE/RL, *Newsline*, July 16, 2007.
85. See Senator Charles Schumer, "Russia Can Be Part of the Answer on Iran," *Wall Street Journal*, June 3, 2008.
86. RFE/RL, *Newsline*, August 15, 2007. In August 2007 Austrian defense minister Norbert Darabos stated Vienna's opposition to missile defense and called the U.S. plans a provocation that rekindles Cold War debates. See RFE/RL, *Newsline*, August 23, 2007.
87. Ibid., June 15, 2007.
88. Vladimir Socor, "Russia Warns of Missile Forward-Deployment in Kaliningrad Region," *Eurasia Daily Monitor*, July 6, 2007.
89. Pavel Felgenhauer, "Two-Plus-Two Talks in Moscow Leave a Big Minus," *Eurasia Daily Monitor*, October 17, 2007.
90. RFE/RL, *Newsline*, November 14, 2007. In June 2007 President Putin and Defense Minister Ivanov threatened to target European sites with missiles if the U.S. proceeded with its program.
91. "Russia Hints Its Ready to Move Missiles to EU Border," Reuters, July 4, 2007.
92. RFE/RL, *Newsline*, December 17, 2007.

93. Ibid., December 18, 2007; and Pavel Felgenhauer, "Baluyevsky Escalates War of Words over U.S. Missile Defense," *Eurasia Daily Monitor*, December 19, 2007.
94. RFE/RL, *Newsline*, February 5, 2008.
95. Dmitry Litovkin, "Without a Cold War, but with a New Missile," Agency WPS, December 18, 2007. See also Maxim Agarkov, "New Threat," *Ekspert*, October 22–28, 2007. Agarkov welcomes a new arms race with the United States, claiming that the previous one proved fatal for the Soviet economy while the emerging one "may provide an impetus for the development of a new Russia."
96. RFE/RL, *Newsline*, April 9, 2008.
97. Pavel Felgenhauer, "Poland Is Caught between Moscow and Washington," *Eurasia Daily Monitor*, April 17, 2008.
98. Andrei Zagorski, "Russia and the U.S.: The Kabuki Dancing Over?" *EU-Russia Centre Review*, no. 8 (October 2008): 106.
99. RFE/RL, *Newsline*, March 27, 2008.
100. Ibid., April 4, 2008.
101. "U.S. and Poland Sign Defence Deal," BBC News, August 15, 2008, http://news.bbc.co.uk/go/pr/fr/-/2/hi/europe/7561926.stm; and "Russian Anger at U.S. Missile Deal," BBC News, August 15, 2008, http://news.bbc.co.uk/go/pr/fr/-/2/hi/europe/7563182.stm.
102. Conor Humphries, "Russia Test-Fires New-Generation Strategic Missile," Agence France Presse, September 18, 2008.
103. "Mr. Lavrov's Offer," *Gazeta Wyborcza*, September 11, 2008.
104. "Russia to Move Missiles to Baltic," BBC News, November 5, 2008, http://news.bbc.co.uk/2/hi/europe/7710362.stm
105. "Treaty on Conventional Armed Forces in Europe Can Be Saved—Germany," ITAR-TASS, July 15, 2007.
106. Reeba Critser, "NATO Forces Closer to Attaining C-17s," American Forces Press Service, August 13, 2008, http://www.defenselink.mil/news/newsarticle.aspx?id=50795.
107. Interview with Lieutenant General Alfred Grigoryevich Gaponenko, in "Russia Former Soviet General Says U.S. Bases in Romania Prelude to 'Resource War,'" *Vremya Novostey*, June 4, 2007.
108. "Poland Wants NATO to Investigate Russia's Air Defence Bases in Belarus," PAP, November 24, 2006. In September 2005 Moscow and Minsk signed an agreement on deliveries of S-300 antiaircraft missile systems. The missiles were deployed near the Polish border. See "Russia, Belarus to Sign New Defense Deal," UPI, November 22, 2006.
109. "Belarus, Russia Stall on Union State Construction—Lukashenko," ITAR-TASS, March 28, 2007.
110. Vladimir Mukhin, "More on Brest Defense Summit: Ministers Cited on Russia-Belarus Air Defense," *Nezavisimaya Gazeta*, November 23, 2006.
111. Vladimir Socor, "Moscow Confronts the West over CFE Treaty at OSCE," *Eurasia Daily Monitor*, May 25, 2007.

Chapter 4. Dominating Europe: Former Empire

1. Svante E. Cornell, Johanna Popjanevski, and Niklas Nilsson, *Russia's War in Georgia: Causes and Implications for Georgia and the World*, Policy Paper

(Washington, DC: Central Asia-Caucasus Institute and Silk Road Studies Program, August 2008), 31.

2. According to a Russian analyst quoted in Carol R. Saivetz, "Making the Best of a Bad Hand: An Assessment of Current Trends in Russian Foreign Policy," *Post-Soviet Affairs* 22, no. 2 (2006): 170.

3. See "The Foreign Policy Concept of the Russian Federation," President of Russia Official Web Portal, July 12, 2008, http://www.kremlin.ru/eng/text/docs/2008/07/204750.shtml. Among the euphemisms justifying Moscow's imperial dominance, according to Graham, the "near abroad" occupies a "special place" in the "Russian psyche" and this emotional yearning needs to be "accommodated." See Graham, "U.S.-Russia Relations: Facing Reality Pragmatically," 12.

4. Wolfgang Gerke and P. S. Zolotarev, "Russian-German Relations in the Context of Global Politics," *International Affairs* 53, no. 3 (2007): 90.

5. Leonard and Popescu, "A Power Audit of EU-Russia Relations," 1.

6. Russia's leaders claim that Russia and its post-Soviet neighbors are "united by centuries of historical, cultural, and economic ties." Putin used this phrase in addressing Russia's Federal Assembly in May 2003. Check de Wilde and Pellon, "The Implications of the European Neighbourhood Policy (ENP) on the EU-Russian 'Strategic Partnership,'" 127. In reality, Russia and its neighbors are "united" by centuries of conflict, conquest, colonialism, and Russification, with a twentieth-century veneer of communist totalitarianism and Soviet imperialism. Moscow flexes its neo-imperial muscle through a language campaign designed to promote Russian as the lingua franca throughout CIS and undermine pro-Western governments intent on reestablishing their national identity and language after years of official Russification. Only Belarus currently recognizes Russian as a state language. See Roman Kupchinsky, "The Russian Language in Ukraine—Resurrecting the Past," *Eurasia Daily Monitor*, June 24, 2008.

7. Rainer Lindner, "New Realism: The Making of Russia's Foreign Policy in the Post-Soviet World," *EU-Russia Centre Review*, no. 8 (October 2008): 30.

8. See James Sherr, "Russia and the 'Near Abroad,' in a Medvedev Presidency," in *Russia after Putin*, 28–29.

9. "Russian Ambassador Plays Down Impact of Ukrainian NATO Membership," Interfax, June 8, 2002.

10. "Russian Ambassador: We Will Not Allow U.S. Presence in Caspian," *Baku Today*, June 12, 2003; Stephen Blank, "Central Asia's Great Base Race," *Asia Times Online*, December 19, 2003, http://www.atimes.com/atimes/Central_Asia/EL19Ag01.html.

11. See "Putin Welcomes Ukraine's EU Bid, Criticizes Bid to Join NATO," ITAR-TASS, June 3, 2007; and "Russia Cannot Be Indifferent to Ukraine Joining NATO," ITAR-TASS, June 4, 2007.

12. Valery Rzhevsky, "Crimeans Rally against NATO in Simferopol," ITAR-TASS, December 16, 2006.

13. Jakob Hedenskog and Robert L. Larsson, "Russian Leverage on the CIS and the Baltic States," Defence Analysis (Stockholm: Swedish Defence Research Agency (FOI), June 2007), 95–96.

14. RFE/RL, *Newsline*, January 24, 2008.

15. For a summary of official threats to the territorial integrity of neighbors see

Vladimir Socor, "Moscow Makes Furious but Empty Threats to Georgia and Ukraine," *Eurasia Daily Monitor*, April 14, 2008.

16. Vladimir Socor, "Russia Setting Up 'Collective Peacekeeping' Forces," *Eurasia Daily Monitor*, October 3, 2007. The mandate of Russia's peacekeeping troops in Abkhazia is automatically prolonged each year by the CIS, even though the CIS is not recognized as a full-fledged international organization and cannot authorize peacekeeping missions. The Russian operation in Abkhazia has no mandate and is purely Russian in its composition. In Transnistria, Russian troops do not benefit from a CIS mandate.

17. See the Constitution of the Russian Federation, http://www.constitution.ru/.

18. Gregory Gleason, "Uzbekistan Charts a New 'Uzbek Path,'" *Eurasia Daily Monitor*, November 21, 2008.

19. Khadija Ismailova and Shahin Abbasov, "GUAM: New Life, New Identity," *Transitions Online*, May 29, 2006, http://www.tol.cz/look/TOL/article.tpl?IdLanguage=1&IdPublication=4&NrIssue=168&NrSection=4&NrArticle=17200. Russian officials condemned the renamed GUAM as the creation of an "anti-CIS." See Sergei Sidorenko and Vladimir Solovyov, "GUAM Puts an End to Its Post-Soviet Past," *Kommersant*, May 24, 2006.

20. Vladimir Socor, "Two Meetings, Two Tones in GUAM," *Eurasia Daily Monitor*, October 20, 2006.

21. See the interview with Vladimir Voronin in *Kommersant*, March 11, 2008. Voronin reportedly wants Moldova's neutrality guaranteed by the EU, the United States, Russia, OSCE, and Ukraine.

22. Vitaliy Martyniuk, "The GUAM after Batumi: A Path to Changes but Which Ones?" *UCIPR Research Update* 14, no. 25/543 (July 12, 2008), http://www.ucipr.kiev.ua/modules.php?op=modload&name=News&file=article&sid=6032521.

23. Jean-Christophe Peuch, "Ukraine: Regional Leaders Set Up Community of Democratic Choice," *Newsline*, December 2, 2005. Kremlin adviser Gelb Pavlovskii described CDC as an overtly pro-American organization that would "serve as an antechamber for Ukraine to join NATO." The CDC was formally established by nine states: Estonia, Georgia, Lithuania, Latvia, Macedonia, Moldova, Romania, Slovenia, and Ukraine, with the EU and the United States as observers.

24. Stephen Blank, "Russia Versus NATO in the CSIS," *In Focus* (RFE/RL), 2008.

25. "Transdniestra Has Long Road Ahead to Integration with Russia—Minister," *Russia & CIS General Newswire*, September 19, 2006. Reportedly, more than 97 percent of voters supported independence and integration into Russia in a referendum conducted in Transnistria in September 2006. See "Moldova's Breakaway Transdniestra Says 'Yes' to Independence," *SeeNews*, September 18, 2006. (Russian spelling of Transnistria.)

26. See Chloe Bruce, "Power Resources: The Political Agenda in Russo-Moldovan Gas Relations," *Problems of Post-Communism* 54, no. 3 (May–June 2007): 29–47.

27. Vladimir Socor, "Putin-Voronin Farewell: An Anti-Climactic Coda," *Eurasia Daily Monitor*, January 25, 2008.

28. "Russia Proposes Suspending New Customs Rules for Transdniestra," *Russia & CIS General Newswire*, March 20, 2006.

29. Vladimir Socor, "Russia Doubling Its Troops in Georgia's Abkhazia Region," *Eurasia Daily Monitor*, May 5, 2008. Russia's troop presence in Moldova and Georgia fails to qualify as a genuine peacekeeping force: it does not have the consent of the state on whose territory it is deployed; it is composed of units from a neighboring country that has a direct stake in the conflict; it is not international but monopolized by Moscow; and it does not abide by the principles of inviolability of borders and noninterference in the internal affairs of the country in which it is deployed. Indeed, the military invasion in August 2008 underscored that Russia cannot be an impartial peacekeeper in Georgia.

30. See Sergei Blagov, "Armenia Seeks Stronger Ties with Russia," *Eurasia Insight*, March 27, 2008, http://www.eurasianet.org/departments/insight/articles/eav032708a.shtml.

31. Haroutiun Khachatrian, "Armenia: Presidential Visit to Russia Sparks Speculation on Turkish-Armenian Relations," *Eurasia Insight*, June 27, 2008, http://www.eurasianet.org/departments/insight/articles/eav062708a.shtml.

32. Maxim Ryzhkov, "Ukraine, Georgia Joining NATO to Affect Relations with Russia," ITAR-TASS, July 6, 2006; and "Ukraine's NATO Entry Will Complicate Ties with Russia," RIA Novosti, December 7, 2006.

33. Oleg Shchedrov, "Russia's Medvedev Warns Ukraine on NATO Bid," Reuters, June 6, 2008.

34. RFE/RL, *Newsline*, October 12, 2007.

35. Russian officials deny that the Soviet government engineered a mass famine in Ukraine in 1932–33 in order to destroy the Ukrainian peasantry and Ukraine's nationhood. Several million Ukrainians perished in the Holodomor as a result of forced grain requisitions. Admitting that Moscow sought to exterminate Ukrainians as a nation would evidently undermine the "Slavic bonds" that Russian propaganda promulgates to keep Ukraine tethered to Moscow. Each year Russian officials prevent the UN from recognizing the Holodomor as an act of genocide. In this way, they avoid admitting that the Russian Federation is the inheritor of a state (USSR) that perpetrated genocide and should be held responsible for appropriate reparations.

36. Roman Kupchinsky, "Sub-Rosa Warfare in the Crimea," *Eurasia Daily Monitor,* July 25, 2008.

37. Jan Maksymiuk, "Is Ukraine Prepared to Maintain Its Tough Stand against Russia?" RFE/RL, August 15, 2008.

38. Nikolay Filchenko, "Foreign Ministry Attempts to Improve Relations with Moldova," *Kommersant*, October 11, 2006.

39. Vlad Spânu, "Russia Prepares to Deliver a Knockout Punch to the Moldovan Economy" (Washington, DC: Moldova Foundation, August 1, 2007), http://www.foundation.moldova.org/news/eng/69.

40. For a full report see "Moldova's Uncertain Future," *Europe Report* no. 175 (Chisinau: International Crisis Group, August 17, 2006), http://www.crisisgroup.org/home/index.cfm?id=43408&l=1. Russia's embargo in March 2006 led to a major economic slump in Moldova, with industrial manufacturing declining by almost 7 percent over seven months. See Aleksey Daryin, "Ban on Imports of Moldovan Wine May Lead to a Budget Crisis," *Kommersant*, August 22, 2006.

41. Vladimir Socor, "Russia in Moldova: A Counter-Example to Ukraine and Georgia?" *Eurasia Daily Monitor*, September 26, 2008.

42. Dmitri Trenin, "The Georgian-Russian Crisis: Objectives, Strategies, and Outcomes" (Moscow: Carnegie Endowment, October 13, 2006), http://www.carnegie endowment.org/publications/index.cfm?fa=view&id=18786&prog=zru; and Sergei Markedonov, "The Paradoxes of Russia's Georgia Policy," *Russia in Global Affairs* 5, no. 2 (April–June 2007): 173–87. For a more official Russian analysis, projecting Moscow's own imperial ambitions onto Georgian policy, see Andranik Migranyan, "Georgia Propelling Its Disintegration," *Russia in Global Affairs* 2, no. 4 (October–December 2004): 118–25.

43. For examples of the EU's studious avoidance of confrontation with Russia see Vladimir Socor, "Euroappeasement: The EU's Answer to Russia's Assault on Georgia," *Eurasia Daily Monitor*, June 4, 2008.

44. According to Russia's deputy foreign minister, Grigory Karasin, in "Russia Alarmed by Prospect of Georgia's NATO Membership," RIA Novosti, April 23, 2007.

45. See Kakha Jibladze, "Russia's Opposition to Georgia's Quest for NATO Membership," *China and Eurasia Forum Quarterly* 5, no. 1 (2007): 45–51.

46. "NATO-Georgia Dialogue Causes Tension with Russia—Official," *ITAR-TASS Daily*, October 16, 2006.

47. Vladimir Soloviov, Olga Allenova, Vladimir Novikov, Vadim Tokhsyrov, "Obliged to Go to War," *Kommersant*, July 18, 2006. In March 2006 Prime Minister Mikhail Fradkov's office informed a joint session of leaders from South and North Ossetia that the federal government had agreed in principle to incorporate South Ossetia in the Russian Federation. See Simon Saradzhyan, "Russia Sees Kosovo as the Answer," *Moscow Times*, March 29, 2006.

48. Dmitri Trenin, *Toward a New Euro-Atlantic "Hard" Security Agenda: Prospects for Trilateral U.S.-EU-Russia Cooperation* (Washington, DC: Center for Strategic and International Studies, July 2008), 9.

49. "Russia Recognizes Georgian Rebels," BBC News, August 26, 2008.

50. See "Russia to Continue Work on Union State with Belarus," RIA Novosti, February 1, 2007.

51. "Belarus Votes, Hopes for Better Ties with West," Reuters, September 28, 2008.

52. A proposal made by Kremlin insider Sergei Markov, reported in Nicu Popescu, Mark Leonard, and Andrew Wilson, "Can the EU Win the Peace in Georgia?" (London: European Council on Foreign Relations, August 2008), 3.

53. "Czechs Say Russian Spies Stir against U.S. Base," Reuters, September 25, 2008.

54. Nataliya Smorodinskaya, "Motives behind Russian Foreign Policy," *EU-Russia Centre Review*, no. 8 (October 2008): 42–43.

55. A. Wess Mitchell, *The Mice That Roared: How Small Powers Are Reacting to, and Shaping, the Transition to Multipolarity* (Washington, DC: Center for European Policy Analysis, July 10, 2008).

56. Quoted in Ryan Miller, "Lithuanian Politics with a Russian Flavor?" *Central Europe Digest,* October 1, 2008.

57. "Latvian Government Resigns," *Stratfor*, December 5, 2007, http://www.stratfor. com/memberships/106210/sitrep/latvia_government_resigns.

58. Stephen Blank, "Web War I: Is Europe's First Information War a New Kind of War?" *Comparative Strategy* 27, no. 3 (May 2008): 1. For instance, in Poland in 2004 a government commission concluded that Russian agents were instrumental in subverting official agencies to sell Polish energy assets to Russian companies.

59. Viorica Marin, "Russia Wants Both Balkans and Black Sea—That Announcement Was Made by President Putin at the BSEC Summit in Istanbul," *Adevarul*, June 27, 2007.

60. Anca Simina, "Putin Turns His Back on Basescu," *Evenimentul Zilei*, June 28, 2007.

61. For details on Russia's policy of subverting the CEE states, see Janusz Bugajski, *Cold Peace: Russia's New Imperialism* (Westport, CT: Praeger, 2004).

62. RFE/RL, *Newsline*, May 23, 2007.

63. Nadezhda Arbatova, "Russia-EU Quandary 2007," *Russia in Global Affairs* 4, no. 2 (April–June 2006): 100–111.

64. According to Russia's defense minister, Sergei Ivanov, ITAR-TASS, February 9, 2007. Under Putin, Russia has reanimated the glorification of the Red Army in its supposed liberation of Eastern Europe during World War II. It has remained silent on the wartime collaboration between Hitler and Stalin to carve up Europe as well as the wide-scale repression that the Red Army brought in its wake as it forcefully occupied half of Europe, murdered or deported tens of thousands of democrats and anticommunists, and imposed the Communist system on Moscow's satellites. Soviet policies retarded the economic and political development of half of Europe for over forty years.

65. Matti Huuhtanen, "Russia, EU Face Fractious Talks; Putin Defends Ban on Meat Imports from EU," Associated Press, November 23, 2006.

66. Anna Smolchenko, "Europe Scolds a Bristling Putin," *Moscow Times*, May 21, 2007.

67. "Removal of War Monument Was Estonia's Way to Show Independence—Premier," Interfax, May 16, 2007.

68. "EU, NATO Build Pressure on Russia in Estonia Row," Agence France Presse, May 3, 2007. According to Russia's permanent representative at the OSCE Aleksey Borodavkin, "the blasphemy committed in Estonia will certainly affect Russia's relations with the EU and NATO." See "Envoy Says Estonia Events May Affect Russia's Relations with EU, NATO," RIA Novosti, May 3, 2007.

69. RFE/RL, *Newsline*, November 15, 2007.

70. Kyrill Dissanayake, "Analysis: Estonia Accuses Russia over Cyber-Attacks," *BBC Worldwide Monitoring*, May 17, 2007.

71. "Estonia Protests to Russia over Airspace Violation," Agence France Presse, June 20, 2007.

72. Lyudmila Aleksandrova, "NATO Expansion Harbours Threat to Russia Security—MP," *ITAR-TASS Weekly News*, March 20, 2004. Baltic and EU officials point out that the Baltic countries will accede to the CFE Treaty once Russia has fulfilled its obligations under the Istanbul Agreement by pulling its troops out of Georgia and Moldova.

73. RFE/RL, *Newsline*, January 22, 2008.

74. Ibid., October 11, 2007.

75. Ibid., October 3, 2007.

76. Information provided to the author by an Estonian government source in September 2008.

77. See the comments by Vladimir Chizhov, Russia's ambassador to the EU in M & K, "The Wedge of Eastern Europe: Friendly Mood and Difficult Atmosphere for the Russia-EU Summit," *Kommersant*, May 24, 2006. According to a GlobScan survey, positive perceptions of Russia have dropped substantially in Western Europe in recent years. In 2005 positive ratings fell from 38 to 22 percent in Italy, from 38 to 27 percent in Britain, and from 30 to 21 percent in France. The figures were compiled before the energy question gained prominence in perceptions of Russia's misbehavior.

78. Russia's import ban on Polish meat products cost Warsaw about $513 million annually and convinced the government to veto talks on a revived EU-Russia treaty. Robert Wielaard, "Poland Claims Support from Partners in Import Ban Standoff with Russia; EU Offers to Mediate," Associated Press, November 20, 2006.

Chapter 5. Dividing Europe: European Union

1. Gerke and Zolotarev, "Russian-German Relations in the Context of Global Politics," 82.

2. The Kremlin does not need to be actively divisive when EU governments adopt contradictory positions toward Russia. The EU displayed disarray over Russia's widely criticized parliamentary elections in December 2007, when French president Sarkozy and Italian prime minister Prodi congratulated Putin on his victory. Their gesture put them at odds with several other EU governments, which questioned the legitimacy of the ballot. The EU's Portuguese presidency issued a mild rebuke over the conduct of Russia's elections. See RFE/RL, *Newsline*, December 5, 2007.

3. Ibid., May 22, 2007. On May 21, 2007, the Gazprom-owned daily *Izvestia* wrote that older EU members needed to rein in the newer ones in their relations with Russia. According to officials, threats to the EU's energy security emanate from CEE as the new members allegedly place their own national interests ahead of EU interests.

4. Ibid., April 25, 2007.

5. Ibid., October 25, 2007.

6. Ibid., May 18, 2007.

7. Eyal, "European Appeasement Will Worsen Russian Aggression."

8. For a recent study of CEE approaches toward Russia and the European CIS see Janusz Bugajski, *The Eastern Dimension of America's New European Allies*, Strategic Studies Institute Monograph (Carlisle, PA: U.S. Army War College, October 2007).

9. Hedenskog and Larsson, "Russian Leverage on the CIS and the Baltic States," 116.

10. Vitaliy Martyniuk, "The East European Union: Developing a New Format of the EU Policy in the East," *Research Update* (Ukrainian Center for Independent Political Research) 14, no.18/536 (May 26, 2008).

11. Based on the author's private conversations with EU officials in Brussels in December 2007.

12. RFE/RL, *Newsline*, October 29 and 30, 2007, and January 14, 2008.

13. For discussion on the Eastern Partnership proposal see Vitaliy Martyniuk, "The EU Membership Prospects of Ukraine in View of French EU Presidency," *Research Update* (Ukrainian Center for Independent Political Research) 14, no. 19/537 (June 2, 2008).

14. Daniel Grotzky and Mirela Isic, *The Black Sea Region: Clashing Identities and Risks to European Stability*, CAP Policy Analysis no. 4 (Munich: Center for Applied Policy Research, October 2008), 5.

15. RFE/RL, *Newsline*, July 20, 2007.

16. Ibid., November 9, 2007.

17. Check Ivan Krastev, *The Crisis of the Post–Cold War European Order*, Brussels Forum Paper Series (Washington, DC: German Marshall Fund of the United States, March 2008), 3.

18. "Russia Sees Germany, France as Partners in European Security," ITAR-TASS, August 29, 2004.

19. Alexander Rahr, "Germany and Russia: A Special Relationship," *Washington Quarterly* 30, no. 2 (Spring 2007): 137.

20. "Russian Deputy Foreign Minister Titov on Cooperation with Germany," *Rossiyskaya Gazeta*, April 27, 2006. For its part, Germany's Foreign Office website entry for the Russian Federation declares that Germany "supports the process of transition in Russia." Unfortunately, it fails to specify what Russia is transitioning toward. See http://www.auswaertiges-amt.de/diplo/en/Laenderinformationen/01.

21. For some examples of Russia's PR toward Germany see Aksel Lebahn, "Russia Is Here Again!" *International Affairs* (Moscow) 53, no. 2 (2007): 22–35; and I. Maksimychev, "Russo-German Relations: What Will Tomorrow Bring?" *International Affairs* (Moscow) 51, no. 5 (2005): 102–10.

22. Gerke and Zolotarev, "Russian-German Relations in the Context of Global Politics," 87.

23. For an analysis of the Putin-Schroeder relationship consult Michael Thumann, "Russia and Germany, Schroeder and Putin—Cabinet Diplomacy 21st Century Style," *Conference Papers* (Washington, DC: German Marshall Fund of the United States, June 30, 2005).

24. According to a letter to the editor authored by Chancellor Schroeder in *Die Zeit*, April 5, 2001.

25. Graham Timmins, "German *Ostpolitik* under the Red-Green Coalition and EU-Russian Relations," *Debatte: Journal of Contemporary Central and Eastern Europe* 14, no. 3 (December 2006): 301–14.

26. Ryan Miller, "Germany's Baltic Betrayal," *Central European Digest*, July 15, 2008.

27. Igor Deyev, "Russia One of Germany's Largest Foreign Trade Partners," ITAR-TASS, October 6, 2006; and "Spokesman Says Pipeline Project High on List of Russia, Germany Priorities," ITAR-TASS, January 16, 2006.

28. Pavel K. Baev, "The Post-War Trajectory of Russia-EU Non-Partnership," *Eurasia Daily Monitor*, September 3, 2008. Baev also points out that the EU is dependent on exports to the growing Russian market; hence, "any shift by Russia toward Chinese or Indian producers threatens to push its manufacturing sector into recession. Minor quarrels about Polish beef or timber to Finland indicate

that European states are awakening to this deepening dependency but have no answer to the massive exposure of their business interests to the risks of Kremlin economic policy, which often is selective and vindictive."

29. Mike Eckel, "Russia, European Union Reach Agreement on Meat Imports after January 1," Associated Press, December 19, 2006.
30. See the article by Vladimir Putin, "Gerhard Schoeder and International Politics," *Vorwaerts*, November 30, 2005.
31. Vladimir Socor, "From Schroeder to Stoiber?" *Eurasia Daily Monitor*, July 9, 2007.
32. "Germany Backs Russia's NMD Initiatives," Interfax-AVN, July 6, 2007.
33. Paul Ames, "Solana: Nations Free to Join U.S. Anti-Missile Program, No EU Plans to Participate," Associated Press, March 1, 2007. Solana confirmed that EU members were free to join the U.S. missile defense system, but the EU as a bloc had no intention of joining.
34. Yevgeny Grigoryev, "Moscow and Berlin Agreed on a Visit of Medvedev," *Nezavisimaya Gazeta*, May 16, 2008.
35. "Russian President Proposes New Comprehensive European Security Pact," *VOA News*, June 5, 2008, http://www.voanews.com/english/2008-06-05-voa24.cfm.
36. Andrei Fedyashin, "When Will the West Answer Medvedev?" *Moscow News*, June 10, 2008.
37. Pavel K. Baev, "Russia and Germany Restart Their Special Partnership," *Eurasia Daily Monitor*, October 6, 2008.
38. Thomas Gomart, "France's Russia Policy: Balancing Interests and Values," *Washington Quarterly* 30, no. 2 (Spring 2007): 147.
39. Martin Walker, "Russia v. Europe: The Energy Wars," *World Policy Journal* 24, no. 1 (Spring 2007): 2.
40. See Natalie Nougayrede, "New Franco-Russian Dialogue," *Le Monde* (Internet Version), June 6, 2006, http://www.lemonde.fr/cgi-bin/ACHATS/acheter.cgi?offre=ARCHIVES&type_item=ART_ARCH_30J&objet_id=992100.
41. Rossiya TV, May 21, 2008; and RIA Novosti, May 21, 2008.
42. Michael Emerson, "Time for a Strategic Bargain with Russia," *CEPS European Neighborhood Watch*, no. 38 (May 2008).
43. David Brunnstrom, "NATO Says Still Backs Plan for U.S. Missile Shield," Reuters, November 17, 2008. Under French direction, the EU also decided to resume negotiations on a new PCA with Russia.
44. Anna Arutunyan, "Russia Stands Firm," *Moscow News*, July 26, 2007.
45. RFE/RL, *Newsline*, July 18, 2007.
46. *Times* (London), July 18, 2007.
47. RFE/RL, *Newsline*, November 6, 2007.
48. http://www.timesonline.co.uk/tol/news/uk/crime/article4265569.ace.
49. RFE/RL, *Newsline*, November 13, 2007.
50. Ibid., October 10, 2007.
51. Ibid., December 17, 2007.
52. Ibid., January 18, 2008.
53. BP subsequently pulled its last technical specialists out of Russia. Peter Sutherland, chairman of BP, said that AAR's actions were doing "enormous damage" to Russia's reputation as a place to do business. Lord George Robertson, deputy

chairman of TNK-BP, asserted that the behavior of AAR was outrageous: "AAR's efforts to wrest control of the company through illegitimate means are damaging the company and, regrettably, Russia's reputation among international investors." "Boss of BP Russia Venture Leaves," BBC News, July 24, 2008, http://news.bbc. co.uk/go/pr/fr/-/2/hi/business/7524153.stm.

54. See MacShane, "Putin's Tories."
55. RFE/RL, *Newsline*, April 18, 2008.
56. "Italo-Russian Relations," Ministry of Foreign Affairs, Rome, http://www.esteri. it/MAE/EN/Politica_Estera/Aree_Geografiche/Europa/I_nuovi_rapporti.htm.
57. RFE/RL, *Newsline*, April 29, 2008.
58. Leonard and Popescu, *A Power Audit of EU-Russia Relations*, 28.
59. Christos Ringas, "Pipeline Deal Highlights Greece's Complex Regional Role," *Southeast European Times*, June 2, 2008.
60. See Boris Maiorskii, "Spain: Cervantes in Moscow," *International Affairs* 48, no. 3 (2002): 167.
61. Valery Shliamin, "Finland: Solving Problems Together," *International Affairs* 50, no. 1 (2007): 79–84.
62. "Russian Democracy Will Head Westwards—Finnish Minister in Prague," CTK National News Wire, May 13, 2008.
63. "German Foreign Minister Upbeat on New Russian Leader," Agence France Presse, March 28, 2008.
64. For a valuable analysis see Ariel Cohen, *The New Cold War: Reviving the U.S. Presence in the Arctic*, Backgrounder no. 2202 (Washington, DC: Heritage Foundation, October 30, 2008).
65. "Security Council of the Russian Federation on Russia's Interests in the Arctic," *EastWeek*, no. 30 (139) (September 24, 2008): 4–5. The Security Council adopted a concept document titled "Assumptions of State Policy in the Arctic to 2020 and Beyond." It states that Russia will seek to develop the natural resources of the region, which is expected to become Russia's key resource base in the twenty-first century.
66. Consult O. Nordsletten, "Norway and Russia: Development of Cooperation," *Military Thought* 10, no. 6 (November 2001): 64–69.

Chapter 6. Energy as Strategy

1. Marat Khairullin, Dmitry Balburov, and Nikolai Vardul, "The Art of Concentrating Forces into a Spearpoint Formation," *Gazeta*, February 7, 2006.
2. "Russia Challenges the World Economic System," *People's Daily Online*, June 18, 2007, http://english.people.com.cn/200706/18/eng20070618_385261.html.
3. For details on existing and planned energy transportation routes see Robert Pirog, "Russian Oil and Gas Challenges," *Connections: The Quarterly Journal* 6, no. 3 (Fall 2007): 82–99.
4. Marshall I. Goldman, "The New Imperial Russia," *Demokratizatsia* 16 (Winter 2008): 10.
5. Anderson, "The HUMINT Offensive from Putin's Chekist State," 271. According to Anderson, KGB officers made an easy transition to businessmen while retaining their "active service" status under a commercial cover (p. 274).

6. Russia possesses about 28 percent of the world's natural gas reserves. For a useful overview of Gazprom see Steve Thomas, "Gazprom: Profile" (London: Public Services International Business Unit (PSIRU), Business School, University of Greenwich, May 2006).

7. According to Nelli Sharushkina of the Moscow Office of the Energy Intelligence Group, quoted in Vladimir Kovalev, "Power Play," *Transitions Online*, March 6, 2007, http://www.tol.cz/look/TOL/article.tpl?IdLanguage=1&IdPublication=4&NrIssue=208&NrSection=4&NrArticle=18379.

8. Tobias Buck and Neil Buckley, "Russian Parliament Vote Backs Gazprom Export Monopoly," *Financial Times*, June 16, 2006.

9. Gazprom has become a state within a state and is able to deploy its own security units to protect its overseas holdings. See Carl Mortished, "Gazprom to Raise Its Own Private Army to Protect Oil Installations," *Times* (London), July 6, 2007.

10. Moscow is greatly reliant on profits from its European operations. Energy sales to the EU account for nearly 50 percent of the Russian federal budget, while Gazprom depends on the EU market for 70 percent of its earnings. The figures are supplied in Roberts, *Russia and the European Union*, 59. In contrast, by 2006 U.S. petroleum imports from Russia amounted to only 3 percent of the total.

11. For a listing of EU members' dependence on gas supplies from Russia, see Andreas Heinrich, "Gazprom's Expansion Strategy in Europe and the Liberalization of EU Energy Markets," *Russian Analytical Digest*, no. 34 (February 2008): 15.

12. See Benita Ferrero-Waldner, "The European Union and Russia—Future Prospects," *Salzburg Global Seminar—Russia: The 2020 Perspective* (Salzburg, April 6, 2008).

13. Carol R. Saivetz, "Making the Best of a Bad Hand: An Assessment of Current Trends in Russian Foreign Policy," *Post-Soviet Affairs* 22, no. 2 (2006): 183.

14. Hedenskog and Larsson, "Russian Leverage on the CIS and the Baltic States," 7–9. The authors believe that Moscow has tactical goals rather than strategic objectives, which they confusingly claim are "*ad hoc* based and only loosely fitting Russia's explicit priorities." Such an analysis views Russian state priorities through a Western prism and not a Kremlin perspective.

15. RFE/RL, *Newsline*, April 19, 2007.

16. J. Michael McConnell, *Annual Threat Assessment of the Intelligence Community for the Senate Armed Services Committee* (Washington, DC, February 27, 2008).

17. See Kovalev, "Power Play."

18. According to Fedun, "in the oil-rich region of Western Siberia, the mainstay of Russian output, the period of intense oil production is over." See RFE/RL, *Newsline*, April 16, 2008.

19. "Russia Bears Its Military Teeth," BBC News, October 2, 2003, http://news.bbc.co.uk/2/hi/europe/3159044.stm.

20. Vladimir Socor, "Russian Energy Policy and Strategy in Europe" (speech given at the Center for Strategic and International Studies, Washington, DC, April 21, 2008). According to some analysts, Russia is unlikely to favor the creation of an international gas cartel similar to OPEC as it may not be able to dictate its policies and would not be willing to abide by its exporting decisions. For precisely these reasons, Russia has refused to join OPEC. See Goldman, *Petrostate*, 164–69.

21. See Ariel Cohen, "OPEC Redux: Responding to the Russian–Iranian Gas Cartel," WebMemo #2118 (Washington, DC: Heritage Foundation, October 27, 2008). On October 21, 2008, in Tehran, the Gas Exporting Countries Forum (GECF), including Russia, Iran, and Qatar, agreed to form a grouping to "coordinate gas policy." The Group of Three is due to meet quarterly to coordinate control over two-thirds of the world's gas reserves and a quarter of all gas production. Iran has the second-largest gas reserves in the world after Russia, and the two together control about half of global gas reserves. They plan to divide consumer markets, including those in Europe, between them by agreeing on export volumes, delivery schedules, gas field development, and construction of new pipelines. The new grouping would provide Moscow and Tehran with significant geopolitical advantage over smaller gas suppliers, such as Azerbaijan, Turkmenistan, Kazakhstan, and Uzbekistan.

22. Robert L. Larsson, *Nord Stream, Sweden, and Baltic Sea Security*, Defense Analysis (Stockholm: Swedish Defence Research Agency (FOI), March 2007), 78–81, http://www.foi.se/upload/english/reports/foir2251.pdf. Goldman points out that Moscow has not hesitated to cut energy supplies to "strengthen its side of a political dispute, a practice it inherited from its forebears in the Soviet Union's Ministry of the Gas Industry and Ministry of the Petroleum Industry." See Goldman, *Petrostate*, 3.

23. Vladimir Socor, "Moscow Forcing Czech Republic to Guess as to Reasons Behind Oil Supply Cut," *Eurasia Daily Monitor*, July 28, 2008.

24. "Russia Looks to Cut Oil Output in Dispute," Reuters, January 9, 2007.

25. Vladimir Socor, "Russia Cuts Oil Supplies to Czech Republic without Explanation," *Eurasia Daily Monitor*, July 15, 2008. The cut may also be related to Moscow's strategic decision to shift a large part of the oil volume from the westbound Druzhba pipeline into the northbound Baltic Pipeline System, for shipment onward by tankers and bypassing the three Baltic states. This shift, planned to occur over the next few years, will increase the vulnerability of all CEE countries along the Druzhba system.

26. Vladimir Socor, "Gazprom Threatens to Reduce Supplies to Ukraine," *Eurasia Daily Monitor*, October 4, 2007. According to Socor, the procedure was as follows: "Gazprom, monopoly buyer of Turkmen gas for Ukraine, sells those volumes to Gazprom's proxy RosUkrEnergo, the monopoly intermediary between Gazprom and Ukraine. RosUkrEnergo sells that gas at the Ukrainian border to its proxy within Ukraine, UkrGazEnergo, a parity joint venture of RosUkrEnergo with Gazprom-friendly elements in Naftohaz and other Ukrainian offices. These arrangements have drastically cut Naftohaz's income while enriching Gazprom's proxies in Ukraine. Moreover, transit and storage service fees for Russian gas passing through Ukraine westward were fixed at deeply discounted levels, thus cutting Naftohaz's income even further."

27. BBC Monitoring International Reports, 5 Kanal TV, Kyiv, September 27, 2007.

28. RFE/RL, *Newsline*, February 8, 2008.

29. Vladimir Socor, "Trans-Black Pipeline: Another Chance for Georgia and Europe," *Eurasia Daily Monitor*, February 1, 2008.

30. "Moldovan President Says Satisfied with Gas Accords with Russia," RIA Novosti, June 22, 2007.

31. "Gazprom Considers Dividing Gas Contract with Moldova, Transdniestra (Part 2)," *Russia & CIS General Newswire*, March 2, 2007.
32. Vladimir Socor, "Shortfalls in Russian Oil Deliveries to Germany," *Eurasia Daily Monitor*, September 5, 2007; and "Lukoil Reduces Oil Supplies to Germany, Again," *Eurasia Daily Monitor*, February 20, 2008.
33. RFE/RL, *Newsline*, August 29 and 31, 2007.
34. Nord Stream's chief executive officer, Matthias Warnig, is the head of Germany's Dresdner Bank in Russia, a former senior officer in the German Democratic Republic's (GDR) Stasi secret police, and Putin's comrade when the latter worked as a spy in the GDR.
35. Nataliya Grib, "Gazprom Can't Wait to Get to the UK," *Kommersant*, October 6, 2006; and Vladimir Socor, "Netherlands Joins Russo-German Gas Pipeline Project," *Eurasia Daily Monitor*, November 9, 2007.
36. Keith C. Smith, "Russian Energy Policy and Its Challenges to Western Policy Makers" (testimony before the Commission on Security and Cooperation in Europe, Washington, DC, June 25, 2007).
37. Vladimir Socor, "More Problems for Russo-German Gas Pipeline Project," *Eurasia Daily Monitor*, August 16, 2007.
38. RFE/RL, *Newsline*, July 13, 2007.
39. Pavel K. Baev, "Kremlin Brings French Total on Board Gazprom's Shtokman Project," *Eurasia Daily Monitor*, July 16, 2007.
40. RFE/RL, *Newsline*, September 21, 2007.
41. Vladimir Socor, "Estonia Will Not Allow the Nord Stream Pipeline on Its Seabed," *Eurasia Daily Monitor*, September 27, 2007.
42. "Baltic Council Opposes Nord Stream Project," UPI, June 5, 2008.
43. Vladimir Socor, "South Stream Gas Project Defeating Nabucco by Default," *Eurasia Daily Monitor*, March 5, 2008.
44. The proposed Nabucco pipeline would originate in eastern Turkey and run through Bulgaria, Romania, and Hungary to Austria, with a projected capacity of 30–35 billion cubic meters of gas annually. The consortium includes Turkey's pipeline company Botas, Bulgaria's pipeline operator Bulgargaz, Romania's Romgaz, Hungary's MOL, and Austria's OMV as project leader. By the end of 2007, the cost of building the pipeline was estimated at €10 billion, as cited in Peter Pogany, "Russia-Ukraine Gas Row—Cacophonic Overture to Nabucco Summit," *Energy Bulletin*, January 12, 2009, http://www.energybulletin.net/node/47703.
45. "Russia Is Conducting Talks with Croatia and Bosnia on Their Participation in Implementing the South Stream Gas Pipeline Project," ITAR-TASS, May 29, 2008.
46. "Austria May Be Excluded from South Stream Project and the Gas Pipeline May Be Built via Slovenia," *Russian Oil and Gas Report* (Russia), April 16, 2008.
47. Vladimir Socor, "Gazprom's South Stream Project Can Be Halted in the Black Sea," *Eurasia Daily Monitor*, March 6, 2008.
48. Vladimir Socor, "Gazprom Takeover in Hungary Looms Behind Possible OMV Takeover," *Eurasia Daily Monitor*, July 25, 2007.
49. Vladimir Socor, "OMV Joins Gazprom to Undercut Nabucco," *Eurasia Daily Monitor*, January 29, 2008. Gazprom has also tempted Vienna with the prospect of Baumgarten becoming the main reference for the gas price in the EU and

creating a European gas exchange, complete with a major financial and trading center. This would be conditional on Gazprom's control of the hub's operations. See Vladimir Socor, "Austrian OMV Deal with Gazprom Threatens Nabucco Project," *Eurasia Daily Monitor*, November 19, 2007.

50. Vladimir Socor, "An Austrian Back Door for Russian Takeover of Hungary's Energy Sector," *Eurasia Daily Monitor*, July 25, 2007. OMV has steadily increased its stake in MOL by working through MOL shareholder Medget Rakhimkulov, the Russian billionaire in Budapest. It also seeks access to hydrocarbon fields in Russia by swapping OMV downstream assets in Central Europe for Russian upstream assets.

51. Vladimir Socor, "France Ready to Leap on the South Stream Bandwagon," *Eurasia Daily Monitor*, October 31, 2008.

52. Vladimir Socor, "OMV Versus MOL: A Test Case for the EU and Its Energy Policy," *Eurasia Daily Monitor*, October 2, 2007.

53. Vladimir Socor, "Hungary's MOL Energy Company Grows in Central Europe and Beyond," *Eurasia Daily Monitor*, August 7, 2007.

54. Vladimir Socor, "The EU Commission between MOL and OMV: Another 'Sleepwalking Case'?" *Eurasia Daily Monitor*, November 20, 2007.

55. RFE/RL, *Newsline*, September 18, 2007.

56. Vladimir Socor, "Hungary's Socialist Government Joins Gazprom's South Stream Project," *Eurasia Daily Monitor*, February 29, 2008; and RFE/RL, *Newsline*, February 26, 2008.

57. Vladimir Socor, "OMV Utilizing and Sabotaging the EU at the Same Time," *Eurasia Daily Monitor*, February 5, 2008.

58. Brian Whitmore, "Moscow Turns Its Attention to the Balkans," *Newsline*, June 28, 2007.

59. RFE/RL, *Newsline*, April 30, 2008.

60. Vladimir Socor, "Agreement to Integrate Bulgaria into Russia's Gas Network," *Eurasia Daily Monitor*, January 24, 2008.

61. Vladimir Socor, "Bulgaria Seduced by South Stream Gas Project?" *Eurasia Daily Monitor*, September 14, 2007.

62. RFE/RL, *Newsline*, January 28, 2008. Naftna Industrija Srbije (NIS) has a monopoly on the distribution of both oil and gas in Serbia.

63. Ibid., January 2, 2008.

64. Vladimir Socor, "Romania Is the Last Target for Gazprom's South Stream Temptations," *Eurasia Daily Monitor*, October 21, 2008. Bucharest can turn down the South Stream offer because it does not need additional gas volumes. Romania consumes 18 billion cubic meters of gas annually: approximately 12 billion from internal production and 6 billion cubic meters imported from Russia. Proven domestic reserves are expected to last for thirty years, giving Romania relative gas supply security in CEE.

65. Vladimir Socor, "Romania Firmly Aboard Nabucco Project, Hints at Leverage vis-a-vis South Stream," *Eurasia Daily Monitor*, November 3, 2008.

66. Vladimir Socor, "Moscow Exploiting the Kosovo Context to Take Over Serbia's Energy Sector," *Eurasia Daily Monitor*, January 10, 2008.

67. Vladimir Socor, "Bulgaria's Ambitions for Caspian Oil Transit," *Eurasia Daily Monitor*, September 13, 2007.

68. Moscow controls most of the export routes from the Caspian Basin and has been buying gas at under $70 per thousand cubic meters (tcm). It has then sold that gas to Europe at almost $300 per tcm. Actual transportation costs do not exceed $5 a tcm. See Keith C. Smith, "Europe's Response to Russia's Energy Policies," *CSIS Commentary*, April 2007. In effect, both Central Asia and Europe were subsidizing the Russian economy. Russia agreed to substantially raise its price for Central Asian gas in January 2009 out of concern that the Central Asians would turn to other customers and break Russia's monopsonistic position.

69. Vladimir Socor, "Vilnius Energy Summit Institutionalizing a Process," *Eurasia Daily Monitor*, October 12, 2007.

70. RFE/RL, *Newsline*, October 12, 2007.

71. Vladimir Socor, "Vilnius Energy Summit Institutionalizing a Process," *Eurasia Daily Monitor*, October 12, 2007; and RFE/RL, *Newsline*, October 12, 2007.

72. Socor, "Gazprom's South Stream Project Can Be Halted in the Black Sea."

73. Vladimir Socor, "Gas Companies Welcome Hungarian MOL's 'NETS' Project for Central and Southeastern Europe," *Eurasia Daily Monitor*, March 19, 2008.

74. Vladimir Socor, "Hungary's MOL Wins Fuel Market Share in Central Europe," *Eurasia Daily Monitor*, October 10, 2008.

75. Joshua Chaffin and Ed Crooks, "Brussels Gas Plan Likely to Raise Temperature," *Financial Times*, November 14, 2008.

76. Vladimir Socor, "Euro-Asian Oil Transportation Corridor Proposed at Kyiv Energy Summit," *Eurasia Daily Monitor*, May 28, 2008.

77. Vladimir Socor, "Transit Space Concept Launched at Kyiv Energy Summit," *Eurasia Daily Monitor*, May 29, 2008.

78. RFE/RL, *Newsline*, August 30, 2007.

79. Vladimir Socor, "Lex MOL Reflects European Rethinking on Energy Investment Regime," *Eurasia Daily Monitor*, October 30, 2007.

80. RFE/RL, *Newsline*, September 20, 2007.

81. Vladimir Socor, "Iranian Gas Eyed in Hungarian Efforts to Resuscitate Nabucco," *Eurasia Daily Monitor*, September 29, 2008.

82. Roman Kupchinsky, "The Price of Gas and Russian Democracy," *Eurasia Daily Monitor*, December 17, 2008.

Chapter 7. Business as Policy

1. *Economic and Social Survey of Asia and the Pacific 2008* (Bangkok: United Nations Economic and Social Commission for Asia and the Pacific [UNESCAP], March 2008), http://unescap.org/survey2008/notes/russian.asp.

2. Attila Mesterházy, "State and Market in the New Russian Economy," Committee Report, 061 ESCEW 08E (Brussels: NATO Parliamentary Assembly, 2008).

3. Alexei Kuznetsov, "Russian Companies Expand Foreign Investments," *Russian Analytical Digest*, no. 34 (February 5, 2008): 2.

4. Although Putin claimed that establishing "state capitalism" was not a goal of his administration, state-controlled conglomerates were created in numerous industries, including oil and gas, aircraft manufacturing, aircraft engine making, airline travel, banking, shipping, shipbuilding, titanium, bearing manufacturing, residential utilities, steel, nanotechnology, and nuclear energy. Preparations have also been initiated for establishing state companies for airports, machine tools,

automobile manufacturing, military electronics, toll roads, investment promotion, grain exports, pharmaceuticals, and fishing. See Jonas Bernstein, "Amid Vows to Limit State Interference, the State's Stake in Business Grows," *Eurasia Daily Monitor*, February 6, 2008.

5. Goldman, "The New Imperial Russia," 13.

6. Vassily Likhachev, "Russia and the European Union," *International Affairs* (Moscow) 52, no. 2 (2006): 106. Russia's GDP reached only 12 percent of the EU's total in 2004 and is only 6 percent larger than that of the ten new EU members combined.

7. Alexei V. Kuznetsov, "Prospects of Various Types of Russian Transnational Corporations (TNCs)" (Turku, Finland: Electronic Publications of Pan-European Institute, Turku School of Economics, October 2007), http://www.tse.fi/FI/yksikot/erillislaitokset/pei/Documents/Julkaisut/Kuznetsov10_07.pdf.

8. See Csaba Weiner, "Russian FDI in Central and Eastern European Countries: Opportunities and Threats," Working Paper no. 168 (Budapest: Institute for World Economics, Hungarian Academy of Sciences, April 2006), 6. Weiner provides a wealth of information and statistical data on Russian business activities in the CEE states from the mid-1990s to the mid-2000s.

9. Fred Weir, "Oil-Rich Russia Eyes Foreign Assets," *Christian Science Monitor*, March 12, 2008.

10. See Andrew E. Kramer, "Russia Creates a $32 Billion Sovereign Wealth Fund," *New York Times*, February 1, 2008; William R. Thomson, "Sovereign Wealth Funds—A Controversial New Power in Global Markets," October 9, 2007, http://www.321gold.com/editorials/thomson/thomson100907.html; and Tim Weber, "Who's Afraid of Sovereign Wealth Funds?" BBC News, January 24, 2008, http://news.bbc.co.uk/2/hi/business/7207715.stm.

11. Sophia Kishkovsky, "Russia Takes Critical Tone on Economy," *New York Times*, June 8, 2008, http://www.nytimes.com/2008/06/08/world/europe/08russia.html?em&ex=1213070400&en=1ff334144331123d&ei=5087%0A.

12. Dmitry Medvedev, speech given at the World Policy Forum, Evian, France, October 8, 2008, http://article.wn.com/view/WNAT339AAB54EFAFF78D5CE4107B23B2211E/.

13. RFE/RL, *Newsline*, February 6, 2008.

14. Roman Kupchinsky, "Gazprom's European Web—The Russian Rubik's Cube" (unpublished paper in author's collection, February 2008), 1–37. Also see Hans-Martin Tillack, "A Tale of Gazoviki, Money and Greed," *Stern*, September 13, 2007. According to Tillack, the Berlin-based Gazprom Germania established a complex network of shareholdings in companies that stretch right across Europe. In the gas sector, they include the Centrex Group, with offices in Austria, Switzerland, Cyprus, and Russia, and active in Italy and Hungary, with privileged access to Gazprom executives.

15. According to a Harris Poll survey released in February 2008, Spain is the only European country out of the five largest EU members in which a majority of the public favors Russian investment. In Britain, 65 percent of the public opposes it. Majorities in all five states also do not trust Russia's reliability as an energy supplier. See "Majorities in Five European Countries and the U.S. Believe Russia Is an Unreliable Energy Supplier," Harris Poll #19, February 20, 2008, http://www.harrisinteractive.com/harris%5Fpoll/index.asp?PID=873.

16. For a listing of Gazprom's joint ventures in Europe, including offshore locations, see Andreas Heinrich, "Gazprom's Expansion Strategy in Europe and the Liberalization of EU Energy Markets," *Russian Analytical Digest*, no. 34 (February 5, 2008): 12–13.

17. RFE/RL, *Newsline*, February 7, 2008.

18. For a useful overview of Russia's foreign intelligence activities under the Putin administration consult Anderson, "The HUMINT Offensive from Putin's Chekist State," 258–316.

19. Heinrich, "Gazprom's Expansion Strategy in Europe and the Liberalization of EU Energy Markets," 8–9.

20. Sectoral and company specific information can be found on corporation websites. Other information for this section was obtained from a wide range of sources, including Weiner, "Russian FDI in Central and Eastern European Countries."

21. "A Bear at the Throat: European Energy Security," *Economist*, April 14, 2007.

22. RFE/RL, *Newsline*, December 19, 2007.

23. "Gazprom and E.ON Sign Agreement to Jointly Develop Yuzhno-Russkoye Oil and Gas Field," *Your Oil and Gas News*, October 3, 2008, http://www.your oilandgasnews.com/news_item.php?newsID=11937.

24. RFE/RL, *Newsline*, November 28, 2007.

25. Jack Ewing and Jason Bush, "Russia Goes West with Its Oil Riches," *Business Week Online*, November 2, 2006, http://www.businessweek.com/globalbiz/ content/nov2006/gb20061102_045202.htm.

26. RFE/RL, *Newsline*, March 26, 2008.

27. For details on the Centrica dispute see "Gazprom's Goal: 10% of UK Gas Market by 2010," *Platts Oilgram News*, November 19, 2004; "Gazprom Arranges Prepurchase for Centrica," *Kommersant*, February 3, 2006; "The New Cold War: Russian Power Giant with Its Sights Set on British Gas Warns the West: Sell Us Your Fuel Firms or We'll Cut Your Supplies," *Daily Mail*, April 21, 2006; and "Hint of Hope for Gazprom on Centrica Bid," *Evening Standard*, April 25, 2006.

28. "France Set to Join Russian Infrastructure Projects," RIA Novosti, December 4, 2007.

29. "Russia, France Put Aside Georgia War Differences," Reuters, September 20, 2008.

30. Vitaliy Martyniuk, "Ukraine's Euro-Integration in the Light of EU-Russia Relations," *Research Update*, June 8, 2007.

31. "Eni and Gazprom Sign Gas Pipeline Accord for EU," *EnerPub*, June 23, 2007, http://www.energypublisher.com/article.asp?id=10031; and "Eni and Gazprom Sign the Agreement for South Stream Project," *Scandinavian Oil-Gas Magazine*, November 23, 2007, http://www.scandoil.com/moxie-bm2/news/eni-and-gazprom-sign-the-agreement-for-the-south-s.shtml.

32. Kupchinsky, "Gazprom's European Web," 26–27.

33. Vladimir Socor, "Lukoil Embarking on a Vast Expansion Program Despite Financial Crisis," *Eurasia Daily Monitor*, December 2, 2008.

34. Ibid.

35. Kupchinsky, "Gazprom's European Web," 22.

36. Ibid., 25.
37. Goldman, "The New Imperial Russia," 12.
38. Rolleiv Solholm, "Gazprom, Total, and StatoilHydro Create Shtokman Company," *Norway Post*, February 22, 2008.
39. "Norilsk Nikel Invited to Norway," *BarentsObserver.com*, June 10, 2008, http://www.barentsobserver.com/index.php?id=4491039.
40. "Russia Offers Gas Link Compromise," *Utility Week*, March 16, 2007.
41. Pavel Simonov, "Cyprus—Russia's Gateway to the Middle East and Europe," *Axis Information and Analysis*, June 9, 2005.
42. "About the Company," Lukoil Baltija R, 2005, http://www.lukoil.lv/index.php?&374.
43. Andrew Neff, "Gazprom Seeks Stake in Proposed Latvia Gas-fired Power Plant," World Markets Research Centre, April 9, 2008.
44. "About the Company," Lukoil Baltija R.
45. "Estonian Local Government Asks Security Police to Study Effect of Russian Investments," Baltic News Service, May 11, 2006.
46. "Vhnestorgbank and B.R.E. Bank S.A. of Poland Signed a Cooperation Agreement," VTB News, April 27, 2002, http://www.vtb.com/rus/web.html?s1=24&s2=17&s3=1&l=2.
47. RFE/RL, *Newsline*, October 12, 2007.
48. For details see Pavel Simonov and Allister Maunk, "Oil Secrets of the Polish Intelligence," *Axis Information and Analysis* (Global Challenges Research), March 13, 2006.
49. "Citigroup Keeps 'Hold' on Austrian OMV," APA-Economic News Service, October 15, 2007.
50. "Gazprom's Vemex Wants to Buy Gas from Czech Producer—Report," *European Spot Gas Markets*, April 11, 2008.
51. In April 1997 Slovak premier Vladimir Mečiar signed a series of agreements in which a Gazprom-Slovak joint venture was created to transport Russian gas to the EU. The exact terms of the joint venture were never published, and the agreements were due to expire in 2008.
52. RFE/RL, *Newsline*, August 31, 2007.
53. "Company Profile," Overgas, http://www.overgas.bg/Page.jsp?language=En&rootunid=94C47EC09199A885C2256FB1005FCC3B&unid=2B19C4BF9AEBAE79C2256FB1005FCC45.
54. "Lukoil's Bulgarian Refinery Assigns 65mln Euro Desulphurization Project to Hellenic Tehnodomiki's Unit," *SeeNews*, March 19, 2008.
55. "Bulgaria Industry: Lukoil to Acquire Petrol Stations and Storage Facilities from Petrol," Economist Intelligence Unit ViewsWire Select, March 4, 2008.
56. "Atomstroiexport Contract for Belene Plant Is Worth 135 Billion Rubles," *Russia & CIS Business & Financial Daily*, May 8, 2007.
57. "Russian Atomstroyexport to construct Belene NPP in Bulgaria," Regnum News Agency, October 31, 2006, http://www.regnum.ru/english/731004.html; and European/Middle Eastern Briefs, *Platt's Global Power Report*, January 24, 2008, 10.
58. "Bulgaria to Establish Giant Energy Firm," *Global English* (Middle East and

North Africa Financial Network), February 14, 2008; and "Bulgaria Industry: Energy Boost," Economist Intelligence Unit ViewsWire Select, February 21, 2008.

59. "Russia's Gazprom Interested in Cooperation with Romanian Gas Company," *BBC Monitoring Europe*, February 19, 2008.

60. "Gazprom Goes on Being Interested in Cooperating with Romgaz for Storehouse at Margineni," *Rompres*, February 19, 2008; and "Russian Gas Firm Gazprom Mulls Acquisition of Romanian Gas Company Romgaz," *Central Europe Energy Weekly*, November 10, 2007.

61. United Nations Conference on Trade and Development, Geneva, November 8, 2005, http://www.unctad.org/en/docs/c3em26d2a4_en.pdf.

62. For details see Roman Kupchinsky, "Is Gazprom Maneuvering to Obtain Romanian Aluminum?" *Eurasia Daily Monitor*, June 6, 2008.

63. Roman Kupchinsky, "Russia and the World Gold Market," *Eurasia Daily Monitor*, November 18, 2008.

64. RFE/RL, *Newsline*, June 15, 2007.

65. "Foreign Trade Exchange Serbia-Russian Federation," Serbian Chamber of Commerce, 2008, http://ino.komora.net/Home/Bilateralcooperation/tabid/2907/Default.aspx.

66. RFE/RL, *Newsline*, June 11, 2007.

67. Ibid., April 4, 2008.

68. Ibid., April 11, 2008.

69. Ibid., June 13, 2007.

70. "Kosovo Status Can Only Be Settled Between Belgrade, Pristina," *ITAR-TASS Daily*, April 20, 2007.

71. Estimated at over $1,000 for each of Montenegro's 650,000 citizens. See Oana Lungescu, "Russians Prompt Boom in Montenegro," BBC News, February 21, 2008, http://news.bbc.co.uk/go/pr/fr/-/2/hi/europe/7255240.stm.

72. *Montenegro 2007 Progress Report* (Brussels: Commission of the European Communities, 2007), 42.

73. Vladimir Socor, "Lukoil Embarking on a Vast Expansion Program Despite Financial Crisis," *Eurasia Daily Monitor*, December 2, 2008.

74. RFE/RL, *Newsline*, June 27, 2007.

75. Ibid., September 19, 2007.

76. "Ukraine Mounts Challenge to Black Sea PSA," *Nefte Compass*, April 17, 2008.

77. Interfax, "Ukraine's Chief Auditor: Deals with RosUkrEnergo Illegal," *Kiev Ukraine News Blog*, February 6, 2008, http://blog.kievukraine.info/2008_02_01_archive.html.

78. "Rosbank Ups Share in Belrosbank to 76.92%," *Russia & CIS Banking & Finance Weekly*, September 2, 2006.

79. For background see "Buying Slavneft Share in Slavnetbank," *Russia & CIS Business & Financial Daily*, September 24, 2007.

80. "Russia's Bank of Development to Extend $30mln Loan to Belnevsheconom-bank," Belarusian Telegraph Agency (BELTA), December 4, 2007.

81. "Russia's VTB Bank to Invest $20mln in Subsidiary Bank in Belarus," BELTA, March 27, 2008.

82. "Russian Group PECO Plans to Set Up a Mortgage Bank in Belarus," BELTA, January 14, 2008.

83. "Gazprom, Belarus Begin Work on Project of New Power Plant," ITAR-TASS, April 1, 2008.

84. Hedenskog and Larsson, "Russian Leverage on the CIS and the Baltic States," 65–67.

85. Vladimir Socor, "Gazprom Touts Agreements with Moldova as 'Models,'" *Eurasia Daily Monitor*, January 4, 2007.

86. Vladimir Socor, "Is Moldova's President Dropping the European Banner?" *Eurasia Daily Monitor*, June 29, 2007.

87. "VimpelCom to Invest $800 Million in CIS Excluding Russia in 2008," Tass English-Language Business Newswire, March 12, 2008.

88. Sergei Blagov, "Armenia Seeks Stronger Ties with Russia," *Eurasia Insight*, March 27, 2008.

89. Haroutiun Khachatrian, "Mixed Media Views of Proposed Russian Ventures," *Transitions Online*, February 20, 2007, http://www.tol.cz/look/TOL/article.tpl?Id Language=1&IdPublication=4&NrIssue=206&NrSection=4&NrArticle=18347. Armenia's former president Levon Ter-Petrossian believes that Russian economic enticements are intended to make sure that Armenia rejects any compromise over Nagorno-Krabakh, maintains its dispute with Azerbaijan, and remains a Russian outpost in the South Caucasus.

Chapter 8. Conclusions: Revitalizing the West

1. Based on presentations and discussions at a CSIS conference on Central European Security in Bucharest, Romania, on April 1, 2008.

2. Ahto Lobjakas, "NATO Commander Seeks Defense Plans for Baltic States," RFE/RL, October 7, 2008.

3. Ronald D. Asmus, "NATO's Hour," *Wall Street Journal Europe*, August 18, 2008.

4. See Mitchell, "America's New Eastern Problem"; and Neil Barnett, "Revisiting Territorial Defense for Central Europe?" *Central Europe Digest,* August 15, 2008. Territorial defense means "an emphasis on something like partisan or insurgent resistance to an invader from the East. The Estonians could provide a model here: their defense policy is based around exactly this principle, in the hope that by pinning down and harassing the (presumably Russian) enemy, they can buy time for more formidable allies to come to their assistance."

5. According to Mitchell, Washington should announce its intention to transfer its entire Europe-based military establishment to new locations in Central Europe. This should include the EUCOM headquarters and the bulk of the U.S. Seventh Army and Third Air Force—upward of sixty thousand troops. Such a signal would inject confidence for U.S. allies both inside and outside NATO that article 5 will be honored. See Mitchell, "America's New Eastern Problem."

6. Max Boot, "Eastern Europe Can Defend Itself," *Wall Street Journal*, August 25, 2008.

7. Consult Cornell, Popjanevski, and Nilsson, *Russia's War in Georgia*, 29.

8. For a far-reaching proposal for globalizing NATO and bringing in willing and capable new members see Ivo Daalder and James Goldgeier, "Global NATO," *Foreign Affairs* 85, no. 5 (September–October 2006): 105–13.

9. Smith, "Russian Energy Policy and Its Challenges to Western Policymakers."

10. Socor, "Russian Energy Policy and Strategy in Europe."

11. As stated by the European Parliament's foreign affairs committee in September 2007. See RFE/RL, *Newsline*, September 5, 2007.

12. Refer to the speech by NATO Secretary General Jaap de Hoop Scheffer in Riga, Latvia, on July 14, 2006, http://www.nato.int/docu/speech/2006/s060714a.htm.

13. See Martti Ahtisaari and Joschka Fischer, "Europe Needs to Assert Itself in the World," *Financial Times*, October 1, 2007.

14. Leonard and Popescu, "A Power Audit of EU-Russia Relations," 5.

15. Vladimir Socor, "What the European Union Can Do about Georgia after the Russian Invasion," *Eurasia Daily Monitor*, August 30, 2008.

16. *Conflict Resolution in the South Caucasus: The EU's Role*, Europe Report no. 173 (Tbilisi: International Crisis Group, March 20, 2006), i.

17. See Dmitry Zhdannikov and Darya Korsunskaya, "Russia Tycoons Bailout Could Turn into Kremlin Trap," Reuters, October 30, 2008. The Kremlin has entrusted the state-owned development bank, VEB, to distribute a $50 billion rescue package that will help Russian companies to refinance a total of $120 billion of Western loans by the end of 2009. VEB disbursed $2 billion to Mikhail Fridman's Alfa Group and $4.5 billion to Oleg Deripaska and his aluminum major Rusal.

18. Yuri Zarakhovich, "Mismanagement of Russian Economy Could Lead to Social Unrest," *Eurasia Daily Monitor*, December 1, 2008.

19. Oleg Shchedrov, "Don't Destabilize Russia, Putin Warns Foes," Reuters, December 20, 2008.

Selected Bibliography

Anderson, Julie. "The Chekist Takeover of the Russian State." *International Journal of Intelligence and Counterintelligence* 19, no. 2 (May 2006): 227–88.

———. "The HUMINT Offensive from Putin's Chekist State." *International Journal of Intelligence and Counterintelligence* 20, no. 2 (June 2007): 258–316.

Aron, Leon. "The Politics of Memory." *Russian Outlook*, AEI Online, September 8, 2008. http://www.aei.org/publications/pubID.28503/pub_detail.asp.

Baev, Pavel K. "Russia and Germany Restart Their Special Partnership." *Eurasia Daily Monitor*, October 6, 2008.

Barysch, Katinka. *The EU and Russia: Strategic Partners or Squabbling Neighbours?* London: Centre for European Reform, May 2004.

Blank, Stephen. "Power Struggles in the Kremlin—How Stable Is the New Regime?" In *Russia after Putin: Implications for Russia's Politics and Neighbors.* Policy Paper. Stockholm-Nacka: Institute for Security and Development Policy, March 2008.

Brzezinski, Zbigniew. "Putin's Choice." *Washington Quarterly* 31, no. 2 (Spring 2008): 95–116.

Bugajski, Janusz. *Cold Peace: Russia's New Imperialism.* Westport, CT: Praeger, 2004.

———. *The Eastern Dimension of America's New European Allies.* Strategic Studies Institute Monograph. Carlisle, PA: U.S. Army War College, October 2007.

Chizhov, Vladimir. "Russia-EU Cooperation: The Foreign Policy Dimension." *International Affairs: A Russian Journal of World Politics, Diplomacy, and International Relations* 51, no. 5 (2005): 134–38.

Cohen, Ariel. *The New Cold War: Reviving the U.S. Presence in the Arctic.* Backgrounder no. 2202. Washington, DC: Heritage Foundation, October 30, 2008.

Cornell, Svante E., Johanna Popjanevski, and Niklas Nilsson. *Russia's War in Georgia: Causes and Implications for Georgia and the World.* Policy Paper. Washington, DC: Central Asia-Caucasus Institute and Silk Road Studies Program, August 2008.

Daalder, Ivo, and James Goldgeier. "Global NATO." *Foreign Affairs* 85, no. 5 (September–October 2006): 105–13.

Emerson, Michael. "Time for a Strategic Bargain with Russia." *CEPS European Neighborhood Watch*, no. 38 (May 2008): 1.

Flenley, Paul. "Russia and the EU: A Pragmatic and Contradictory Relationship." *Perspectives on European Politics and Society* 6, no. 3 (2005): 435–61.

Forsberg, Tuomas. "The EU-Russia Security Partnership: Why the Opportunity Was Missed." *European Foreign Affairs Review* 9, no. 2 (2004): 247–67.

Gerke, Wolfgang, and P. S. Zolotarev. "Russian-German Relations in the Context of Global Politics." *International Affairs* 53, no. 3 (2007): 80–107.

Goldman, Marshall I. *Petrostate: Putin, Power, and the New Russia.* New York: Oxford University Press, 2008.

Grotzky, Daniel, and Mirela Isic. *The Black Sea Region: Clashing Identities and Risks to European Stability.* CAP Policy Analysis no. 4. Munich: Center for Applied Policy Research, October 2008.

Hedenskog, Jakob, and Robert L. Larsson. *Russian Leverage on the CIS and the Baltic States.* Defence Analysis. Stockholm: Swedish Defence Research Agency (FOI), June 2007.

Jibladze, Kakha. "Russia's Opposition to Georgia's Quest for NATO Membership." *China and Eurasia Forum Quarterly* 5, no. 1 (2007): 45–51.

Kagan, Robert. "The End of the End of History: Why the Twenty-First Century Will Look Like the Nineteenth." *New Republic*, April 23, 2008.

Karaganov, Sergei. "The New Epoch of Confrontation." *Russia in Global Affairs*, no. 4 (October–December 2007).

Kovalev, Vladimir. "Power Play." *Transitions Online*, March 6, 2007. http://www.tol.cz/ look/TOL/article.tpl?IdLanguage=1&IdPublication=4&NrIssue=208&NrSection=4 &NrArticle=18379.

Krastev, Ivan. *The Crisis of the Post–Cold War European Order.* Brussels Forum Paper Series. Washington, DC: German Marshall Fund of the United States, March 2008.

Kuznetsov, Alexei V. *"Prospects of Various Types of Russian Transnational Corporations (TNCs)."* Turku, Finland: Electronic Publications of Pan-European Institute, Turku School of Economics, October 2007. http://www.tse.fi/FI/yksikot/erillislaitokset/pei/ Documents/Julkaisut/Kuznetsov10_07.pdf.

Kuznetsova, E. "Will the Roadmaps Lead Russia to Europe?" *International Affairs* 51, no. 4 (2005): 67–71.

Laruelle, Marlene. *Russian Eurasianism: An Ideology of Empire.* Washington, DC: Woodrow Wilson Center Press, 2008.

Lebahn, Aksel. "Russia Is Here Again!" *International Affairs* 53, no. 2 (2007): 22–35.

Leonard, Mark, and Nicu Popescu. *A Power Audit of EU-Russia Relations.* Policy Paper. London: European Council on Foreign Relations, November 2, 2007.

Likhachev, Vassily. "Russia and the European Union." *International Affairs: A Russian Journal of World Politics, Diplomacy, and International Relations* 52, no. 2 (2006): 106.

Lindner, Rainer. "New Realism: The Making of Russia's Foreign Policy in the Post-Soviet World." *EU-Russia Centre Review*, no. 8 (October 2008): 28–37.

Lucas, Edward. *The New Cold War: The Future of Russia and the Threat to the West.* New York: Palgrave Macmillan, 2008.

Lynch, Dov. "Russia's Strategic Partnership with Europe." *Washington Quarterly* 27, no. 2 (Spring 2004): 99–118.

McFaul, Michael, and Kathryn Stoner-Weiss. "The Myth of the Authoritarian Model." *Foreign Affairs* 87, no. 1 (January–February 2008): 68–84.

Merkushev, Vitaly. "Relations between Russia and the EU: The View from Across the Atlantic." *Perspectives on European Politics and Society* 6, no. 2 (2005): 353–71.

Nowak, Andrzej. *History and Geopolitics: A Contest for Eastern Europe.* Warsaw: Polish Institute of International Affairs, 2008.

Nygren, Bertil. *The Rebuilding of Greater Russia: Putin's Foreign Policy towards the CIS Countries.* New York: Routledge, 2007.

Piadyshev, Boris, Aleksandr Bessmertnykh, and Boris Shmeler. "Realpolitik from Munich." *International Affairs* 53, no. 3 (2007): 50–80.

Pirog, Robert. "Russian Oil and Gas Challenges." *Connections: The Quarterly Journal* 6, no. 3 (Fall 2007): 82–99.

Powell, Bill, and Li You. "How the KGB (and Friends) Took Over Russia's Economy." *Fortune* 158, no. 5 (September 10, 2008): 84–94.

Roberts, Cynthia A. *Russia and the European Union: The Sources and Limits of "Special Relationships."* Carlisle Barracks, PA: Strategic Studies Institute, U.S. Army War College, February 2007.

Rose, Richard, and Neil Munro. *Elections without Order: Russia's Challenge to Vladimir Putin.* Cambridge: Cambridge University Press, 2002.

Sherr, James. "Russia and the 'Near Abroad,' in a Medvedev Presidency." In *Russia after Putin: Implications for Russia's Politics and Neighbors.* Policy Paper. Stockholm-Nacka: Institute for Security and Development Policy, March 2008.

Shevtsova, Lilia. "Anti-Westernism Is the New National Idea." *Moscow Times,* August 7, 2007.

Smorodinskaya, Nataliya. "Motives behind Russian Foreign Policy." *The EU-Russia Centre Review,* no. 8 (October 2008): 42–43.

Socor, Vladimir. "Euroappeasement: The EU's Answer to Russia's Assault on Georgia." *Eurasia Daily Monitor,* June 4, 2008.

———. "From Schroeder to Stoiber?" *Eurasia Daily Monitor,* July 9, 2007.

———. "South Stream Gas Project Defeating Nabucco by Default." *Eurasia Daily Monitor,* March 5, 2008.

Timmins, Graham. "German *Ostpolitik* under the Red-Green Coalition and EU-Russian Relations." *Debatte: Journal of Contemporary Central and Eastern Europe* 14, no. 3 (December 2006): 301–14.

Tolz, Vera. *Russia: Inventing the Nation.* London: Arnold, 2001.

Treisman, Daniel. "Putin's Silovarchs." *Orbis* 51, no. 1 (Winter 2007): 141–53.

Trenin, Dmitri. "Russia Redefines Itself and Its Relations with the West." *Washington Quarterly* 30, no. 2 (Spring 2007): 95–105.

Trenin, Dmitri, and Bobo Lo. *The Landscape of Russian Foreign Policy Decision-Making.* Washington, DC: Carnegie Endowment for International Peace, 2005.

Volkov, Vadim. *Violent Entrepreneurs: The Use of Force in the Making of Russian Capitalism.* Ithaca, NY: Cornell University Press, 2002.

Walker, Martin. "Russia v. Europe: The Energy Wars." *World Policy Journal* 24, no. 1 (Spring 2007): 1–8.

Wegren, Stephen K., ed. *Russia's Policy Challenges: Security, Stability, and Development.* Armonk, NY: M. E. Sharpe, 2003.

Weiner, Csaba. "Russian FDI in Central and Eastern European Countries: Opportunities and Threats." Working Paper no. 168. Budapest: Institute for World Economics, Hungarian Academy of Sciences, April 2006.

White, Stephen. *Russia's New Politics: The Management of a Postcommunist Society.* New York: Cambridge University Press, 2000.

Wilson, Andrew. *Meeting Medvedev: The Politics of the Putin Succession.* Policy Brief. London: European Council on Foreign Relations, February 2008.

———. *Virtual Politics: Faking Democracy in the Post-Soviet World.* New Haven, CT: Yale University Press, 2005.

Zagorski, Andrei. "Russia and the U.S.: The Kabuki Dancing Over?" *EU-Russia Centre Review*, no. 8 (October 2008): 102–10.

Index

About the Author

Janusz Bugajski is the holder of the CSIS Lavrentis Lavrentiadis chair in South East European Studies and the director of the New European Democracies Project at the Center for Strategic and International Studies in Washington, D.C. Bugajski runs the South-Central Europe area studies program at the Foreign Service Institute, U.S. Department of State, and has been a consultant to the U.S. Department of Defense and the U.S. Agency for International Development, among other organizations. His most recent books include *Atlantic Bridges: America's New European Allies*, with Ilona Teleki, and *Cold Peace: Russia's New Imperialism*. He lives in Silver Spring, Maryland.